INNER READING
AND
INNER HEARING

RUDOLF STEINER (1913)

INNER READING AND INNER HEARING

& How to Achieve Existence in the World of Ideas

Two Lectures Cycles, Followed by Two Christmas Lectures
Dornach, October 3–7 and December 12–20, 1914
Dornach, December 26 and Basel, December 27, 1914

TRANSLATED BY MICHAEL MILLER
INTRODUCTION BY CHRISTOPHER BAMFORD

RUDOLF STEINER

SteinerBooks

CW 156

SteinerBooks
Anthropsophic Press

610 Main Street
Great Barrington, Massachusetts 01230
www.steinerbooks.org

Translation by Michael Miller

This book is volume 156 in the Collected Works (CW) of Rudolf Steiner, published by SteinerBooks, 2008. It is a translation of *Okkultes Lesen und okkultes Horën* published by Rudolf Steiner Verlag, Dornach, Switzerland, 2003.

The drawings in the text were done by Hedwig Frey and Lenore Uhlig, based on the stenographer's sketches of Rudolf Steiner's blackboard drawings.

Library of Congress Cataloging-in-Publication Data

Steiner, Rudolf, 1861-1925.
[Okkultes Lesen und okkultes Horkn. English]
Inner reading and inner hearing ; and, How to achieve existence in the world of ideas : two lecture cycles, followed by two Christmas lectures, Dornach, October 3-7 and December 12-26, 1914 and Basel, December 27, 1914 / Rudolf Steiner ; translated by Michael Miller ; introduction by Christopher Bamford.
p. cm. – (The collected works of rudolf steiner ; v. 156)
Includes bibliographical references and index.
ISBN 978-0-88010-619-1
1. Anthroposophy. I. Steiner, Rudolf, 1861-1925. How to achieve existence in the world of ideas. II. Title. III. Title: How to achieve existence in the world of ideas.
BP595.S8656513 2008
299'.935–dc22
2008038737

Printed in the United States

CONTENTS

PART II
How to Achieve Existence in the World of Ideas

INTRODUCTION

CHRISTOPHER BAMFORD

If one reads them carefully, despite their vast quantity—the figure usually given is around 6,000—Rudolf Steiner's lectures rarely fail to astonish and surprise; and always for unique reasons. No matter how many lectures one has read, one always finds new insights, either because the research is new or because Steiner's mood or disposition in relation to his audience shades his remarks in a way that brings out previously hidden nuances or perspectives not available elsewhere. Such is the case with the three short lecture cycles printed here. The year is 1914; the months October and December: a fate-filled moment both for Anthroposophy and Western civilization.

The year before (1913) had seen the expulsion of the German Section from the Theosophical Society and the establishment of the Anthroposophical Society. This finally gave Rudolf Steiner the untrammeled freedom to form his own spiritual movement without the constraints that working within the Adyar-based Theosophical Movement had inevitably imposed. On February 3, the first constitutive General Meeting of the new Society took place and by the middle of the year, it numbered over 3,000 members, active in 85 working groups. That same month, a second, equally epoch-making event occurred when it was finally decided that the "Building," which in 1918 would be renamed the Goetheanum, but was then still known as the "Johannesbau" or "John Building" after John the Evangelist, would be located in Dornach, Switzerland, rather than in Munich, Germany, as had been previously considered. This decision, long in coming, was made on May 18, and on September 20 the Foundation Stone was laid. By November construction was underway. Clearly, the spiritual world was seeking to found something, as may also be seen from the deeply esoteric lectures Steiner gave during this period—such as those on *The Fifth Gospel, The Secrets of the Threshold,*

The Esoteric Foundations of the Bhagavad-Gita, and *Christ and the Spiritual World: The Search for the Holy Grail.*

By the following year, 1914, as if prophetically preparing for the wartime years, the center of Anthroposophical work had shifted to Dornach, where construction was in full swing and Steiner oversaw all aspects of the work. As a consequence, he was forced to reduce his lecturing activity, though he continued to research and speak on the Fifth Gospel, as well as on life between death and a new birth. It had been his hope to open the Johannesbau by December. However, with the inception of hostilities, following the assassination of Archduke Franz Ferdinand in Sarajevo on June 28, that of course did not happen. Events moved very fast, as the world caught fire. By the end of July, Austria-Hungary had declared war on Serbia, and Russia had ordered the mobilization of troops. On August 1, Germany declared war on Russia; on August 3 on France; on August 4, Germany invaded Belgium and Britain declared war on Germany. The die was cast.

Rudolf Steiner had long recognized what was coming. He understood that humanity was entering a great test. Since the deed of 1879, when the Archangel Michael—according to both Steiner's research and esoteric lore—overcame the Dragon, throwing him to Earth, and assumed the regency of the age, offering himself to human beings as their mediator and helper, the spiritual world had sought fiercely to manifest itself on Earth. Human beings meanwhile, for their part, sunk deeper into materialism and into the dragon's clutches. Evil had entered the world in a new way. Yet the call was to rise upward—to work one's way in freedom toward the spirit, thereby dissipating the evil, which in so many ways and in so much in human life now drew humanity evermore downward. From this point of view, the war came—or ought to have come—as a form of "hitting bottom." If ever an event should bring human beings to change their way of thinking and being, this was it. During the first six months of the year, therefore, Steiner, while continuing to focus on the building that would be the living manifestation of the anthroposophical spirit, sought above all to strengthen his students' spiritual resolve.

The reality of war had indeed changed everything. Suffering and death began to fill the air. Spiritual research, of the kind that Rudolf

Steiner had been doing, became difficult, if not impossible. In response to people's very heartfelt needs and the great confusion in the spiritual world, his focus narrowed. Thus, over the next few years, we find a greater emphasis on the vital connections between the living and the so-called dead, as well as on the esoteric historical currents underlying the ongoing carnage. On a more mundane level, travel, too, became more difficult. Steiner had to curtail his lecturing activity. Steiner's orbit would gradually become limited largely to Dornach and Berlin. Personal changes also ensued. His wife Anna (Schultz) Eunike (Steiner) had died in 1911. This left him free to marry his longtime co-worker and spiritual collaborator, Marie von Sivers, who was still a Russian citizen. With the War, the long-planned event became a necessity. Rudolf Steiner and Marie von Sivers were married on December 24, which meant that Marie Steiner, now with an Austrian passport, could travel freely to Berlin with her husband, Rudolf Steiner.

At the same time, Providence, establishing the new center outside the war zone, in Dornach, obviously provided a haven. While witnessing the horrific events going on in the rest of Europe, those in Switzerland were protected from them. This made it all the more important, as Steiner repeatedly stressed, for those whose fortunate karma had granted them this asylum to uphold with all their strength their spiritual ideals, manifesting them in their lives in the full existential resolution that the "Spirit will triumph."

The time for theory was over. The path to spiritual knowledge must be lived and practiced. Such is the context of the lectures collected here.

"Inner Reading and Inner Hearing," the first cycle, was originally intended to contain fourteen lectures. They were to be given during the rehearsal of Steiner's new Mystery Drama, which would have carried the previous four plays to a new level. This fifth play was to have been written during rehearsals in Munich, but the War made rehearsals impossible. It was never written. Nevertheless, in response to requests that he give the lectures anyway, Steiner gave what he had previously conceived of as a major and extended cycle of fourteen lectures in the shortened form of four lectures. Though, as he says, the War now made it impossible to say what he would have said in Munich—"it is just not possible to speak the highest truths into the storm"—what he did say, perhaps precisely because he was forced to speak at a "lower" level, is unusually clear, astonishing, and enormously instructive.

The tone is intimate. Steiner is speaking here not just as teacher, but also as friend and colleague, a coworker in a shared enterprise at a time of common—indeed, from a European point of view, near universal—grief and foreboding. But the War and its desolation are present only between the lines. Steiner's explicit theme is essentially meditation: the path to the spirit, to entering into relationship with spiritual beings—in the first place with the dead, but also with the angelic beings. Rather than instruction, he gives advice in the most remarkable, forthright, touching way, speaking not theoretically but directly from his experiences—which are often the most valuable teachings.

He begins with the in-itself-astonishing statement that "the essentials of spiritual science have been won basically through inner reading and inner hearing." That is to say, inner reading and inner hearing constitute the primary method of spiritual research. They are the way we come to and experience spiritual reality.

Such an "inner" phenomenology and hermeneutics, however, is very different to what we habitually practice in relation to the "outer" world. Steiner gives the example of someone who suggested that "seers" be gathered together to observe a group of people, each of whom was instructed to think and feel certain things. If then, based on seeing their auras, all the seers agreed and were correct in perceiving what the members of the group were experiencing inwardly, the validity of the seers' inner perceptions would be proved. In other words, this person has proposed a typical scientific experiment. But inner perception does not work like that. The spiritual world is not at the behest of our desires and intentions. Quite the contrary: it is always a gift: not a generic gift, but a gift given by a specific giver, a spiritual being. For the spiritual world is a world of beings—from the highest angelic hierarchies to the so-called dead. Spiritual knowing is not something we can take. It must be received. Therefore, to approach such knowing-receiving, we must silence our desires, purposes, and intentions and present ourselves in devoted, expectant, attentive, empty waiting. Whatever comes originates in the spiritual world, not in us. And that world is nowhere else but here, where we are. But we are unaware of it; we do not see it.

> Where are the beings of the elemental world; where are the beings of the spiritual world; where are the beings of the upper hierarchies? They are right where we are. They are all around us—where the table and the chairs are, where you yourselves are. They are everywhere all around us, but they are so thin and evanescent compared to the relationships and processes of the things of the external world that they escape our attention. We continually go straight through the spiritual world and do not see it; we are inattentive to the spiritual world because our disposition is not prepared for it.

The same, in fact, is also true for a right perception of the so-called physical or outer world. When we think, feel, and will in relation to the outer world, we usually think of ourselves as over "here" and the world as over "there." But, though we can certainly develop valuable capacities in approaching it in that way, reality is not like that. With regard to our soul and spirit, we are not skin-bound. When we see a rose, our astral body and our "I" are *in* the rose; and this experience is *reflected* back to us by our organism or body. We do not produce what we experience inwardly; we only reflect it. "With our soul-spiritual nature we are truly within the part of the world we observe, and we see it because our organism reflects it." But in ordinary daily life what we see is more or less ourselves reflected back to us. It is *maya* (or illusion) because we do not realize we are within what we see.

Perception of the spiritual world is even more complex, because (as stated in the above quotation) it is so fleeting and mobile compared to the fixity of the physical world. To begin to experience it, we must learn to forget ourselves as we do in meditation. Suppressing the *self-ness* of the "I" enables us to sink down into the so-called astral body. But to have access to what we experience there, this experience too must be reflected—in this case, not by the physical organism but by the so-called etheric or life body, which is a body, we might say, of living thinking. To do this is more difficult than "reading" what our physical organism reflects, for what the etheric reflects is in continual movement—as it were, non-dual movement, outside space and time. This movement is a sign, which must be read or interpreted by "diving down" from the astral into the etheric body, "which is experienced as a fall into an abyss," in the process of which we separate into three parts (thinking, feeling, and willing), each of which has access to an "inner hearing" which reveals the meaning of what we have "read." The state of consciousness involved is akin to a conscious sleep state. It is the state of living consciously in the astral body, which enables us to experience the reflection of the spiritual world in the etheric body. But since this "reading" is actually a "descending into," the reading becomes something closer to "hearing." Then we realize how different true reality is from what we experience in the state of ordinary sensory-physical consciousness.

The process involved is one of identification. The fleeting world through which we encounter the spiritual world is one of images. First, we must clearly separate ourselves from these images. Then, in freedom we must plunge down into them, become one with them—in Steiner's striking metaphor "eat them." We enter their reality. Through this reality, the truth is heard. The phenomenon of "inner hearing" arises. But, in fact, it is not we that hear; more accurately, the image we have become "hears." This is a living process through which we really hear an objective spiritual being—Steiner's example involved communicating with the so-called dead—spiritually.

Much more, of course, is involved in all this than may be recounted here. Only the bare bones may be given. These lectures, in fact, which require close reading and even closer rereading, take us on a profound journey—one described in such precise and vivid language that we can sense something of the transformative magic that those listening to Steiner must have felt—from the sensory world into the experience of the spiritual researcher or meditant, and then back into the sensory world again.

Of central importance in the whole process is an experience of the Zodiac and the planets. When we dive into an image and identify with it, the image itself disappears. At the same time we feel diminished or reduced: we feel that we are only "a piece" of what we were before. As Steiner tells it, our experience is, as it were, a twelfth of what it had been: we feel ourselves in a circle, of which we occupy a twelfth. In other words, we have transformed ourselves into the Zodiac, through which the spiritual being, having penetrated through the image, speaks to us. We gaze, as it were, from the periphery inward—not, as in sensory perception, from the center outward—and discover there seven voices, corresponding to the planets. In other words, the astral body contains a twelvefold reflecting capacity and the etheric body a sevenfold reflecting capacity. Steiner then likens these two—the outer (astral, star-body) Zodiac and the inner planets—to vowels and consonants. In summary:

> We can say that we perceive a series of images. First we stand outside the series; then we dive down into it. In that process, through our devotion and sacrifice, we form a world sphere around what we wish to perceive. This world sphere contains within itself, like seven planets, the vowel system through which the being in question can speak with us when we ourselves, through the twelvefold nature of our being, form the system of consonants.
>
> We can only come into relationship with a being of the spiritual world by enclosing it; enclosing it in such a way that the enclosing gesture forms the cosmic consonants; the being itself can then address us in the cosmic vowels. And when the cosmic vowel system can work together with the cosmic consonant system, which we ourselves have formed, then reading and hearing work together. Then we penetrate into a particular region of the spiritual world.

These experiences must be reflected in the etheric body, where they may be cognized in the diluted, shadowy form of thoughts and ideas. If they were not so reflected, and we returned still bearing them into the physical, we would die: our body could not contain it. Indeed, Steiner stresses throughout that in the process of meditation and the encounter with the spiritual world, the threshold of death is ever-present, a danger that must be navigated cautiously and carefully.

What does it mean, we may ask, that we cannot directly apprehend spiritual realities? It means that we are protected; but even more it means that we are called to realize them in other ways, which takes preparation, a kind of continuous moral awareness, beginning with "the constant practice of loving interest in everything that surrounds us in the world." We must forego interest in ourselves. All the exercises in *How to Know Higher Worlds*, for example, have this as their consequence. Here Steiner gives some others, taking as his example ways of developing interest in other people. At a certain point in our development, we can enter into a completely different relationship with others, for instance, by taking a selfless, loving interest in their physiognomy, or the play of expression in their faces, or their gestures. Entering deeply into these three common realities, in fact, we have manifestations of three cosmic vowels. Later, Steiner will give clues to two more.

Throughout the first four of these lectures, Steiner speaks directly and candidly of his own research experiences—above all with the dead, but also, as the lectures unfold, with higher spiritual beings—in astonishing depth and detail. The lectures, therefore, ought not to be read for mere information about the spiritual world, but read and reread as a guide to our own inner and outer lives. Read in this way, readers will find them of almost inexhaustible wealth. In the last lecture, however, his tone changes. It is as intimate as before, but now it becomes more personal, as Steiner speaks, this time more out of his own life experiences than his research experiences, of the mission and task of Anthroposophy or spiritual science. What shines through here in a remarkable way, suffusing the text with a glow of warmth, is Steiner's enormous love for humanity, for the human project, and for individual human beings.

The second set of lectures, "How to Achieve Existence in the World of Ideas," follows on from the first, taking up several already-established themes, while giving them a somewhat different emphasis.

The call or injunction shifts from meditation and serious inner work to the consequences of such work for ordinary daily life. Common to both is the insistence that Anthroposophy not remain theoretical. One way of doing so is clearly to take up meditation. Another is to take up the spiritual realities discovered and articulated by those able to do the inner work, and put them into practice in one's life. Steiner is here concerned that Anthroposophists do not simply take up Anthroposophy as just another system of ideas to be schematized and philosophized about only intellectually. For him, Anthroposophy is nothing if it is not existential—if it does not change how we live. The second set of lectures thus builds in a new way on some of the spiritual realities touched upon in the first, as well as introducing others. It tries to show how, if people live their lives out of the conviction of their reality, their lives become different. Every spiritual fact adduced by the spiritual researcher has its application or extension in daily life. To live out of such conviction—in thought, feeling, and action—in fact constitutes a kind of second-order spiritual research. For when we take a spiritual fact as if it were a directive for life, and try to extend its reach by ordinary thinking, remarkable ethical and epistemological consequences appear in our lives and in our relationships with those we live with. They are changed fundamentally. Not nearly as dense as those preceding them, these lectures in their own way are equally astonishing. Time and again, as we read them, one senses "This is something I could do," and a new insight dawns.

The collection ends with two extraordinarily moving—and relevant—Christmas lectures—Steiner's first Christmas lectures of the war. Then, as now, as he puts it, "one can hardly think of a sharper mental contrast" than that between the desperate state of the world and the angels' proclamation to the Shepherds:

> Divine Revelation in the heights and Peace on Earth for people of good will.

Truly, these days the birth of the Christ child cannot simply be celebrated as usual; some deeper recognition is required, namely, that we face the reality that what entered the world at Christmas—and how it did so—is still not understood. The full meaning of Christ Jesus—and His birth, life, death, and resurrection—still eludes us. Though it has been slowly moving and evolving in human consciousness for two millennia, the reality and meaning of Christ's incarnation still has not penetrated humanity. It is perhaps the most difficult reality to grasp—and always has been. Historically, certainly, this is the case.

In the first centuries following the Mystery of Golgotha, for example, Mithras and the Mithraic Mysteries enjoyed great popularity. But Mithras was a very different being than Christ. Mithras could be encountered only in clairvoyant vision. He, too, was conceived of as a mediator between the spiritual world and the human soul, but he could not be conceived of as incarnating in a human body. He came down to Earth, but only in the imaginal realm. Ancient clairvoyance knew "The Future and Coming One," a Sun Being, Christ, and knew that he was approaching the Earth to dwell there, but it could not grasp that He would actually take on a human body and that the future of the Earth and the cosmos would thereby be transformed. People could not experience that "the great gift of cosmic Love, the Christ, from the God whom one calls the Father" had come to dwell with them, to unite His being through that deed with the whole future meaning of earthly evolution. For this, people had to learn to love Christ Jesus as their brother: they had to develop a relationship of the deepest intimacy with Him.

To some extent, indeed, over the centuries, human beings slowly did create such a relationship of intimacy and friendship, but now this intimacy—which is only half of the picture—must be broadened to include the cosmic and divine dimensions of Christ's work. Now Christ's cosmic nature must also become part of the new Christianity.

Ancient clairvoyance knew of the Cosmic Christ's work before Golgotha, but the Mystery of Golgotha itself came, as it were, as a stumbling block, which was aggravated by the general decline of spiritual vision. Thus, the great Mani, the third century founder of Manicheanism could see how Christ descended from the spiritual heights, but could not comprehend that He had penetrated the earthly world and dwelt in a human body, changing everything. And after Mani, even that knowledge of the descent grew weaker until it disappeared.

Ancient Gnosis, too, knew these things and its testament, as Steiner shows, is still most moving, but spiritual science can now see further and more deeply. In this spirit he gives a beautiful verse, which is far from the ancient Gnostic view, but oriented, like theirs, toward the living Cosmic Christ:

Light is love ... Sun-weaving
Love-radiance of a world
of creative beings —

which, through ages unheard-of,
holds us to its heart,
and which at last has given us
its highest spirit in the sheath
of a man for three
years: then He came into His

Father's legacy, which is now the Earth's
innermost heavenly fire:
that it, too, may once become Sun.

Now the task is to unite the Christ of Heaven and the earthly Christ in a single path of love, walked individually by each one of us. The attempt to do so, as Steiner says, will fill our souls, not only with love, but also and above all with humility. For by walking this path, we will begin to understand the enormity of the task of humanity, now and into the future: namely, "that human beings, as they go from incarnation to incarnation, must come more and more deeply to the understanding of what Christ really is."

To know Christ is always the most intimate, personal matter. It is the most inner affair and it occurs only gradually. Christ must be born in one's heart. That is why, as Christ becomes truly known, institutional Churches will wane and lose their purpose. For each individual must make the relationship, so as to give birth to Christ within; which means that the relationship is direct and requires no mediation. This path is contained in a verse of Angelus Silesius, much loved by Steiner:

> If Christ be born in Bethlehem a thousand times
> And not in you, you remain in eternal perdition.

INNER READING
AND
INNER HEARING

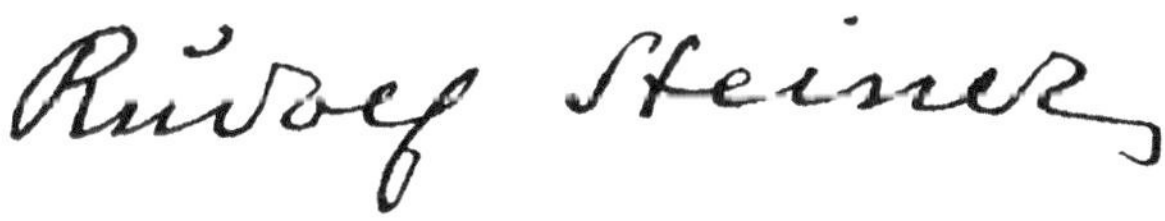

PART I

INNER READING AND INNER HEARING

1

The Human Being in Relationship to the World

DORNACH, OCTOBER 3, 1914

You should not expect that these four lectures will be a substitute for what was intended for Munich.† I will try to give a sketch here of something of what the content the Munich lectures should have been, but the most important and essential things that should have been said there must be held for less turbulent times. I am amazed that some people think that the strenuous effort required to speak about spiritual-scientific subjects of the highest importance (which is indeed what should have happened in Munich) could be mustered in times like the present. The time will come when people will understand that it is just not possible to speak the highest truths into the storm.

When karma permits, I will in the future give a cycle of lectures on the substance of my theme that will take the place of the Munich lectures. However, since the wish has been expressed to hear something on this theme anyway, I want to accommodate that as far as possible over the coming days.

The essentials of spiritual science have been won basically through inner reading and inner hearing. And when spiritual researchers speak about the nature of *inner reading* and *inner hearing*, we hear something about the methods by which they come to their results. Truly, the most absurd opinions one could possibly conceive prevail today regarding how spiritual-scientific results are obtained.

As an introduction before I move on to my main topic, I want to mention a triviality—trivial in relation to what our spiritual movement wants to be. Some professor, a present-day research scientist, wrote a review of my book *Theosophy*.† The review came out several years ago, and its author was evidently most annoyed by what my book says about the human aura, thought forms, and the like. Among many things I don't care to mention now is one that is perfectly understandable from the point of view of a research scientist, such a typical modern thinker. The review says that if one believes there really is something to this stuff about the aura and thought forms, then some of the people who can see auras and thought forms should subject themselves to an experiment in which they would be brought together with a group of people who have certain thoughts, feelings, and sensations within themselves. Then the seers should be asked, "What do you see about the people standing or sitting there in front of you?" And, in the opinion of the writer of this review, if these seers say what the people being observed subsequently confirm that they have truly thought and felt, and if in addition the seers agree with one another in their statements, then one can really believe them.

Nothing is more natural, more self-evident than this objection. One could almost say that a thinker familiar with the natural science of the present day must raise it, because it would have to appear to be the most rational thing that could be said. However, one thing remains true. The man in question must have read the book before he wrote the review. One must assume this, since the review gives the impression of honesty. But it is impossible that he read it. As self-evident and natural as it is that one will make this objection as long as one does not know the truths contained in the book, it should be equally self-evident that one who has read the book with understanding will not make such an objection. With these words I am saying something dreadful for all normal scientific thinkers of today, because that is incomprehensible for them; they cannot understand it at all. Among the many things in the book is the following: if seers really want to look into the spiritual world and see the truth, they must above all first practice a self-education that enables them to immerse themselves in things in an utterly selfless manner, so that they can silence their own desires when they present themselves to the spiritual world. But if five or six people come together to make an experiment according to scientific method, as is demanded in the review, they sit down with the desire to arrive at some results according to very particular methods demanded by natural science. There everything is done according to wishes and desires, as in ordinary life—which is precisely what should be overcome. It is obvious that every perception of the spiritual world would be extinguished in such an experiment made entirely according to the ordinary thinking of the physical plane. These thoughts of the physical plane, along with all their wishes and desires, must be overcome.

One can reply to such objections in only a positive way. Such an experiment could certainly be arranged, but it should not be arranged according to the methods of the physical plane; rather it should be arranged according to the methods of the spiritual world. How should it take place? Above all the intentions should lie in the spiritual world and not originate in the head of some curious professor. If the intention is that people who are seers on the physical plane should experience something of the thoughts and feelings of other human beings, that intention should originate in the spiritual world. And it should come from the spiritual world, through karma, that a handful of people should be brought together—through the dispensation of fate, not through the methods of a professor. On the other side, also the seers must be brought together by destiny. Then the experiment would be arranged by the spiritual world, and the seers would be able to reveal what lives in individual people as feelings, etc. If the experiment were arranged in this way it would most definitely succeed: it will always succeed if so arranged.

One who truly reads *Theosophy* with understanding will know what I have just said, but will recognize as a self-evident truth of the spiritual world that an experiment of this sort is not possible in our time. One must take that into account. And because I learned from the above-mentioned review that people are not in a position to read the book in such a way as to find this thought for themselves, I have spelled out what I have just said word for word in a note in the sixth edition,[†] the galleys of which lie before me. One of the most essential conditions of a book that has grown out of spiritual science is that one assimilates more than its content—that is the very least of it. In addition, in assimilating the book, one in a certain way alters how one thinks and feels and senses things; one progresses in relation to the standards and criteria otherwise used in the ordinary world. The difficulty confronting the understanding of spiritual-scientific works even today is that people read them like other writings and believe they can absorb the content in the same way as in other writings; whereas in fact something in themselves must be transformed if they have understood a true esoteric book really thoroughly.

Hence it is understandable that most people in our time reject real esoteric books. For what must take place in people who read such a book in the present day? These people who approach the book are obviously very clever, as are all people these days. They know that they can judge the content of the book, that there cannot possibly be a better judge of the book. They know that up front. And after reading it should they be able to judge things differently? They obviously cannot. They are indeed clever and have the best manner of forming judgments. They will not submit to changing something in their judging. Therefore they will get no feeling for the goals, the intentions of the book. At best they can conclude that they have learned absolutely nothing from the book, and that it's all merely a game of words and concepts. That is entirely obvious, and so must it be if one does not keep the inner nerve of spiritual science in view, that in whatever way, no matter how small, one will arrive at a different manner of feeling and judgment regarding the world by reading a true spiritual-scientific book.

One point should be considered if the words "esoteric reading" and "esoteric hearing" are to have any meaning at all. We must first to a certain degree say goodbye to the ordinary manner of judgment in relation to the physical plane. I have emphasized more than once that although one is acquiring a new form of judging, thinking, and feeling for the spiritual world, obviously one must remain a rational person and hold on to a common sense judgment for the events and entities of the physical plane. But for the higher worlds something is necessary that is not valid for the physical plane. I will begin with a topic familiar to you.

We are accustomed to relating to the things and entities of the physical plane through our thinking, feeling, and willing. When we think and form concepts, we acquire definitions and concepts of the things and entities of the physical world and the processes occurring there. In that way we make that which, in our opinion, exists in space and takes place in time into our mental property, so to speak. We learn to know about things through our thinking and forming of concepts. It is the same with feeling. We approach any sort of thing, for example a rose. We are cheered by the rose, and through our feeling transfer something in the outside world into our own soul. In this way we make something that comes from the rose and affects us into the property of our own soul. In the case of willing, we incorporate into the outside world something that lies in our intentions.

When we consider our manner of being on the physical plane we see only relationships between ourselves and the outside world. Everything we apply in thinking, feeling, and willing, everything we do when we engage the exterior world for ordinary physical, bodily matters, is of no use to us—in the form in which it is carried out on the physical plane—in knowing something of the higher world in some way. Rather everything that is useful to us, in knowing something about the physical world—the ways of feeling and the ways of forming concepts so as to know about the physical world—can serve only as preparation for spiritual-scientific research.

Take note: In the physical world what we do when we think, feel, and will serves us directly in knowing something of that world or in doing something in it, but for the higher worlds everything that serves us so directly in the physical world is only a preparation. What we are capable of thinking about the physical world, no matter how acutely we think, gives us no knowledge about the higher worlds. Through thinking, however, our soul is prepared, or brought up, so to speak, in such a way that it gradually becomes capable of penetrating into the spiritual world in the right way. What we can will and feel about the physical world is useful merely for the self-education of the soul, as preparation for its penetration into the spiritual worlds.

To make myself clear, let me put it this way: Scholarly researchers learn through their scientific method something about the external world and then are accustomed to say that they know this or that about the external word. This method of researching, of thinking, is of no use in entering the spiritual world; its only significance is as an exercise for the soul forces. Through thinking and pursuing research the soul becomes more capable of living within itself and activating its power, and only this is effective for penetrating the higher worlds. The activities normally carried out in the physical world are applicable for the spiritual researcher only as a cultivation of the soul.

I want to choose one more comparison to make the matter clearer. Let us assume that a man is a carpenter. He has learned carpentry and intends to make this or that object. Through daily activity as a carpenter he makes this or that, year after year. That is the nature of his job. However, things are being made that are useful not just for the physical plane; something else appears as an extra. He becomes more dexterous; his use of his hands becomes more nimble; and as he becomes more skillful and nimble he acquires something for his own organism, a corollary. It is the same with intellectual activities. Take, for example, a botanist. If I am active as a botanist and make amazing efforts decade after decade in the field of botany, that is a fine thing on the physical plane. However, all this effort has a secondary effect: I become more agile in thinking; my thinking becomes, so to speak, trained. (Do not take the expression in the ordinary, trivial sense of the word.) Spiritual researchers must enter into this training and use what is used in ordinary life in the service of external knowledge to make the intellectual powers more agile, more supple. For when, instead of applying these powers to usefulness and advantage in the physical world, we use them in the service of self-education, as happens in meditation, concentration, and the exercises received, then we are preparing ourselves to penetrate into the spiritual world. The phrase "we are preparing ourselves" is exceptionally important, for basically we can do absolutely nothing else than prepare ourselves to penetrate into the spiritual world; the rest is a matter for the spiritual world, which must then meet us halfway. It does not, however, meet us halfway when we are only as we ordinarily are on the physical plane.

Only if we have transformed our soul forces in the manner described can we hope for the spiritual world to come to meet us. It cannot be like research in the physical world, where one approaches things so easily. We can only prepare ourselves, so that when the things of the spiritual world approach us they do not escape our notice, but rather really make an impression on us.

Therefore, we must say that all we can do for researching the spiritual world is to prepare ourselves worthily, so that when karma is willing for it to meet us, we are not blind and deaf to it. We *can* prepare ourselves, but encountering the spiritual world is an act of grace on its part and must be understood as such. Hence the answer to the question of how we can succeed in penetrating the spiritual world is that we must prepare ourselves with everything that makes our thinking and feeling more supple, more agile; whatever trains our thinking, so to speak, whatever makes our feeling, our sensing finer, more devoted. And then wait, wait, wait! That is the golden word: be able to wait in quietness of soul. The spiritual world does not allow itself to be attained in any way other than by making oneself worthy of it and then developing an expectant mood in peacefulness of soul. It depends on that. An expectant mood is the essential. We earn the spiritual world for ourselves when we make ourselves ready for it in the way I have described many times in my books. But then we must also acquire absolute peacefulness of soul, the only thing that makes it possible for the spiritual world to approach us.

Once in my lectures I used the following image. In the physical world if we wish to get a look at anything, we go to it. Anyone wishing to see Rome must travel to Rome. That is perfectly natural in the physical world, because Rome is not going to come to us. In the spiritual world it is exactly the opposite. We can do nothing except prepare ourselves through the methods described to receive the spiritual world in a worthy manner. Peacefulness of soul, persistence in our position—then it will come to us. We must wait for it in peacefulness of soul. That is what is important in the matter. Where is what will come to us? Where is it? I have already spoken often on that subject also and will mention it only by way of introduction so that we will have a good foundation to build on over the coming days.

Since you know our anthroposophical literature, I will ask the question in this way: Where are the beings of the elemental world; where are the beings of the spiritual world; where are the beings of the higher hierarchies? They are right where we are. They are all around us—where the table and the chairs are, where you yourselves are. They are everywhere all around us, but they are so thin and evanescent compared to the relationships and processes of the things of the external world that they escape our attention. We continually go straight through the spiritual world and do not see it; we are inattentive to the spiritual world because our constitution is not prepared for it. Moreover, if we have the opportunity to penetrate that world, as is the case at night in sleep, then our consciousness proves too weak, too dull, to perceive the spiritual beings around us. We human beings are in the spiritual world—in this fine, fluctuating world—from the onset of sleep until awakening, but we do not perceive it because our consciousness is too dull to perceive it.

What must happen for us to learn to perceive this world in which we have always been living? To understand what should happen we need to discuss several important points. Above all, we must not lose sight of something I have attempted to present more exactly for the general public in the final chapter of my book *The Riddles of Philosophy*.† I want to see whether people who are not a part of the Anthroposophical stream can understand it.

How does external perception actually take place? It is true, is it not, that people—especially those who consider themselves to be very clever—usually think that external perception takes place because things are on the outside, and we human beings live inside our skin; these external things make an impression on us, and through that our brain produces an inner image of external objects and forms. Now it is most certainly not like that; the situation is entirely different. In truth, human beings are not at all within their skin with respect to their spirit and soul. When, for example, we see a bouquet of roses, we are in reality inside the bouquet with our "I" and astral body, and our organism is a reflecting device that reflects things back to us. We are in truth always spread out above the horizon we are observing. Moreover, in waking consciousness we exist with a significant part of our "I" and astral body within the physical and etheric bodies as well. Here is what the process is really like, as I have mentioned often in my lectures: Imagine you are walking around in a room with a number of mirrors on the walls. You walk through the space, and where you have no mirror, you do not see yourself. However, as soon as you come to a mirror, you see yourself. In a place without a mirror you don't see yourself; when a mirror is there once again, you see yourself once again. That is also how it is with the human organism. It is not the producer of the things we experience in the soul—it is only a reflecting device. The soul is united with things on the outside, for example here with this bouquet of roses. Whether the soul sees the bouquet consciously or not depends on whether the eye, in connection with the brain device of the soul, reflects what the soul is living with. Moreover, during the night we do not perceive, because, when we sleep, we pull our "I" and astral body out of our physical and etheric bodies, which as a result cease to function as a reflecting device. Going to sleep is like taking away a mirror that was in front of you. As long as you can look into the mirror you have your own face in front of you; take the mirror away and immediately nothing of your face is left there.

With our soul-spiritual nature we are truly within the part of the world we observe, and we see it because our organism reflects it. At night this reflecting device is taken away, and we see nothing more. The part of the world we see is ourselves.

One of the worst things about *maya* is that we believe our spiritual-soul being is within our skin. It is not. In reality we are located in the things we see. If I face other people, I am located within them with my "I" and my astral body. Were I not to place my organism over against them, I would not see them. My organism is responsible for the fact that I see them, but with my "I" and my astral body I am inside them. The failure to recognize this is one of the most disastrous aspects of maya.

In this way we get an idea of the nature of perception and experience on the physical plane. Let us now look at the spiritual world, which I have said is so fleeting, so highly fluctuating and mobile in comparison with the processes and things of the physical world. We also live within that world, but we do not experience it in the same way as the coarse things of the physical world, because it is too fine. If we want to experience this fluctuating fineness, we first have to properly tone down our ordinary "I," the bearer of our individuality, our *self-ness.* We do this through a correct meditation. What does this meditation consist of? We take up any subject of thought and give ourselves entirely over to it. We forget ourselves and live in this thought, while we suppress the self-ness of our ordinary daytime consciousness. We exclude everything connected with the self-ness of daytime consciousness. And since we as earthly human beings are accustomed to applying self-ness to the physical plane, we first have to suppress all self-ness. Instead of living in the physical and etheric bodies, we gradually succeed through this suppression of self-ness in living in the astral body alone.

Please note that what matters is that when we meditate, concentrate, the first goal is always to strive not to live in self-ness—it may not provide physical experiences—but to endeavor to force [our consciousness] down into the astral body. When it is in the astral body, it is not reflected in the physical body. When you see the bouquet, you are in truth inside the bouquet. The physical body is a reflective device; you see the bouquet because the physical body reflects it for you. When you suppress the "I" with its self-ness, you will be in the astral body. The astral body is now so delicate that you can consciously perceive the fine, fluctuating things outside in the external world. But in order really to perceive them, they must first be reflected.

Here is something you must consider. Many of you are loyally and truly devoted to meditation, through which you succeed in suppressing ordinary self-ness and begin to experience in the astral body. However, reflection must join this experiencing before you can perceive consciously in the astral body. Many of you have already gone so far in meditation that you experience in the astral body. Now it is a matter of the reflection. And just as in ordinary life we receive experiences mirrored by the physical body, so, when we want to perceive in the spiritual world, must the experiences of the astral body be reflected by the etheric body.

But what happens when a person's experiences in the astral body are in fact reflected in the etheric body? Something happens then that is totally different from seeing in the physical world. In the spiritual world one does not have the easy time of it that one has in the physical world. A bouquet standing here before me is an object contained within itself. I can take pleasure in it. I can take it home with me, put it in a vase there, and so forth. It is not at all like that with what one encounters as astral experiences, reflected through the etheric body. Everything there is living and weaving. Nothing is at rest, even for a moment. But how a thing appears when reflected is not at all the thing in question. In the case of this bouquet it is a matter of what it is. I take the bouquet, and then I have it. When something is reflected to me through my etheric body, I cannot just take it as it is and be satisfied with it. It simply is not at all what it seems.

I have often used a comparison for this fact as well. If strokes are made here, and I could not read [the letters BAU are written on the blackboard], I would say I see lines that are fitted together in a particular pattern. I cannot take what is on the blackboard home with me as I can the bouquet. In that case, I would have nothing. And even when I can read what is on the blackboard—BAU [building]—I still do not have the thing in question. The thing in question for me is the building outside.† That is what I express through these lines and signs: building. Even when I read the sign, I do not have the thing in question. I only read the signs; I do not have the building itself. In ordinary reading I do not have the thing in question in front of me; rather I have only the sign for it.

That is how I should understand what I experience in the astral body and then receive reflected in the etheric body. I comprehend it correctly only as a sign that stands for something else. To contemplate what is reflected in my etheric body from my astral body does not suffice any more than in the case of the lines here in BAU. It is a question of what the signs mean. I must first learn to read them. In the same way, I must first learn to read what I perceive in the spiritual world. What are reflected in my etheric body are the signs for the truth. That means I must learn to read in the spiritual world. The only way we can experience anything from the spiritual world is to understand that we must take what it offers us as letters and words, which we must learn to read. That is it. And not to learn, to believe that we can spare ourselves learning to read the esoteric script, would be just as clever as someone taking a book and saying, "There are fools who say that something is expressed in this book. I thumb from page to page in it and see only pretty letters." Those who cannot read the letters absorb only what they see and are unconcerned about what is expressed.

One who does not pay attention to what I have just said comes to an entirely unbalanced relation to the spiritual world. There it is a matter of learning to interpret and read what one perceives. We shall learn in the following lectures how this interpretation and reading is meant.

Now I can say that I have clarified, at least in an introductory manner, the preliminary concept of esoteric reading. It occurs when we experience ourselves in the astral body as we otherwise do in the "I" in the physical world, so that the experiences of the astral body are reflected in the etheric body, rather than the experiences of the ego in the physical body.

We must consider something else. We are not only, as I have said today, in outside things; in a waking state we send something of the "I" into the physical body, drawing it out of the physical body again only during the night, in sleep. This means that in order to perceive in the physical world we must be able to dive into our physical body with the "I." In order to perceive in the spiritual world, to read the spiritual world, we learn first that we can experience things in our astral body and that we can receive the reflections of things we experience in the astral body in the etheric body.

Now, we must ascend to the point of being able to dive down into the etheric body, just as we dive into the physical body when we awaken. Pay attention to what follows. It is necessary to dive down into the etheric body with the astral body when we learn to read in the spiritual world. Just as we dive down into the physical body when we awaken, so must we, without diving down into the physical body, dive down into the etheric body. Esotericists, rightly so, call this diving down into the etheric body a fall into the abyss. It is necessary that one is not stupefied during this fall into the abyss, that one presses down with one's consciousness and finds oneself during the fall. For this diving down into the etheric body does not proceed as comfortably as diving down into the physical body. It is in fact something like a mighty plunge into the abyss, for one is now split into three parts, as I have described it in my book *How to Know Higher Worlds.*† One is split apart, divided, dissolved into a tripartite entity. You cannot consciously descend into the etheric body without being divided in the way indicated.

When we sleep, we are outside the physical and etheric bodies with our "I" and astral body, and our consciousness is too dull to perceive the spiritual world. When we dive down into the physical body, which reflects the physical world to us so that we perceive that world, that is also a kind of falling into the abyss, only it is made so comfortable for us that we do not feel it as a shock. When we progress through our exercises to the condition in which we can perceive something in the spiritual world, we learn to "read." That is comparable to a sleeping state that has become conscious. We also learn to recognize the falling into the abyss, the splintering into three parts, when we are submerged in our etheric body. If we maintain our consciousness, we are able to dive down into things and processes in the spiritual world that are outside us.

When we live in the astral body and receive things as reflections in the etheric body, we learn to read, as when we read a book. As soon as we are submerged in the etheric body, we splinter ourselves into three parts. And we can send out the three parts, which can then wander about consciously in the spiritual world. In their wandering about there, they experience what we call "esoteric hearing." Esoteric hearing begins as soon as we have plunged into our own etheric body. Now we really penetrate into things. Now we notice that we can experience what we have previously learned to read.

Let us repeat: Through esoteric exercises we are enabled to suppress our self to the point that we can learn to live consciously in the astral body. Then, gradually, the processes and entities of the spiritual world are reflected by the etheric body. If we are able to interpret this reflected world in the right way, as we shall hear in the following lectures, then we have learned the art of esoteric reading. If we progress and are able to read not only from outside the etheric body, but dive down to awaken in the etheric body, we send the three parts from us out into the world and hear the processes in their inner nature and activity. At this stage we *hear* them.

We can gradually develop the faculty of esoteric reading and esoteric hearing in such a way that through it we bring about something very particular. We can actually penetrate the reality of things. For what occurs on the physical plane is not reality, truly it is not. A simple deliberating can show us everywhere that what we experience in our immediate surroundings is not reality, that we interpret everything incorrectly.

Someone once said to me on the banks of the Rhine, "That is the ancient Rhine." That is certainly a very beautiful, deeply felt thing to say. But what is actually ancient about the Rhine? The water that one sees flow by? Certainly not. It is constantly flowing and in the next moment is no longer there. The ancient thing could at best be the channel the water has carved in the soil. However, that is not what one means when one says "the ancient Rhine." What is it really that we denote with the expression "ancient Rhine"? We do not say about the sea, that it is an "ancient sea"; and in the sea there are also channels dug out by the water, and likewise in the sea there are currents. When the Gulf Stream flows through the ocean, not only is the water changed every moment, but also the channels are different.

What, then, in the physical world is permanent? Nothing, absolutely nothing. That is true of the entire physical world. Your own organism is constantly in flux: eight years ago you did not have the flesh and blood you have today. Nothing in the physical is permanent. Everything is flowing, and what we refer to with the word, we do not have before us.

To speak of the "ancient Rhine" only makes sense when we mean what is permanent in it: the elemental beings who actually live in the Rhine, the river god Rhine, a spiritual being who is ancient. Only then have we said something with any meaning. We must mean something spiritual with the expression "ancient Rhine," or we speak thoughtlessly. It is profoundly true that we only come to true realities when we hold fast to the spiritual worlds. Only then do we penetrate the true realities. The fact and the means of our entry we shall see tomorrow and the next day, when we discuss esoteric reading and hearing in detail, as far as is possible.

2

Identification with the Signs and Spiritual Realities of the Imaginative World

DORNACH, OCTOBER 4, 1914

We want now to take another close look at what I said yesterday about the true relationship of human beings to the world. I said it is in fact an instance of maya, a delusion, to assume that we, as soul-spiritual human beings, are within our skin and the things are all around us, and that we take the representations of those things into ourselves, so to speak. In truth, as soul-spiritual human beings we live inside the things, and we would not be able to perceive them if we did not receive our experiences of them as reflections from our organism. And indeed, as we live within the ordinary physical world, things are reflected to us by our physical organism, by its entire system of senses, from its system of thought, its system of feeling, and its system of willing.

Therefore our organism is in truth a mirroring device, and what we experience is not produced in us by our physical organism—an erroneous idea of materialism—but is reflected. Our organism no more produces what we experience in our souls about things than a mirror produces what we see in the mirror. Materialists who assert that the brain or another organ produces our soul experiences are saying the same thing as those who would assert that the image they see of their own face in the mirror does not belong to them, but is instead produced by the mirror.

The truth of the matter must be experienced when one attains to inner reading in the manner described yesterday. After we have prepared ourselves, we experience the more evanescent (that is, in regard to the physical being), fluctuating beings and occurrences of the spiritual world. We see them inasmuch as we experience them in our astral body, reflected by our etheric body, and we experience these reflections as images. I said yesterday that in general we can regard the images experienced in this way only as signs of spiritual reality. And I attempted to make clear through a comparison the error people would commit if they regarded as reality what was experienced directly as dream images—though vastly more lively than ordinary dream images. That would be exactly the same as taking the word "BAU" as reality instead of as a sign of a building. We must imagine that when we have attained the condition of receiving those delicately evanescent images of the spiritual world reflected through our etheric body from outside inward, we are so to speak standing before an open book, a book that has been opened for us, which we must first learn to read properly.

That is correct, on the whole. But one thing is much more valid for experiences of the higher worlds than for the experiences of the physical world: everything that is correct is subject to exceptions. And what I have just said is particularly subject to exceptions. You must know this; otherwise you cannot find your way in the spiritual world. What I have said is true in general, but it is subject to exceptions. To what extent it is subject to exceptions, I will explain more concretely.

I begin with a very particular case. Let us assume that someone who has to a certain extent developed clairvoyant powers is eager (let us take a case that is familiar to many people) to call up in the spiritual world a dead person, a person who recently or further in the past has gone through the portal of death and now lives in the spiritual world in that life we have described as the life between death and a new birth. Now, an encounter of this sort depends (as you can already understand from yesterday's lecture) on being blessed by the spiritual world, in order actually to behold the person in question. Normally, mere curiosity will not be satisfied by an enterprise of this sort. Whoever undertakes from the beginning the business of calling up a dead person in the spiritual world merely with the purpose of satisfying curiosity, must either see nothing or be exposed to all sorts of errors. However, let us assume that would not be the case, but that a reason, recognized by the beings of the spiritual world as justified, exists for one to meet this dead person. Assuming that everything is in order, to use a common-place expression, one should to some extent meet the dead person. Now (once again, I am speaking entirely in generalities) it will not happen so easily that the clairvoyant in question transports himself or herself into the spiritual world and then directs his or her wants, desires, or thoughts toward the deceased, in order to be graced to some extent by that person's appearance. If it were undertaken or presupposed that a result of this sort could occur, one would be in error. As a rule something entirely different happens.

Please realize that one can only describe specific cases; that one cannot use general, abstract theories when discussing, as I am now, such a topic about the spiritual world. I can only give an instance, an example.

Let us assume that a seer might have a justified reason to come into contact with a particular dead person and through meditation, through concentration, finds measures to contact this dead person. To describe these measures would lead us too far today, but let us assume that they are the right ones. In that case, if through meditation, concentration, the soul is really in the condition in which the departed can be perceived by the seer, the seer will perhaps then see something that he or she—if not already experienced in this area—could be very easily inclined not to regard as the appearance of the dead person or as something related to the dead person. The seer perhaps sees a world of images spreading out, a living world of images, which are much livelier than the images of ordinary dreams.

I must emphasize this over and over again, because it is usually portrayed erroneously. Ordinary dream images are chimeras, while these images are signs of the higher, spiritual world. You must first learn to understand the world of signs. You experience within yourself moving images, happenings of all sorts, connected with this or that personality. That is what you experience; you can at first discover hardly any resemblance between what you have striven for and the images you then experience. However, one thing appears if you have not taken a false path. Within this animated world of images you will experience something that seems to be the most important point in it. You will think that other images contain something familiar to you; they remind you of all sorts of things, which could possibly be bobbing up from your memory, and although you could never have had precisely these incidents among your recollections, they could still, because they depend on what you have experienced, possibly be the memories of such experiences, which have been invaded by fantasy images.

Particularly here true clairvoyants must be attentive. They must not forget that they are involved with a world of images, which could have constituted itself from their memories. But at a certain point something appears that hides no recollection of this sort. One must distinguish exactly between what could be constituted from our fantasy and what among the images is the one thing around which everything else comes together. You must recognize that it would never have come from memory, also that it could never have entered your field of vision from the dream world. Naturally you have a certain practice in order to distinguish dream images from reality and to observe this distinction precisely. But then you come to the point of recognizing that something is there around which everything else is gathering. Normally (I am trying to speak precisely) the situation is that this one thing in the middle of all others can appear in a certain sense paradoxical, even absurd. The situation is that something remarkable, something very strange, appears in a sequence of images of this sort—which is otherwise so beautiful, so magnificent, so powerful. Now, it will very often happen that this kind of thing flows away again, goes away, so that the seer can more or less get nowhere with it. Then you must of course take up the experiment once again from scratch, and usually those who have a certain practice in the visionary art will once again be successful. They will see such a series of images one after another, perhaps a new series of images of a completely different sort. But once again something will show itself in the midst, which is the same as what one has already seen as the midpoint of a series of images.

To find the right thing amongst the series of images on the first or second attempt, you must have attained a certain degree of seeing. When you have the series of images before you, you must become completely calm and self-aware and really live within the image with your self-consciousness, so that it does not escape like a dream picture. You must confront it just as you do an object in the external world. You must have control of yourself so that you know it is you yourself who perceives, and that the image is over there. You must be able to differentiate yourself from the image and not become absorbed by it.

In order to achieve this, one would do well first to try, while the image is still there, to alter something within it. Let us suppose, for example, that the image is there and that you have successfully distinguished yourself from the image. Then suppose that a certain personality who looks disagreeable, unfriendly, appears in the world of images. Try to capture the feeling of how it would be if you were really nice to this personality, so that it would look at you in a friendlier way after giving you such a dirty look. If you succeed in consciously altering something in the world of images, then you have an easier time establishing your position in relation to that world.

The next step must be (it is difficult to find an expression, for the things of the spiritual world are so different from those of the physical world) that you must really identify yourself with all the images there. You must dive into them, must become one with them. For by becoming one with them, you fulfill an important truth. To use a trivial expression, you must spiritually eat the whole series of images, gulp them right down, assimilate them, identify with them, dive down into the series of images. That means you must know that you have differentiated yourself from the series of images and maintained your position outside them, and now you dive down of your own free will into them, as if you were jumping into water to swim in it.

And now comes the most important thing, for now you experience in your own soul everything that is expressed in this series of images. If, for example, one person fights or wounds another, you experience yourself as the inflictor of the wound and also as the soul that is wounded or attacked. You are everything in these images. You are utterly within them. If you had an image in front of you in which a beheading is depicted, you experience yourself at the same time as the person who is beheaded and the person who does the beheading. That is how you experience yourself within this very fluctuating world of images. You yourself are every image and every movement in it.

The image as such, as an imagination, becomes invisible, but the inner experiences become so much more significant. You now cease to see the image, but you are in the midst of a rich experience in it. If you really succeed in living within the images, then the second act of the whole affair begins. However, it does not necessarily follow immediately.

From this point on, many discouraging things may befall the visionary. It can happen that when you decide to dive down into the image, to swim in it, it takes off like a dream or something you have forgotten. That is entirely possible. Only in the rarest cases will it happen that one immediately has the experience I will now talk about. Most of the time the situation is that the image appears to have totally vanished, like a vanished dream.

Now, as true clairvoyants we must clearly understand that it does not have to be the case that the image has disappeared. It can be that what in the rarest cases happens right after the disappearance of the image does not come until much later. It can come out of day or night experiences, right in the midst of them. For it is very often the case that what you have eaten must first be digested in the soul, which can take a while. However, when it has been sufficiently digested, sufficiently unified with you, then you know that you are in connection with the personality, with the individuality of the dead person, and it sends its own thoughts into you. Now you think the soul experiences of the dead person. You are in connection with that person, who now speaks with you, and you hear.

In truth it is the image you have united with, or the series of images that you have taken up, carry within, and are now one with that really hear the truth and take up the truth. And usually it is the case that this hearing, as spiritual hearing, is no longer tied to images, but is carried by the consciousness that the soul of the visionary has connected with the dead person in question, allowing it to say what is no longer heard with the ear, nor noticed by the physical gaze, but is directly taken up by thought: you know it is not your thought; it is what the dead person is speaking to you.

As you can see, a certain preparation is required to approach a dead individuality, a preparation that can be described as I have just done. If you have reached the stage of hearing the dead person after identifying with the image, then any delusion is impossible. For a delusion could appear only in the same way as a delusion on the physical plane, when you meet a certain person and mistake him for another. Usually you won't do that. You recognize a person on the physical plane through that person him- or herself. When, for example you run into Mr. Low on the physical plane, you do not need to prove to yourself from theoretical principles that it is Mr. Low. The being one meets reveals that. Likewise in the spiritual world you also know that you are facing a being when it speaks to you in an obviously spiritual manner, communicates in a spiritual manner.

What I have just described is the transition from reading an extremely ambiguous sign—not by interpreting it with the intellect, but by taking it within yourself, becoming one with it, devouring it, in a manner of speaking—to spiritual hearing. Through the living process you effect through uniting with the image in your soul, you prepare yourself to really hear the objective being spiritually.

Reading is a living process, a process that is really alive. You must throw your soul into the matter. Something much different is demanded of you than what is demanded on the physical plane. It is most comparable to the situation we would be in on the physical plane if someone gave us a book and demanded that we should eat it in order to read and understand it. If we were set up to digest an *A* in a different way than an *I*, because we had different inner processes in digesting the letters *A* and *I*, this process would be comparable to the spiritual processes described. We do not approach a spiritual process or a spiritual being before we have devoted our entire soul to understanding the being or process in question. We must ourselves become one with the sign or letters of the spiritual world. We must read them and then, while we read them, hear them in spirit.

I said that this is valid in general. One must in fact speak very precisely in the field of spiritual science. I said in general, for there are indeed exceptions. It can, for example, happen that a seer in the condition of spiritual beholding not only experiences a series of images, as I have just described, but really experiences as an image, as an imagination, something that is similar to the dead person in question as he or she was in outward appearance in life. The seer in question can of course know that it is the dead person, but can never know it for certain. It can be right, but it doesn't need to be entirely right. To explain this, I will reach for a comparison. Our ordinary writing, printing or cursive, consists of signs. When I write the word "BAU" [building], the word has no similarity with our building out there. However, it was not always so in the course of the development of writing. If we go back to ancient times, we find pictograms. Back then people made pictures, which were still similar to the objects the pictures were supposed to represent; and from this picture-writing, the first writing in signs and letters developed.

The situation is the same with the relationship between the clairvoyance we strive for with our Rosicrucian method and the atavistic, more or less primitive clairvoyance that can appear in many people through certain preconditions. Just as our writing consisting of signs and letters is something that has evolved, and pictograms are more primitive, clairvoyance in our sense is something that has evolved and the sight that brings the vision to expression in dream images is more primitive. Precisely the evolved clairvoyance will often not be able to behold the vision in an image. The situation for developed clairvoyance will usually be as I have described. However, exceptions do indeed occur, and people without particular development, purely from the resources of their organism, may become clairvoyant and perceive many more images that are similar to spiritual processes than the developed clairvoyant who has first carried out all the procedures I have described. But through primitive clairvoyance they can never get to the point of learning anything with certainty; and even what can be learned with certainty in this manner are only events that depend on earthly life.

Let us say, for example, that someone has died and has left behind a will without being able to tell anyone where the will is deposited. The person dies. A personality with the preconditions of untrained clairvoyance arrives on the scene and possibly, in a trancelike condition of imagination, is brought into relation with the dead person in question. And the untrained seer can then perceive the thoughts of the dead person about where the will was deposited, seeing the image of the place, a cabinet for example. That can happen. But these cases always depend on the external physical plane, on something that happened on the physical plane. The things involved could be more complicated, but they are always dependent on the physical, the earthly plane. One will not get much further in this field of primitive clairvoyance. In order to proceed further and have contact with the spiritual world in a truly clear and certain way, the preparations I have spoken of are indeed necessary.

Now I must tell you something still more precise so that in the following lectures we can go into the particulars of spiritual reading and hearing. I said that what lies behind the maya of outward experience, what is inside things, becomes a truth the moment we enter the spiritual world. It becomes a truth, as I have explained to you in each concrete incidence. It is not enough that we perceive any particular image through clairvoyance, and see the image in front of us as we see entities of the physical world. That is not enough. We must arrive at the point of diving down into the images, of really casting ourselves into them. We must consciously do what we also do in ordinary life, only we do not do it consciously in that case. We must really go into the image. If I perceive a series of images with the midpoint I have described, I must go outside of myself; I must enter into this series of images, must devour them, swallow them up; I must be right in them.

Now, what I have described can appear as a spiritual experience, but we do not yet really understand it. To understand it, we must be able to exercise spiritual self-observation during the process of diving into it. When we dive down into such a series of images, something happens in us that we sense in ourselves. Reflect now on exactly how it is when you first understand your position in relation to imaginative images, and then on how it is when you dive down into the series of images. The feeling is entirely different when we consciously stand before the images than it is when we have dived down into them.

I will try to describe how these two feelings are different. The moment we dive into the images, we know that we have made them disappear because we have identified with them. In that moment we are seized by a feeling of insufficiency concerning ourselves. We become aware—these things are hard to describe—that we are indeed really now only a piece of what we were when we stood in our previous standpoint. We are only a piece of it.

We must of course make this observation often so that we enter entirely into things and achieve the ability to interpret them correctly. It is best to characterize such things through analogies. Let us say it feels as if you had a weight of twelve kilos, which, without anything else happening, suddenly became only a one-kilo weight. You feel as if you are only a twelfth of yourself, and the other eleven twelfths are outside in the world. You can draw a symbol of what has happened to you. You feel yourself somewhere outside in the world, but you do not feel yourself there with your entire being; rather you feel that eleven-twelfths of yourself are out there in the world, that you have been split up. You can express it symbolically by saying that you are at one point on the circle and the other eleven-twelfths are divided up over the rest of the circle. Here you are [*a* on drawing], and there [2, 3, 4, and so forth] are the other eleven-twelfths.

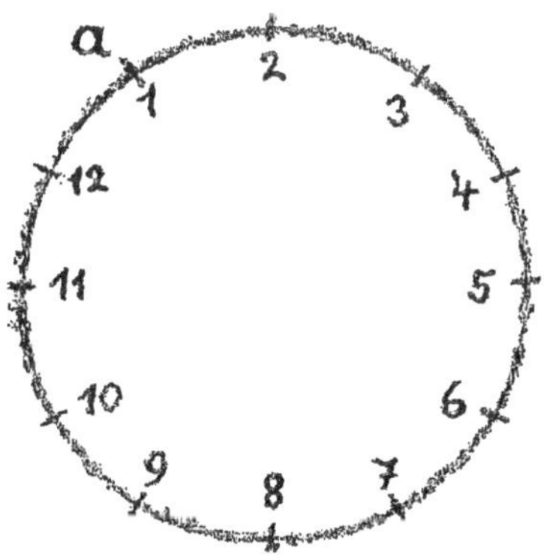

Now it is really quite true that you are out there in the world: you have become a twelfth of yourself and have left the other eleven-twelfths lying in a circle, so to speak.

We can give it a name with an expression from esotericism: You have transformed yourself into the zodiac; you have yourself become the zodiac. And from now on what you hear comes to you from within this zodiac. Therefore, using the earlier example, the dead person speaks to you from within the zodiac.

Consider what is present here in contrast to perception in the physical world. In the physical world we are enclosed in our skin, and things are on the outside; they apparently come into us when we gaze at them. In the case of spiritual perception we stand on the outside, at one point, a twelfth of the horizon, and we gaze inward from there. Now we have the world we are looking at within the zodiac. We are gazing from the outside inward. In ordinary life we look outward from within. And we perceive what we encounter there inside us as a spiritual voice with which the dead person speaks to us, because we become accustomed to listening in different ways, to paying attention in different ways.

I will speak more precisely on this subject, but first I want to explicate it for you through the symbol. We can, for example, get the feeling that we can best perceive what the dead person is saying when we direct our spiritual ear in the direction toward the spiritual number five [see drawing.]

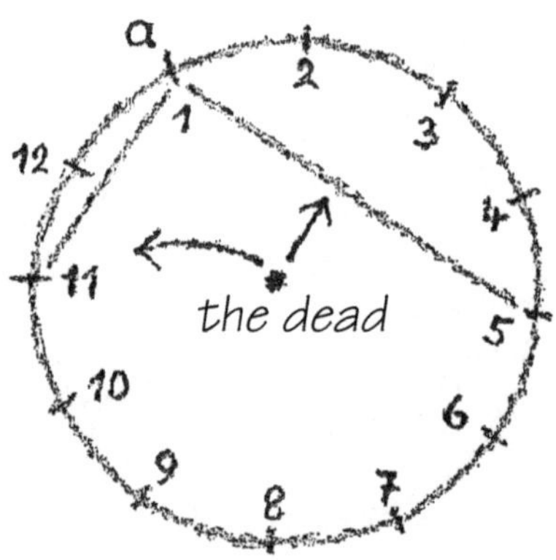

Now the entity stops speaking at that point, but we hear it when we direct our spiritual ear to another point [11]. We learn gradually to recognize that we must distinguish within the circle seven voices, which are so different that we perceive them in a different way according to whether they are heard from one or another point. Everything we perceive speaks as if it were coming from seven voices within the circle.

We can also express it this way: We have gone into the periphery of the world. What we are to perceive is within this periphery. We must learn to feel ourselves as a part of the periphery and must, I will say, in cosmic humbleness, not make any demand to be anything other than a twelfth of the periphery. However, we must ask the other eleven-twelfths for aid and must assume that they are outside of us ourselves. We must attempt to acquire a power of discernment for what speaks to us there. We must discern how everything a cosmic being can say to us can vary in the most differing ways.

Here we once again clarify the subject through a comparison. We can in fact call what speaks to us within this circle, *spiritual vowels*. And everything we ourselves are in the circumference of the circle, and what lies in the circumference, are *spiritual consonants*. Consonants and vowels work together. Consonants remain still because we have poured out our own being into the universe. And vowels, because they move about inside, thereby bring to expression what needs to be said.

Once again I come back to our example of seeking to meet with a dead person. I get to the point that a series of images appears, and in the middle of this series is something that appears to me to be paradoxical, something that seems absurd. I understand perfectly well that it is something I could not have received from the sources of the inner being of my soul. I get to the point of diving down to become one with the series of images. While I am diving down into the series, I am in this particular point [point *a* on drawing], and all around eleven-twelfths of my being have released themselves.

For that reason I said (remember that one must speak precisely when speaking of esoteric things) that the series of images belongs to us. We have nothing inside us other than the "enjoyed" series of images; it stands there in the one-twelfth (see drawing on the following page). The rest, which cannot become one with this series of images, distributes itself outside in the periphery. And then we can

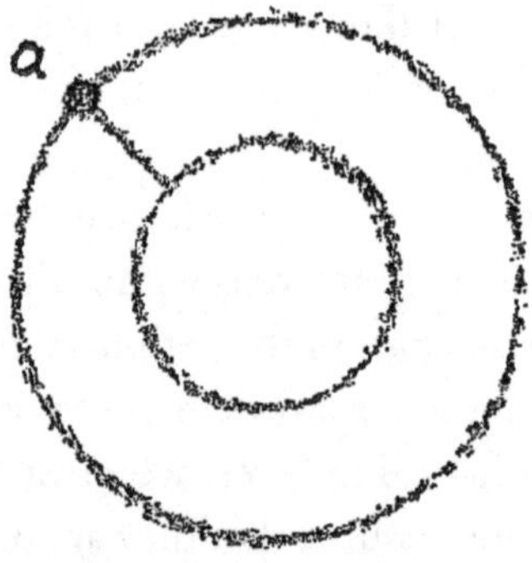

succeed, sooner or later, in receiving in truth the spiritual voice, the communication of the dead. Then we actually hear the dead person speaking from the periphery we have formed around what we wish to connect with.

What have we done, really? We have gone outside ourselves and have become one with the world, but only with one part of the world. We have grasped what we wish to perceive with all our being. We have, so to speak, formed a spiritual aura around the dead person. We cannot form it completely, however; we can stand only at one point and must form the aura out of what we are not.

We can say that we perceive a series of images. First we stand outside the series; then we dive down into it. In that process, we form, with what we have devoted, sacrificed, a world sphere around what we wish to perceive. This world sphere contains within itself, like seven planets, the vowel system through which the being in question can speak with us when we ourselves, through the twelvefold nature of our being, form the system of consonants.

We can only come into rapport with a being of the spiritual world by enclosing it, enclosing it in such a way that this enclosing forms the cosmic consonants; the being itself can then address us in the cosmic vowels. And when the cosmic vowel system can work together with the cosmic consonant system that we ourselves have formed, then reading and hearing work together. Then we penetrate into a particular region of the spiritual world.

I ask you now not to let yourself be led, by what I have just said, to the erroneous conclusion that what I have described relates in any way to the physical zodiac or the seven planets. That is not the case; it wasn't meant that way. Rather it is true that during each time, we form, so to speak, a world sphere in the twelvefold part around the particular being we wish to perceive. We form everywhere a world for ourselves.

It is indeed true that if we wish to know something completely on the physical plane, we must look at it from many sides, from many points of view; we must go all around it. In the spiritual world, it must become for us a reality that we do not go around it with our whole being; rather we must divide up our being, so that we create a periphery around what we wish to perceive. Every time a real spiritual perception occurs, we have created such a spiritual periphery. And only because the divine beings we have come to know in the higher hierarchies have done this macrocosmically, has the zodiac appeared before us.

Suppose now that what I have described has occurred, that communication with the dead has taken place, and imagine that such a communication could be in a particular moment—now, let us say—kept and hardened. This hardening would represent a human being, a spiritual human being obviously, divided up into twelve parts, twelve fixed stars. If what has been perceived were kept in a fixed form, it would represent a planetary system. Because the gods did this with an especially great plan, our universe came into being. While we create something transitory in each individual act of clairvoyance, our entire universe is the fixed and retained clairvoyance of the gods, of the higher hierarchies. For this reason also, we can only know this world when we know it in its spiritual foundations.

The physical is something that is not at all real, as unreal as the flowing water of the Rhine I gave as an example yesterday. Only the spiritual is real. We must become acquainted in reality with the solar system by deciphering in spiritual reading and hearing what lies behind it. In many respects we have already done that.† Tomorrow we will speak about what is yet to be said concerning this.

3

The Vowels and Consonants of the Spiritual World

DORNACH, OCTOBER 5, 1914

FROM the considerations we developed yesterday and the day before, you will have realized that esoteric reading and esoteric hearing consist in experiences of the human soul. I have used various analogies to present how we must first become one with the signs that offer themselves to the seer in the imagination, and then, obviously, with what meaning these signs convey about spiritual realities.

I want to give you first a more precise idea, as far as possible in these few lectures, of what is necessary to rise from unordered clairvoyance to disciplined, real clairvoyance that we can actually call esoteric reading and esoteric hearing. The first topic I will discuss could be called the vowel system of the spiritual world. (It is of course expressed fundamentally by analogy.) How one learns to hear and read the vowels of the spiritual world is obviously a much more inward process than are any processes of ordinary life, and only through many circumlocutions will we be able to approach what we could call the experience of the vowels, the vowels of the cosmos. From what I alluded to yesterday you will have understood that one can speak of seven such vowels; for we can symbolically establish a parallel with the planetary system.

Now let us return once again to what I mentioned yesterday as an example: the seeking of one who is dead. I started with that and attempted thereby to explicate the kind of experiences through which we gradually grow into the experience of the spiritual world. We have heard that we, through the different preparations the visionary must first work through, see a series of images. We actually stand in relation to these things fundamentally as one would toward the things in the outside world. We also stand in relation to a dream image in the same way as to the things of the outside world. Only gradually do we succeed in getting to the point, as we have seen, where we can identify ourselves with the images—devour them, so to speak—where we become one with the images and live entirely within them.

However, we must keep firmly in mind that when these images finally lead us to finding the dead person or some other event or being in the spiritual world, they are the signs of spiritual realities. As images they are in fact themselves realities; by themselves they express a spiritual reality.

They are there, these images. The question must now arise: Are these images only there when the seer prepares appropriately and gets to the point of seeing them? They are not there only then, and this is very important to keep in mind. Assume that you are standing or sitting in some place and are sufficiently prepared to see something. A series of images, so wavering, so ephemeral, appears before your soul. Now, suppose that instead of a seer, another person arrives at seeing this series of images, someone who hasn't a trace of the seer's gift and sees only ordinary images from the physical world in the surroundings. Are these images then not there? They are always there. They are rightly and properly always there.

Expressed in another way, as I did in my discussion the day before yesterday: we are indeed inside the bouquet; our perception of it rests on the reflection through our own organism. The moment prepared seers get to the point of having a related spiritual being in their imagination before their soul, they are also inside it. Through the subsequent procedure of identifying themselves with it, they accomplish only a process of consciousness; in truth they are inside the being. But not only seers are inside it: any time individuals encounter an object with ordinary physical eyes and physical imagination, they are not only within the physical object—which indeed, as we have seen, is nothing other than an illusion—but are also inside the spiritual being. We are always inside spiritual beings that are not physically incarnated. Therefore, we are always inside the images seen, in part, by seers. The images are also constantly in our surroundings, and we are always inside them. They remain imperceptible, invisible, because human powers of perception are too dull and too coarse to perceive these subtle weaving beings and formations with their ordinary coarse senses.

That is expressed abstractly. We can come up with still another question: Why can't we perceive what is flowing about in the world, within which we in fact exist? Why is that? We first learn this when we begin to identify ourselves with the imaginations, when we really carry out the process I discussed yesterday. Then we learn why we human beings cannot be conscious within the spiritual world, which is nonetheless all around us. How does one learn it?

Let it be said once more: a series of images stands before the soul. We try to identify ourselves with it, to digest it, so to speak; we unite with the series of images and are inside it at this stage. In this moment we know the answer to the question about why we must in fact remain outside our body; why we must, so to speak, go outside our body and identify ourselves with the series of images on the outside if we wish to perceive it, and why we can only receive the images, as we have seen, reflected from our own etheric body. We learn why it is necessary, why it is so arranged.

Through what we experience with these images when we have identified ourselves with them, we know the following directly: if, after identifying ourselves completely with the series of images, we were to go back into the physical body, if we did not remain outside and wait until the etheric body reflects the essence of the images, we would carry everything we have become one with into our physical body, into the space enclosed by the skin—and we would immediately destroy the physical body to the point that it would be ripe for death. It would immediately be the seed of death in the physical body. When death does make its entrance in earthly existence, the soul has reached the point that it can identify itself with what in the normal course of life lives outside as imagination. Then death really does enter.

So you see, we can take seriously in the deepest possible way something that permeates all esoteric considerations like a powerful motto. It is the statement made by all those who have become esotericists in the true sense of the word: The moment one arrives at true clairvoyance, the experience is that of standing in the company of death. One reaches the portal of death. I have often stressed this from other points of view: One learns to recognize what it is like for a person who steps through the portal of death. One cannot arrive at clairvoyance without going through this serious, powerful moment, which esotericists designate as standing before the portal of death.

But we learn something else as well. I have already alluded to it once in a series of lectures held in Munich,† but from another point of view. We learn to pose from then on, in deepest seriousness, a vital question of spiritual science. We learn to ask: How is it really with us human beings since we still fundamentally live constantly in a fluctuating web of spiritual entities that we cannot bring into our physical bodies without bringing in the seed of death? Outside, we are always surrounded by imaginations, we are right in the middle of a sphere of imaginations—but they must not come inside us. What then comes into us from these imaginations? Shadowy images, reflections, mirror images, as our thought, as our ideas. On the outside are the full-blooded, real imaginations. They reflect themselves in us; we experience them in the diluted, shadowy form of our thoughts and ideas. If we were to bring them into us in their full-bloodedness instead of merely bringing them to reflection, we would stand in every moment before the danger of death.

What is really going on in this? Nothing less is going on than that we are protected by the world order from experiencing the spiritual entities and processes surrounding us in their full-blooded state. We are protected because in our ordinary, everyday consciousness only shadows of these full-blooded spiritual entities touch us. And yet, a great many of these imaginations belong to us, belong to the powers that are creatively active in us. In this world of imaginations the creative forces live in us. We may not experience them in their original form, but only in the shadowy form in which they are in us as thoughts. That can only be so because someone takes away, in ordinary experience, this experience of the imaginations that belong to our thoughts. But they must be experienced. Because we cannot experience them, they must be experienced by stronger beings than we are, by beings that can support them in their spiritual and soul organism without coming into mortal peril. While we think, while we live with our soul, we must be continuously ruled by a being that takes away from us the imaginations lying at the foundations of our thoughts and ideas. If you have any thought, anything at all that you experience in your soul, a world of imaginations outside corresponds to that experience. And a being must have control over you that protects you, looks out for you, and watches over you—a being that takes away from you what you cannot accomplish.

Now we are at a place where we can speak in a more real sense than has hitherto been possible about the entities of the next higher hierarchy, about the angels. Now these beings are within our grasp. We see how they must watch over and protect what we ourselves cannot accomplish. However it can happen, and for seers it must happen, that they perceive what I have just said much more clearly. That is what happens when they progress one level further in their visionary powers.

We mentioned yesterday what leads to our identifying with the imagination: the series of images that appears before us. This identifying is experienced in such a way that we digest the imaginations, which exist outside us, but we experience ourselves in them; we are one with them. But the matter can go even further. I will begin first with the description of the subjective experience. I said yesterday that we arrive at it, as I have described over and over again, when we immerse ourselves in meditation, in concentration. There we get to the point of experiencing a series of images with which we can identify ourselves. I also said yesterday that when one has called up such a series of images through mediation and concentration, and has tried to get into them, then esoteric reading and hearing, the real perception of the spiritual essence of the dead person one seeks, do not necessarily arise immediately. The process may break off just as a process in a dream breaks off, and whatever should appear as a consequence can appear later.

However, if we progress further, if we have the necessary patience and endurance to progress ever further in esoteric development through meditation and concentration, then we experience the process in yet another way. We can experience it in the following manner: We set before us the task of observing a being, a process in the spiritual world. We establish ourselves in meditation, in concentration, thereby drawing ourselves out of the physical body. We then pass into the condition where the content of the soul, which we ourselves have called up through meditation, ebbs away. We sense the transition and notice that it is growing dark, in a way. What we have called up in our soul ebbs away and there emerges a series of images that are much livelier than those in dreams.

Now we are consciously in the presence of the series of images, and when we know we are in its presence, we dive consciously into them. And again a moment may come when we know that we have identified ourselves with the series of images; we have become one with it, we are within it. However, we no longer feel ourselves; we feel as if we were going under in the universe, the cosmos, and as if we were in general nothing within it. We have identified ourselves with the series of images, have totally dissolved them, and have received nothing in their place. However, through the practice of meditation we must acquire the strength not to quail, not to despair, not to believe that we are now dissolving into nothingness. We have the confidence not to come to the feeling of total abandonment we might easily come to. In brief, we are diving, as if we were swimming into nothingness, into the universal cosmos. And then it is like awakening, not from sleep, but rather from something fully conscious. In the moment of waking we know that it was not sleep. We have not lived through it as we live through the void of consciousness in sleep. It was something else. In it something occurred in the interval, something at which we were present. And now we have woken up again, and events that we could not experience in a fully conscious state are coming into our consciousness—and we know very clearly afterward that we have experienced them. It is like a recollection. We remember something that we have not worked through with the ordinary self, but have experienced in such a way that we were raised out of our ordinary self.

And when it enters our consciousness, we experience the thing we set out for, the thing we set as our task.

Now we know that we have lived through something—we could say lived *as a thinking being* through something ("thinking," however, here has a much higher significance than in the physical). We have thinkingly lived through something. However, no matter how far developed we are as human beings, what we can be as a human being cannot approach what we went through while we were in the relative nothingness. Human beings cannot think through that; they cannot thinkingly live through it. For that reason, in the time between the diving under and resurfacing, another being must have taken over the function of thinking for us, of thinking inside us. We could not think on our own; we can only remember afterward what this being, this angelic being, thought in us. We know that in the interval we were interwoven with our angelic being, which thought for us while our consciousness was suppressed. Now we awaken and remember with ordinary thought-experience what the angel experienced and thought in us.

That is the process. It is the way spiritual experiences are usually attained. We attain them in such a way that we know we must first arrive at a state in which a being of the next higher hierarchy enters into us, identifies itself with us. Then what we could not in our own weakness achieve, we are capable of achieving through the being of the next higher hierarchy—but with muted consciousness. We are not permitted the immediate experience; it comes later in memory, in the full "I"-consciousness.

So in actuality the spiritual experiences we are granted are experienced at one time and become conscious to us at another. For example, I have related something I experienced concerning our dear friend Christian Morgenstern[†]—a real experience of this sort. But it first became conscious only after the experience, because during the experience a being of the next-higher hierarchy had to take over the function of knowledge.

Once again you can reflect on why it must be so. Were we actually to bring what a being of the higher hierarchies experiences into our organism, then not only would we kill our own organism, but we would burst its organization apart into its atoms. We would bring about not only its death, but also its simultaneous cremation.

Now you see once again that our seership brings us into a relationship with what we call the portal of death. We can say that we can only really see what death is, what death means, by raising ourselves into moods of the soul that emerge through the described experiences.† For through that we understand human individuality outside the physical body and know how it must be immediately taken up outside the physical body into the bosom of the beings of the higher hierarchies, so that it does not become destructive or lethal to our own being on the physical plane. And the feeling of the human soul resting in the bosom of a being of the higher hierarchies will become real, infinitely real. Then, for the first time, we will know how it looks beyond death. We will know that here on Earth we are surrounded by the mineral kingdom, the plant, animal, and human kingdoms. Beyond death we enter into the bosom of the higher hierarchies, to whose environment we belong, as here we belong to the environment of the physical beings that surround us. A certain feeling of communality with the beings of the higher hierarchies comes into our soul. We can permeate ourselves with this feeling. And we learn properly that a true penetration into the spiritual worlds is not at all possible without bringing with us certain feelings, which can be called religious and pious feelings, feelings of devotion to the higher spiritual world.

The feelings I have just described are so nuanced that they elicit a particular mood in the soul, which I can only express as a mood of resting in the bosom of spiritual beings. This soul mood is needed for any real experience of the spiritual worlds, just as in the physical human world, to be understood by other people, we need to produce an *I* sound through the larynx and the other organs of speech. [The German *I* is pronounced like a long *E* in English.] In the higher worlds the soul feeling flowing from devotion brings about what makes it possible to produce an *I* in ordinary human speech. The experience of this kind of devotion is one of the vowels of the higher worlds. And we can experience nothing, read and hear nothing in the higher worlds if we cannot maintain this soul mood—and then wait for what the beings of the higher worlds have to communicate because we offer them this mood of the soul. From such soul moods, from such a way of meeting the higher worlds, the vowel system of the cosmos is composed.

You may have the feeling that the world surrounds you, but you cannot live in this world with your feeble human powers. You feel that what surrounds you while you live in your human body can only be perceived in the shadowy forms of your thoughts and ideas; or, better said, they reflect themselves from inside you. You may also come to feel that you cannot experience these imaginations directly; your protecting angelic being in ordinary life must reduce it. And when you feel all of this inwardly with the necessary tone of inner piety, then you have the ability to perceive one of the vowels of the spiritual world.

A next level depends on the development of something I alluded to in my book *The Threshold of the Spiritual World.*† We live ourselves into the spiritual world, as I have described there. The process shows that we come out of ourselves, identify ourselves with something else. But that is still not enough, not at all enough. We must not only be able to identify ourselves with other entities; we must also be able to transform ourselves into those entities, so that we really do not remain only what we were when we set out. We must be able to transform ourselves into other entities, to really become what we enter.

A good preparation for becoming able to do that is the constant practice of loving interest for everything that surrounds us in the world. One can certainly not say how infinitely significant it is for the budding esotericist to see more and more that loving interest awakens us toward everything around us in the world. This statement, unfortunately, is not usually taken seriously enough. This is the reason the results achieved in esotericism are often disappointing. It is only too natural that people generally are interested only in themselves with the necessary degree of interest. Even when we aren't willing to believe it and give it another name, we are still mostly interested in ourselves and far less in anything else.

Now it must also be said that in any case the world order has taken care that you must constantly have an interest in yourself. We must really make an effort not to be permanently interested in ourselves, for life on the physical plane inherently brings with it the condition that one be interested in oneself. I will disregard the fact that obviously when an illness occurs, or this or that hurts us or is not in order, we are naturally interested in ourselves. This is in the order of things, and we cannot act any other way. It is possible that even in such a case, through effort, one might achieve not being interested in oneself, but that is extremely difficult. It could be that one is attacked by an illness and is not particularly interested in the fact of having the illness, is quite indifferent to it, but is interested in how such a thing could arise out of the entire universe as this process. It could interest a person that at one point in the universe something happens that now lies inside his or her skin; consequently that person becomes interested in a serious disease as something that is outside the self.

You will admit that what I have described is quite difficult. And it is no different with most things that one experiences on the physical plane. It is in fact very difficult to take the most ordinary thing that our senses and our thinking experience, as if we were outside our skin and to look at it as an object. But that is exactly what we must attempt; only because it is so terribly hard is it generally not attempted at all. Whoever conscientiously and enthusiastically performs the exercises described in *How to Know Higher Worlds* will gradually succeed in attaining such a point of view. You will only reach it by detours, because it is infinitely difficult; but you will attain it to a certain degree in exactly the same proportion as your interest in yourself is diminished, so that you are no longer an interesting subject for yourself, but merely an interesting object. You can do that; it does no harm, and it is even very useful to be interested in yourself if you have become an object. However, you should not confuse becoming an object of your own subject with the subject itself.

In the same proportion in which we begin to become an object for ourselves, we begin to become interested in everything outside of us, in what surrounds us. Then we really gain the loving, interested devotion to the world and its manifestations. And when one cultivates this loving devotion of oneself to the world and its manifestations further and further, then this mood can attain that degree in the soul necessary for us to go out of ourselves and transform ourselves into other entities, to metamorphose ourselves. We gradually attain the ability to accomplish such things. But such things are really difficult for the human soul, so to make this loving devotion possible we must try to find supports of all kinds.

I will offer one support here that can really help a person. We can in fact begin by using the physical world, which is given to us first, as the occasion for a sort of esoteric reading. I have often used an image that is a good one to start with. When we look at the countenance of a person we encounter, it is clear that what our eyes see—the boundaries, the contours of the skin—is not what matters. What matters is the soul that lives behind this facial expression. If we were to represent the facial lines in paper-mâché, the lines would not be what matters; the soul is what matters, what gives the lines form. In this way we can also look at what surrounds us in external nature as if it were an external physiognomy. The materialistic researcher and the ordinary person approach the things in external nature as if they were studying only the external form of a person. It is as if one were to say about a person that whatever soul is within is neither here nor there; it is a misguided superstition of fanciful people, and I am only concerned with what the forms are, which can be measured and investigated with precision. That is how ordinary people investigate external nature. However, we can also realize that just as it is easy enough to see the human countenance as an expression, a physiognomy, of the soul, so we can also regard all external nature not merely as it ordinarily reveals itself, but rather as the physiognomy of what lies behind as spiritual entities. Therefore it is good to look at the entire animal kingdom as a physiognomy of nature.

In any case another mental inquiry is necessary in order not to see what one usually sees, but to see instead something that can be described in this way: An eagle is flying in the air, rising toward the Sun; that is, the upward direction, into the heights, into the spiritual worlds. I will take the eagle as the symbol of one's raising oneself into the spiritual worlds. I see behind the human brow the thoughts that strive upward with presentiment, like an eagle, into the spiritual worlds. I see how this upward-striving expresses itself in the eagle as it rises upward, just as the human soul expresses itself in physiognomy. The eagle belongs to the physiognomy of external nature. I feel something in the eagle as it flies upward—something that gives the impression of the forehead in human physiognomy.

I look at a bull, lying there and chewing away, bound to physical nature, to earthly matter; in reality it only lives in its element when it is totally absorbed in digestion. In all its life processes it remains bound up with what it takes out of the earth. It appears to me to be as ponderous as the earth. I look at people and feel in my spirit that there also is something as heavy as earth, but it is kept in balance by the quality of the eagle. The bull-like quality isn't noticeable. I feel how the bull nature dwells in the human being, but doesn't make itself known to me in the same way as in the bull itself. This bull nature, this external earthly heaviness, becomes a physiognomic trait for human beings. It is just the same with leonine qualities. Physiognomically, the heart is for the human being what the lion is in external nature. And it can become the same for the entire higher and lower animal kingdom.

Those who have connected the eagle, the bull, and the lion with the nature of the human soul have given us a replica, a symbol. They have attempted to read what is written out for us in the external animal kingdom, and from it to understand, separated into individual characters, individual letters, what is experienced in combination in the human being. In brief, one could say that the physiognomy of the natural world is the animal kingdom.

But physiognomy is not the only thing that interests us about the human being. When we try to enter souls more intimately we are interested in what we call the countenance, or the play of expression—what arises when the physiognomy comes into movement. In this case we stand closer to the soul we perceive through the play of expression than to the soul we perceive only through physiognomy. And once again we can seek out how the play of expression relates to the spiritual world lying behind it, in this case by observing the realm of plants in a way similar to what we saw in the animal kingdom. We observe the blossoming of the plant realm in spring and all that it does through the summer; on the one hand the Earth sends it out, and on the other hand the forces of the spheres penetrate plants and lure out the living life that appears in the endless nuances of blossoms, growths, and greenings with their teeming and weaving. When we observe plants in this way and connect them with the spiritual reality of the cosmos that lies behind them, just as we relate a person's play of expression to the soul, then we are once again practicing what we should be. As a result we can say that the realm of plants is the countenance of nature.

What further of the soul that we see, what goes beyond the play of expression, are gestures, the movements that flow out from the soul. Just as we can designate the animal kingdom as the physiognomy of nature, and the plant realm as the countenance of nature, we can regard the forms of the mineral world as the gestures of nature. And one of the most beautiful things a person willing to practice meticulously esoteric reading and esoteric hearing can experience is to experience the mineral world in such a way that everywhere you can gradually assimilate the infinitely varied gestures of the spiritual beings of nature in the form of the limiting surfaces of the minerals and their peculiar relationship to the external cosmos in their translucence and transparency; in the crystalline glow of quartz, calcite, emerald, chrysoprase.

When we do exercises of this sort and get to the point that we really can experience what is expressed in the otherwise dead realm of stone, it is the same as when a soul brings, through a living gesture, what is alive in it to expression. Practice in this way helps us to acquire a loving interest for all beings that are outside us. Then, gradually, we can rise to a stage in our development in which it becomes possible—if we attain the gift of seeing as well—to transform ourselves into the entities that exist outside ourselves. We realize that we have the power to do so. We can transform ourselves into all other people. The human being is capable of infinite transformations in this regard, but practice in the way described is necessary.

Once again we can pose a question, but before doing so I want to stress the element of feeling in what I have discussed. The first thing I mentioned brings us to a consciousness of being protected, to a feeling full of piety. The feeling that we can transform ourselves into the most diverse entities brings us to esteem the humanity of the human being, to value it at its true value—not the humanity that we have within ourselves in the physical world, but the humanity we find only when we become another. Attaining the feeling of the capacity for transformation cannot lead us to an arrogant attitude, for every single transformation tells us that we are not worth as much as the being into which we must transform ourselves. Having the awareness of the ability to transform ourselves brings us to humility. A feeling of deepest religious piety is linked to the awareness of the capacity of transformation.

We can pose another question: let us say we call out these powers of transformation from within ourselves. Are they not always within us? Yes, just as the powers of imagination are always within us, the powers of transforming ourselves are always within us. We must however call them forth in order to perceive spiritual beings. And in order to possess them consciously, we must develop them in the described way. In every moment we are not only ourselves, but also every other being; only we don't develop ourselves to expand our consciousness as far as the other being. Why is that so? This will become clear when we consider one of the situations in life in which people transform themselves into another being on the ordinary physical plane.

It does happen on the physical plane that we use the powers that are otherwise powers of transformation. We use that power, without knowing anything about it, every time we do our fellow human beings the injustice of making our own will lord over theirs in an unjustified way. It begins already when we tell lies to others. Through this we attach a wrong to them. One wins a certain power over them, because the lies continue to work within them.

The same is also true when we do something bad. The powers with which we do something bad are in fact the powers of transformation, only applied in the wrong place. Everything bad in the world is the unlawful application of these powers of transformation. We can make deep insights into the secret of existence when we know where the injustice, evil, crime, and destruction that happen in the world come from. They happen when one applies the best, most holy powers that exist, the powers of transformation, in a wrong way. There would be no evil in the world if there were no transformative powers. Once in a public lecture I even alluded to this peculiarity, that evil is a wrong application of powers that, used in the proper place, would lead to the highest good.† A certain mood is present in our soul when we know it contains something that on the one hand can transform itself into all people and beings, and on the other hand can transform itself into egotism. We must be able to hold this mood up to the cosmos if we wish to hear in a spiritual sense. That is a second vowel.

The mood we can have in relation to the secret of evil as I have presented it is the third vowel—what we experience when we know how a person can become evil. If we know this secret, that there are very lofty powers that can be used in a wrong way, then we have the mood of a third cosmic vowel. We must experience these moods, for that is the heart of the matter.

So we have spoken today of three cosmic vowels. We will speak of others tomorrow. I had to explain first the principle, which is crucial if we are to produce the inner relationship with the cosmos in our inner experience through which we, in the dedication of our own soul powers, become listeners and readers of what happens out there in the spiritual world.

4

Inner Mobility of Thought

DORNACH, OCTOBER 6, 1914

YESTERDAY I attempted to speak of several inner experiences that we could call "the vowel-system of the spiritual world." We saw in particular how esoteric reading and esoteric hearing are living inner experiences, to which the entire personality, the entire being must be committed. I mentioned three such experiences, for which one must prepare painstakingly. The first comes about when we gradually learn to transport ourselves consciously into the supersensible world, in which we are always present unconsciously, and by that means reach the portal of death. Further, I also spoke of the experience we come to when we acquire the so-called capacity for transformation into other beings. And then I attempted to show how the evil in the world can be so present to us that we recognize that its origin arises from a misuse of higher spiritual powers which are—in their place and in their way—fully justified.

Another experience of this kind occurs when we take entirely in earnest something that is connected with what has just been discussed. We must transform ourselves into something else, but in the process of this transformation we must be able to hold on to the thread of our inner experiences. If we cannot hold on to these threads, we would find ourselves in the same situation as people on the physical plane who cannot remember what they experienced in physical life yesterday, or the day before that, or years previously. Just as we must hold on to the continuity of consciousness in normal physical life, so must we hold on to our memory through our transformations in the spiritual world. When we have transformed ourselves into a particular being or a particular process, we could lose ourselves outside our soul, unless we retain something like a higher, purely spiritual recollection of other forms, processes, and entities of the spiritual world. In other words, we must be a multifarious being, must be able to split ourselves up, break ourselves into pieces, go into multiplicity. This inner experience produces a peculiar feeling, the feeling that you are there, you are this being, yet you are nonetheless another being: you exist within separate entities.

Without this developed feeling of multiplicity we would certainly not be able to attain a true spiritual concept, for example, of the nature of the higher hierarchies. We can still, on the path we took up yesterday or on the paths we have followed on other occasions, gain an idea of the nature of the first hierarchy that stands just above us, of the entities of the angels. But to reach a more accurate spiritual idea of the entities of the archangels we must, through inner feeling, understand something about multiplicity. For we learn only gradually to understand the true situation of these entities of the higher hierarchies. We learn to understand it only gradually, because all human conceptualization, all human thinking, is bound to the ordinary relationships of space and time, and entirely different space and time relationships are present when we ascend to the entities of the hierarchy of the archangels.

If we start out from ordinary physical consciousness, we always have a certain fundamental feeling, a feeling that is entirely natural for physical consciousness. For example, when, through the visionary gift, I wish to get to a person who lives between death and a new birth (by "I" I do not mean myself, but in general a person who has visionary power and seeks a dead person), I first have the feeling that the dead person is there, together with me just there, and in relation to time I can seek the dead person out, just as on the physical plane I can seek out another person I know to be alive at that time—I need only to find the way to that person. When we are seeking a dead person,

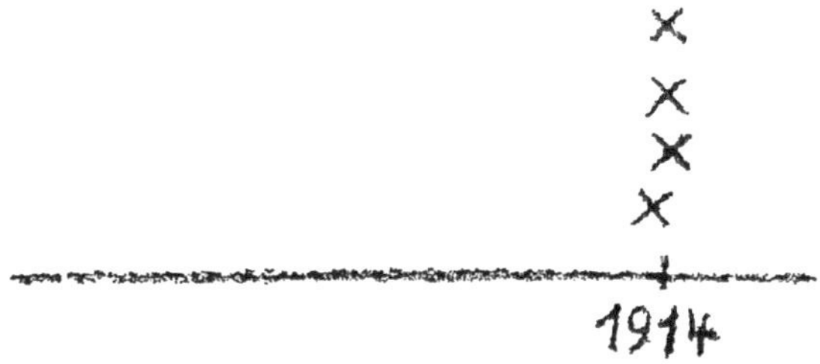

this idea is perfectly correct. It is in a certain sense still correct when we wish to find an entity from the hierarchy of the angels. But it is no longer correct when we wish to seek out in the same way an entity from the hierarchy of the archangels, because an entity from that hierarchy has concentrated its consciousness in a very precise time.

Let us assume that this line [see drawing] represents the course of time. A seer who lives at this point in time, 1914, would be able to find a dead person or an entity from the hierarchy of the angels anywhere in the spiritual world in the same time. However, that doesn't work when we want to seek out a particular entity from the hierarchy of the archangels. In that case we must go outside of time; we must overcome simultaneity. For example, to find a particular archangel, one must go back, let us say, to the fifteenth century. Therefore we cannot say that we will stay in our own time. It may be that we have to go back—back for us—to the year 1465 or thereabouts, and then look for the archangel [see drawing]. If this entity is

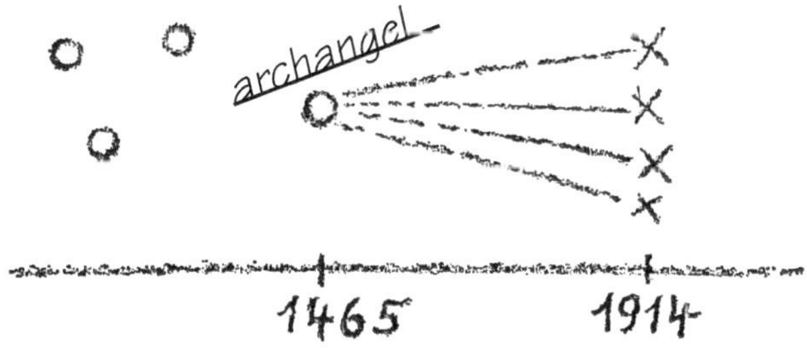

not to be found in the present, its effect radiates nonetheless into our own time. However, we find in our time only its effect; we do not find the entity itself in its own selfhood.

Other archangels must be sought for at other points in time [see drawing: circles]. We have to go outside of time. This is a difficult concept, but one must reach it.

We must be clear that archangels always bear their name rightly. We actually first know why they bear this name when we get to their essence, in the sense I have just characterized. They are called "angels of the beginning," which means they are always to be found at the beginnings of time periods; when peoples originate, when peoples enter into world history for the first time, there are the archangels, present with their full consciousness, with their own selves. That remains present in the future in their effects. The effects flow into time. And if we wish to find them, we cannot merely remain in our time; we must go out of time, seek out temporal beginnings. No one who wishes to live as a soul only in, let us say, October 1914 is in a position to find anything like all the archangels—perhaps not even one of them. That is possible only for those who are able to transport themselves in their soul-being back into other time periods in such a way that those periods become open to their direct experience, so that they themselves live in those other times. But when we transport ourselves into other time periods, it is necessary not to forget how we entered them, no more than we may in the physical world forget today what we did yesterday. That is something like a law of multiplicity, of the outpouring into plurality.

Now, we find the primal origins, the spirits of personality—the archai—only when we have transported ourselves back into the Lemurian epoch, when the Earth was at the beginning of physical development. There we find the archai in their own selfhood. We cannot find them if we remain in the present.

You see therefore that the entire relation of the soul to time must change if we want to penetrate the spiritual world consciously. What we experience in this way—or in fact if we only form an idea of these things and progress further and further in the inner experience of the idea—creates a mood in the soul of inner devotion, something like being poured out into actual spiritual reality. Here we have yet another vowel of the spiritual world.

You can understand how in this further experience I have described, we become more and more independent of the space or time in which we stand in the physical world. You see that we not only go out of ourselves, but that simultaneously with this outgoing we also enter the weaving and being of the universe—and not just one-sidedly as we expand ourselves in spatial spheres, but many-sidedly, as we experience ourselves in time as a living being, who has within itself the points of consciousness of the entities of the higher hierarchies. When we therefore no longer live only in ourselves and, what is more, no longer live in the space and time we refer to as a physical being, but instead have accepted space into our body and time into our soul—take note of this expression; we learn to understand it in its full significance only gradually, when we have meditated on it a great deal—then we have united ourselves with what is not a general abstract feeling, but rather a living weaving and being in a cosmic existence full of meaning. Everywhere one transports oneself has meaning. And everywhere we transport ourselves, meaning sprouts in our soul. And from individual meaning universal meaning constitutes itself and weaves and exists in the world. The meaning of things blossoms forth like fruit out of many centers. And the spiritual content that blossoms forth in individual meanings from individual entities weaves itself together into a universally meaningful Cosmic Word. We weave and live within the Cosmic Word. This weaving within and living within the Cosmic Word is yet another vowel of the spiritual world—the most primal vowel of the spiritual world. With this experience of the Cosmic Word, which we must conceive in its manifold livingness and not merely as spiritual hearing, everything resides that one can call inspiration in the higher sense. With this inspiration we can say: "What I know in this Cosmic Word, the world knows in me; I am basically innocent in everything I know in this way, for the world knows it in me. I can fall short in knowledge of the Cosmic Word only because I am an imperfect instrument that allows this Cosmic Word to resound in me merely as fragmentary radiations. But it is the Cosmic Word that resounds in me." And the more modest we have become, the further we have progressed toward being selflessly devoted without having any pretensions about our own actions, thinking, feeling, and willing, the more we have progressed in allowing the Cosmic Word to rule in the weaving of our own being;[†] then the more objectively we reproduce, through the Cosmic Word, what flows secretly through the world.

So we have once again spoken of a vowel, of the fifth cosmic vowel. I wanted to awaken in you a concept, if only a very primitive one, of what the vowel system of the universe is.

Now, when we have progressed as far as being versed in our inner being in the kinds of feeling I have described through these five cosmic vowels, when we can experience in our soul what is, so to speak, a condensation from the spiritual world, then the soul can listen to what is occurring in the spiritual world; then the spiritual world can speak to it.

What happens, then, when communion with the spiritual world is truly cultivated on the path that opens through what I have described? Our astral body and our ego—the ego, however, has been raised to a higher level by being selflessly muted in the previously described manner and has descended into the astral body—are outside our physical and etheric bodies. Indeed, we are outside our physical and etheric bodies with our ego and astral body when we are perceiving spiritually here in the life between birth and death, but we are still looking back at the etheric body, and it is the etheric body that reflects the vowel system.

The etheric body has the possibility of sevenfold reflection. I have mentioned five of the reflections, five vowels. There are still two other vowels, which should be discussed more thoroughly on another occasion. But the characteristic ebb and flow of the etheric body, what it reflects in its life processes when we are outside ourselves, presents itself as these vowels. That means that something happens in the etheric body when we develop feelings like those we can experience through preparing to stand at the portal of death, or preparing to face evil with understanding, or living and weaving within the Cosmic Word. According to whether one holds one thing or another thing out to the spiritual world, something different is reflected in the etheric body we are looking back at. It is hard to describe, but I will say that the entities of the world are reflected sevenfold in the etheric body.

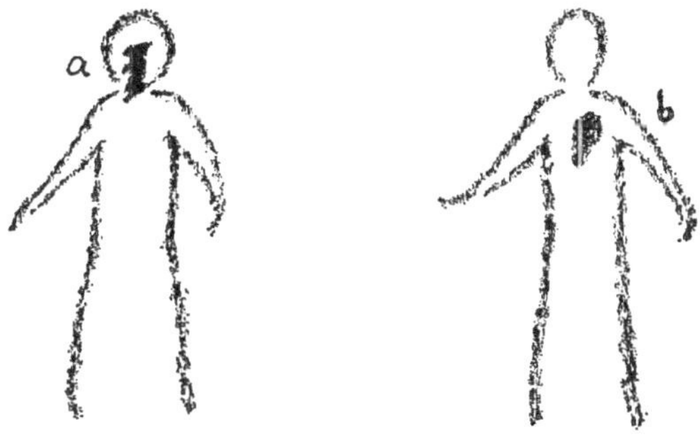

I will represent it schematically like this [see drawing]. This represents the etheric body of a person—very schematically. When we experience the feeling that arises through preparing to stand at the portal of death, the etheric body will be drawn together here in the uppermost region [see drawing, a] and receives a certain radiance and resonance. And from this radiance and resonance something emerges that we can call a vowel of the spiritual world.

If we now develop another feeling, the etheric body draws itself together in another region, let us say the region of the heart [b]. Then one sees another radiance and perceives another kind of resonance, as from within a being into which we have transformed ourselves with the ego and the astral body.

What I have said up until now refers to the vowels of the spiritual world. Just as there are seven vowels, there are also consonants of the spiritual world, twelve in number. We approach these twelve consonants most easily when we comprehend the physical body in the same way we have grasped the etheric body in its vowel-nature. The physical body reveals itself then as a twelvefoldness.

The time here is insufficient even to mention anything of how we can approach the twelvefoldness of the physical body in the same way we approach the sevenfoldness of the etheric body. But this I must say: When we are outside our physical and etheric bodies, they become something entirely different from what they are when we are living in them. When we are living in them, the etheric body is what sustains our life processes, what makes us living organisms, and the physical body is what builds our organism of senses. There we are, inside it. We need our etheric and physical bodies in order to be such people on the physical plane as we actually are. However, as soon as we are outside the physical and etheric bodies in the sense that has already been indicated in this lecture, we relate to them as we would to signs. The etheric body is then indeed a living entity, but it shows nothing of the duty, the function that it has as the life-principle at the foundations of our physical organism. It reveals itself as a sign of the seven vowels. It becomes something objective, which we contemplate and which in its changeability is a reflection of the vowel system of the entirety of the universe. We become as alien to our etheric body as we are to the vowels of the physical external alphabet. And we become as alien to our physical body—which has now become a totality of the twelve signs brought together in it—as we are alien to the consonants or the ordinary alphabet. And just as consonants and vowels permeate the words of the ordinary alphabet, enabling us to read this or that word according to how vowels and consonants are connected, so do we read or hear in the spiritual world something different according to how the etheric body, which can manifest itself in seven different ways, harmonizes with or is connected to one or another of the consonants of the physical body. When we meet people on the physical plane we can communicate because they speak to us and we have eyes to observe and ears to hear the word, to let their language penetrate our souls; everything that forms a relationship with another person is transmitted by our senses. Something similar transpires in the spiritual world.

Let us say we are preparing ourselves to find a human soul who is living between death and a new birth. We know through inner experience that we are now united with this soul, that we are experiencing with it at the same time and in the same place in the spiritual world. Just as we need sense organs in the physical world to communicate with other people, in the spiritual world we need the faculty for looking back at the etheric body and the physical body. They reflect back the interplay of the vowel processes of the etheric body and the consonantal processes of the physical body. And the interplay expresses what one is speaking with the dead person and is therefore necessary for communication with the dead person.

Imagine you are united with a dead person in the spiritual world, with a soul living there between death and a new life. You observe the human physical form in which you yourself live on the physical plane, and you observe your human etheric form. You look back at these, and through them is reflected everything the dead person has to say to you, to communicate with you, what that person is thinking, feeling, and willing. The human physical body and the human etheric body have become one comprehensive sense organ. And we can say: We have received the physical and the etheric bodies in our physical life so that we may have sense organs for the spiritual world. We are made aware once again that life in the physical world is not merely life in a vale of tears from which we must yearn to free ourselves, as a false asceticism would have it. We realize that life in the physical world has a great, an exalted, divine mission. Within physical life we are adapting ourselves for what will develop into sense organs for the spiritual world.

You will understand it more exactly if I tell you how perception of spiritual entities and processes takes place when we ourselves are in the time between death and new birth, when we do not perceive the spiritual world clairvoyantly from within the physical world, but are united in the spiritual world with spiritual beings. As long as we wear a physical and an etheric body as our raiment, we have something that reflects, for they serve us as sense organs. When we lay them aside in death, naturally we no longer have these sense organs as external reality. You could now easily ask: Can we not perceive what we experience in relation to the other entities and processes in the spiritual world between death and new life? Yes; then it is in fact different, and we perceive it in another way. Even visionaries must receive what they experience in the spiritual world as a reflection in their physical and etheric bodies here in the physical world. That is how it is as long as they are here in the physical world, as long as the physical body has not been lost through decomposition and the etheric body through dissolution into the spiritual world. When we are in the spiritual world and no longer have physical and etheric bodies, then we are able to sketch out for ourselves, from the substance of the spiritual world, the world of signs from which the physical body and the etheric body were correspondingly composed. We draw everything into the spiritual world.

Assume you are living as a soul between death and a new life together with another human soul. What you say to it or what it says to you, everything that would otherwise have been reflected in your physical and etheric bodies, is now impressed into the Akashic Chronicle in the spiritual world. What would otherwise have expressed itself in the reflected image of the physical and etheric bodies, in vowels or consonants, you now actually inscribe with your own power into the spiritual world, into the Akashic Chronicle, erasing it yourself when it is no longer necessary.†

I gave the first indication of these things in my book *Theosophy*,† at the beginning of the chapter about the so-called realm of spirits, where I said that individuals in a particular stage of development in Devachan, in the realm of spirits, see their previous incarnation lying out before them on the "continent-area" of the realm of spirits. That is an inscription of a spiritual writing.

The ideal would be for a book like *Theosophy* to be studied so eagerly that many readers would arrive at something like what is being discussed now. A great deal is contained in these books, and those who read them with the heart, with all their inner soul experience, could get to that point entirely through their own reading. However, books on spiritual science are usually not read with the required attention. They really are not, for otherwise, after *Theosophy* and *How to Know Higher Worlds*, and perhaps also *Outline of Esoteric Science*† had been written, all lecture cycles could have been written or delivered by someone other than me. Basically everything is in these books, only people generally don't believe it. And how much could be written if everything contained in the four Mystery Dramas were extracted! I do not say it to promote myself—I have already spoken sufficiently about the humility of the esotericist, of the spiritual scientist—I say it to get you excited about a true reading of these writings, which had to be given particularly in our time, and from which there was, in fact, as little personal credit given as possible.

You see then that human beings, as they live on the physical plane, develop something in reference to the spiritual worlds that is the seed for the experiences of the higher worlds. The etheric body here in the physical world is not just the life-principle of humanity; it is at the same time a means of preparation to experience the sense for the vowels of the spiritual world. And the physical body is a means of preparation for experiencing the consonants of the spiritual world.

We can accomplish much if we seriously attempt to free ourselves from the purely materialistic conception of the human body. Through that we can accomplish much to prepare ourselves so that feelings for the vowel and consonant systems of the cosmos awaken these inner experiences and impulses in the soul. We must only call forth in ourselves a feeling for this preparation for development into higher worlds, which is really similar to what a child must do in the physical world to learn to read and understand the words of our external physical human speech.

The materialistic conception of the human physical body takes it just as it presents itself physically. It is taken the same way as symbols written on a blackboard—say INK—would be taken if we investigated them by looking at the curves and strokes, noting that they go up or down or bend around like so, and so on. In brief, we would describe the forms of the letters. That is just how we approach the physical body today. We describe it anatomically, physiologically heart, lung, liver, and so forth, just as they present themselves on the surface. It is the same as if we were to describe a word by the strokes it consists of; however, the only person who gets anything out of it is the person who has learned to read the word "ink" from the strokes.

We must advance on the physical plane to reading in the spiritual worlds. What we call esoteric reading and esoteric hearing is really a matter of individual experience. We are preparing ourselves for it when, while still in the physical world, we attempt to comprehend the physical body in its character as a sign. What does that mean? I will give you a brief example of this recognition of a sign-like character, but I must leave what is really meant by it to your own meditation and serious reflection. For language really does not suffice in many cases to make oneself understood on these topics. It will only suffice when spiritual science has done its task in the world for a while and has changed language so that words are formed in such a way that they link with what is spiritually real and essential. Language must become much more supple, but that will only be possible when spiritual science has been at work in the world over several centuries, and people have become accustomed through daily involvement with it to take words differently than is the case today—when they are only applied to things and processes on the physical plane.

What occurs in the human head is enclosed in the bone formation of the physical skull; there it is, so to speak, inside. There it is, with few exceptions, physically enclosed from all sides. Schematically we can represent it in this way:

The head, when we begin to interpret it and not simply to describe it as it presents itself to the senses, is terribly significant, because in its interior complicated processes take place that are virtually enclosed on all sides by the hardest human material, bone material. Thereby a part of the overall human entity is shut off. It is, however, a part of the human entity, of the human organism. The human being is really not such a simple physical being that one can speak of a mere human being. The primitive ideas about this subject prevalent today are shown by the criticism of my books [regarding the fact that] they speak of a sentient soul, an intellectual or mind soul, and a consciousness soul; whereas the concept of the soul as a unified organ has been taken as magnificent progress. It is understandable that our materialistic culture prefers the commonly received wishy-washy mish-mash about the soul that is called psychology today to the description of the real elements of the entity found in spiritual science. Dividing the soul into the sentient soul, intellectual or mind soul, and consciousness soul is not based on abstract thinking; they belong to different ages in relation to their creation and are connected with different states of being. We can understand why the present intellectual culture finds something like that to be foolish, but in doing so that culture characterizes itself, and not what it criticizes.

The physical organism of the human being is indeed quite a complicated entity, and by investigating it one can develop the following thoughts, which of course may appear foolish to scientists today. To be sure! But Saint Paul says that many a thing that is foolishness before man is wisdom before God.† So much of what science sees only as foolishness could be "wisdom before God."

Consider this idea—What is the situation with our hands? Our hands are most decidedly connected with our soul being. And when we have a living feeling for what is going on in the hands, it is not without significance how people express what they are saying in the gestures of their hands. There is something to be said for that. Now I will omit many transitional steps and leave it to your own discretion to fill it all in. Suppose now that, not through a process from the human side, but through one rooted in the world being, our hands were not formed in such a way that we could move them completely freely and let them follow our will. Suppose that instead they were connected to us in such a way that we had to keep them entirely still, that they were affixed to us by external nature. What would it be like then, if we had hands, but we could not move them? Even if we had hands we couldn't move because they were affixed to us, we would still develop the will to move them. Even when we could not move them physically, we would in the moment we want to move them, tear off the etheric hands and move those. That is what we do with our brains in reality. Certain lobes of our brain that today lie enclosed within the covering of our skull were still freely movable during the Moon phase of evolution. Today they are bound together, they cannot physically move. But etherically they move, when we think. We move the etheric brain when we think. If we had not received this fixed brain-pan or cranium for the brain that holds the lobes of the brain together, we would reach with our brain lobes and would make gestures with them, as we do now with our hands. However, for us to be able to learn to think, the lobes of our brain had first to be restrained physically, and the etheric part of the brain had to receive the possibility of tearing itself free.

What I am saying is no play of the imagination. A time will come when our hands will be grown solid, when much else besides will be a solid part of the middle of our body; what now appears to be a free part of us near the heart will then be enclosed by a sheath, just as the brain is now enclosed by the cranium. That will be in the Jupiter age. That which is most visibly expressed in our hands is being prepared to become eventually an organ of thought. At present we have preliminarily only rudimentary organs, which are small, not fully grown. Just as once we only had pieces of the cranium here in front on the forehead, we now have lying flat behind our shoulder blades what will eventually enclose our future brain. You interpret the shoulder blades in the human body correctly when you regard them as little pieces of bone that really belong to a skull which is closing up; only it has not yet grown into its full form.

So you have, so to speak, a second human being enclosed in the first. And now I will say something quite paradoxical. There are yet other organs in the human organism that are pieces of a further cranium; these are now tiny in relation to the rest of the organism and will not be fully grown until a yet later time. These organs are the kneecaps. The kneecaps have only made it as far as little surfaces. They are as of yet only suggestions of something that in another direction will become a thought organ for people. We are learning to interpret the human organism when we can say (this is only an example torn out of context) that the human being has in fact three craniums. One is fairly well formed, closed off on all sides. The second is so far present only in two pieces, the shoulder blades. The third cranium consists of nothing more than the kneecaps. The latter two, the shoulder blades and the kneecaps, which now exist only in part, can be completed in thought, rounded out into spheres. Thus we get three brains. What will one day be our second brain is hardly developed in our external human form. Now it shows itself externally; later it will become an interior brain. When you make gestures with your hands today, you are preparing later thoughts, thoughts that will conceive the processes of the elemental world in as real a way as you now conceive thoughts of the physical world with your head. As curious and paradoxical as it sounds, what lies outside the kneecaps, the calves, and the feet are entirely unfulfilled organs related to the Earth's gravity. The knee-caps are preparing themselves, in conjunction with what they absorb spiritually from the Earth today, to become one day, when they are no longer present as physical organs, spiritual organs that will lead the way into the spiritual world when the Earth will be transformed into the Venus state. For that to happen, the present physical form must fall away, and something else must take its place.

You see, there is a lot inside the esoteric observation of the world. The most important thing is not that one knows of this or that book that says this or that about the higher worlds. That is not the most important thing. We must acquire all that, because that is the only way to find what is right. But the most important thing is a certain manner of soul mood, a certain attitude of the soul, through which we learn to approach the world in a new way and to take things in a different way from that used in the past. The important thing is that we be prepared through what we read with inner mobility of the weaving of thought, the experience of thoughts-in-themselves, in order to contemplate everything, even what is given physically in the world. For in their external form things are not at all as they really are, as paradoxical as that sounds. Our shoulder blade is not merely a shoulder blade, as you observe it externally. That is maya; that is false. The shoulder blade completes itself for us if we make a point of conceiving it in reality as a more extensive organ.

When we see people kneeling we can gradually get the impression that it is entirely wrong to regard the kneecaps as they exist there only as little parts. That is entirely wrong. The people kneeling in prayer are preparing themselves to live in the sphere that will surround them some day when their kneecaps will spread out, expand into a mighty vault like the surface of a ball, of which they are now only small parts. Praying human beings show us already in their form what human beings will one day become when the Earth is in the Venus stage.

In this way we gradually learn to read in the physical world. We do not merely look at a kneeling person or at some other gesture of the person. We learn to recognize how what we see about a person, what presents itself directly to us, although it is reality, can be false and untrue. We learn in the alphabet what the cosmos wants to express, not in its present state of being, but in its becoming. In this way we gradually learn to decode, interpret, read substantially the essence, and comprehend what the world truly is. The physical world is nothing more than a written page that lies before us. If we only gape at it, we don't understand what it is all about. We must learn to read. We know equally little about the world when we regard it only with what physical perception provides and do not become aware that we must decode it and penetrate into it. We must read it to understand its meaning.

If we become more and more conscious that the world is a book that the hierarchies have written for us, so that we may read in it, then we first become human in the fullest sense of the word. And fundamentally the building we are raising here,[†] in its form and configuration, should elicit such feelings, such intimate attunements and compositions of the soul, that we become capable of reading the world, of hearing the secrets of the world. For that reason the structure must be as it is, so that it can elicit what lies within us, at least a certain little part of it.

It is good, my dear friends, to form often in meditation an idea of what task spiritual science can have in the world in relation to what is now already in the world; what must develop out of it, how it should adapt itself into what should develop historically. If only there could exist among our friends in the Anthroposophical Society a circle that is carried by the living consciousness that such a thing must be worked and woven into the development of humanity!

It was not merely to convey truths, but to arouse such a feeling in souls that I have given lectures such as these.

5

Times of Expectation

DORNACH, OCTOBER 7, 1914

We will begin this evening with a reading of a few poems left behind—and not yet printed—by our dear friend Christian Morgenstern; and with them a few more poems from the recently published volume.† A musical presentation will follow, and then we will view a few pictures of our building, followed by another piece of music. And for those friends who still wish to stay, I will offer in conclusion a few observations, in which I will fit in a brief comment about our eurythmy for those who expressed the desire to hear something about its nature.

To take the opportunity over and over again to bring Christian Morgenstern's verses before our souls—especially those which lay so close to his heart in the final period of his physical life when he was so intimately tied to us—seems to be a holy duty. It is also something truly intimately linked to the entire nature and path of our spiritual-scientific movement in the present. Still, one may simply say that Christian Morgenstern's manner of living his way into what spiritual science wishes to announce to the world has also in a spiritual sense become felicitous for our movement, which indeed is still at the beginning of its growth.

Most of the friends gathered here know from various cycles and individual lectures I have given here and there in recent months that being together with Christian Morgenstern after his death was one of my most significant esoteric experiences in recent times. And I have not held back, especially with the experience connected with Christian Morgenstern that is so significant for the blessing flowing to our movement from the spiritual world: that a poet could tie his soul so intimately to our movement which to a certain extent the cosmic tableau belonging to the elements of his present nature in the spiritual world, reveals, with the means of the cosmic world and at the same time like an inherent part of Christian Morgenstern, the truth of the very thing we have to recognize and to teach. That is something exceptionally significant, something that can in an astonishing way pour trust into the inner truth and also into the inner power of our movement. We know that something like the confluence of the cosmic All is now bound with Christian Morgenstern's individual being. Just as one beholds in a great canvas of a painter many of the secrets of the physical plane combined into one, so is the whole being of Christian Morgenstern bound together with this, I should like to say, cosmic painting in which he now lives in the spiritual world, because there individuals have to give not only their abilities to what they manifest, but their entire being. And one of the most moving experiences one can have is to see that he now lives, for the first time, with his true nature. It is most moving when one sees how this human being, who lived here in the physical world hemmed in by physical constraints of the most diverse kinds, can now freely unfold himself (those who love him can intuit, can experience this) in the spiritual world. It is moving how we can only fully get to know such a being when we understand him in his significance after death.

So after his death Christian Morgenstern appears to me as the spiritual leader of many people who have, in a recent period of the spiritual development of humanity, gone up into the spiritual worlds and are experiencing through this a tremendous boon, because in the physical world they were endowed with inner yearning for the spiritual worlds and could not find it. They brought this yearning up with them. We have indeed spoken of these yearnings on the day of the laying of the foundation stone in reference to a particular person, Herman Grimm.† I showed how close he was to a comprehension of the spiritual world, and yet was still not able to find it. For him and for many others it means a tremendous benefit that they can now be convinced of what they sought but could not find—convinced because they have it before them in the soul of Christian Morgenstern. It is not as though they could not find it otherwise in the spiritual world, but it is something else to have it right in front of them in this way. That is the huge blessing of the fact that Christian Morgenstern bound himself to our movement in spirit and consequently was able to carry it up, so that those beings who yearned to see such a thing could see Anthroposophy in the spiritual world.

Especially in my connection with Christian Morgenstern after his death, I had often to think of two facts. One is connected with one of the greatest representatives of modern spiritual life, with Goethe. Now, all of us know Goethe as the poet of *Faust*, as one of the truest poets of all times, because he had fought through and suffered through what he showed in *Faust*. You all know that the second part of *Faust* closes with *Faust* going up into the spiritual worlds. Goethe showed this, but in Goethe's time the possibility was not available to find the images that correspond to the truth as it must be seen today. In this connection it makes a tragic impression when we read Goethe's conversation with Eckermann in which he speaks of his difficulties in completing the second part of *Faust* when he was working on visualizing this passage up into the higher worlds.† He says there:

> After all you will admit that the conclusion, where the saved soul goes up, was very hard to do, and that with such supersensible, barely imaginable things I could have lost myself very easily in vagueness, if I had not given a benevolently limiting form and firmness to my poetic intentions through sharply delineated Christian and Catholic figures and ideas.

We know that Goethe found it necessary to reach for these outmoded Christian Catholic forms, that he had to clothe the passage of the soul into the supersensible world in these forms. We know, however, also that the yearning lived in him for what we are attempting today to bring in new forms, forms appropriate for our time.

For that reason it is of infinite significance that our movement found right at the beginning a poet like Christian Morgenstern, who was in the position to transfer everything this movement could give him directly into personal feelings, which resonate for us particularly with such warmth and, magnificently, love from the poems he left behind. That it was possible for him, right at the beginning of our movement, to absorb what it could give so directly into personal terms, is of vast importance, because Christian Morgenstern has raised everything personal into a superpersonal sphere related to the points of departure of our movement. That such a thing is possible is truly related to the confidence we can have in our movement.

I must be ever mindful of another fact these days. I mentioned once in a Berlin lecture that I had a conversation with Herman Grimm,† which was so close to all the yearnings that could lead to an understanding of the supersensible worlds in our fashion. In the conversation I attempted to touch on these things. He had only a gesture of rejection for it; he didn't want to let it come near him. There was something deeply disturbing about seeing this peculiar behavior of Herman Grimm, of all people, toward this fundamentally characteristic form of spiritual life for our time—Herman Grimm, whom I want to call the accredited representative for Goethe in the second half of the nineteenth century. All the strivings of our movement go in the direction of pointing out to just such spirits who are now in the spiritual world what Christian Morgenstern can say to them. You see then how we seek to raise what we feel as our connection, our relation, our love for Christian Morgenstern to a super-personal sphere. I have attempted to indicate this in a few words.

If you pursue with your feeling what will be presented to you now, you will feel through the words of Christian Morgenstern yet another experience: what he is for our movement and is still to become. At one place in particular we will feel ourselves moved deeply in the heart with respect to the events of these times. Even if Christian Morgenstern obviously meant, as he wrote the little verse, an entirely different war than the one we must experience today, what this little poem contains still goes deep into the heart in regard to the events of the present day.

So we will now proceed, before I continue these observations, to hear something from the poems left behind by our dear friend Christian Morgenstern.

(Recitation by Marie Steiner-von Sivers, "Aus den nachgelassenen Gedichten von Christian Morgenstern" [From the poems left behind by Christian Morgenstern]. Which poems were recited is not recorded, but among them were certainly the two following.)

Anthroposophy

Oh World,—you pitiful human,
you who do not know
what here in your midst exists.
The true greatness of this muddled time
is here alive, humanly lived forth,
a piece of the loftiest history unrolls
here before us—and in it we are with it together.
Oh great World, you pitiful mother-being—
who (once again—Oh, you dreamer!)
does not know, does not imagine
what is coming to birth in you.

(1911)

I

I watch how the ancient World
rises up in me and endlessly makes war,
and how the new over it gently glides,
alternately dimming and glowing.
I look on. How ends the war?
Will the thick smoke fall to earth
and over it morning brilliance dawn?
"I" looks on at me. This perhaps declares the victory.

(1909)

(Music. Presentation of pictures of the Goetheanum construction. Music.)

Perhaps you have already gleaned from many things said here and also in other places about the field of spiritual science, as well as from the introductory talk about our dear friend Christian Morgenstern, that it matters somewhat to me to take all our efforts, therefore also what is connected to our efforts, as a whole, as something unified; and that it matters to me particularly that this whole, which is to be incorporated into the evolution of humanity as an impulse toward a new spiritual culture, really connects to the yearnings, the hopes, the expectations for a spiritual culture of the immediately bygone period. I have indeed attempted to emphasize this particularly here, at the celebration of the commemoration of the laying of the foundation stone of our building. We should therefore regard our spiritual science and its endeavors, and also what will live itself into our cultural context as eurythmy, as a unified whole, but also as something that is not only a whole in itself, but that joins onto something we have expected. And when I previously attempted to draw a line with a few words from Goethe to Christian Morgenstern through Herman Grimm, it should be a double example that, on the one hand, there is real reason to believe with rather profound optimism in a progress in the development of humanity and that, on the other hand, spiritual factors, spiritual impulses constantly intervene in the development of humankind. I attempted to lead before your souls how Goethe in the conclusion of his *Faust* was compelled to represent the ascent of Faust into the spiritual worlds with old Christian Catholic forms; and I observed, in addition, how in the poet Christian Morgenstern, one who found his way to us has made a beginning in molding spiritual life, the supersensible worlds, in new forms necessary for people today. From many of the posthumous poems and from much of what I have said, you will have again perceived how poetry can make itself one, most intimately one, with what the spiritual life, as we mean it, desires: that a new relationship be found between the life of the human being on the physical pane and its being connected with the spiritual worlds, and how spiritual factors intervene in the further development of humanity. I tried to make it clear (daring to express what may be expressed among true Anthroposophists) that Herman Grimm, who may be called the accredited representative of Goethe in the second half of the nineteenth century, may to a certain extent now find, in what Christian Morgenstern was able to carry up to the spiritual worlds, what he could not find on Earth in his physical body. There we see the synergy of the spiritual with the physical development of humanity.

And are we not seeking, my dear friends, with everything that is expressed in our building, a new form of the old beauty? After all beauty signifies still much more than what one usually would connect to this concept. We must have a clear idea of how many-sided the progress of humanity is if we wish to be aware of what it means that in any particular age like ours, new forms of beauty, new forms of the entire mood of the human soul should emerge. Humanity must arrive at the point where something develops from the impulses of spiritual science that signifies a progress in relation to what was earlier, that goes beyond what Goethe himself could have intended in *Faust*. We must hope for something of the sort. Goethe, when he felt the longing to immerse himself in beauty, could do nothing other than go to Rome, to relive Greek beauty in his soul. Basically the entire nineteenth century could do nothing other than go to Rome to gain secondhand experience of Greek beauty. But the age has arrived in which we must not merely go to Rome, not merely immerse ourselves in classical Greek forms of beauty; we must enter the spiritual worlds to find new forms of beauty there. And value must be placed on the fact that the bygone age to a certain extent thirsted for such an approach to a period of spiritual experience. More than the present age can imagine, this is all expressed particularly in a spirit like Herman Grimm, this representative of Goetheanism in the second half of the nineteenth century. Not to say something about Herman Grimm, but rather to show by his example what is expected of the spiritual life of our present day, I will fit this link, Herman Grimm, into the development of humanity as it has proceeded from Goethe to us, who may regard ourselves as living and striving in the middle of what Goethe willed in the deepest recesses of his heart, in the deepest recesses of his soul. The way in which spiritual life progresses in the evolution of humanity is complex and accessible only to deeper contemplation.

You know I mention personal matters only when there is an objective reason to do so. I often, when I turn my attention to the evolution of humanity, think of a feeble attempt I made as a very young person. In only the second essay I ever had published,† I attempted—naively, obviously, for I was just twenty-three or twenty-four years old—to form a clear idea of the progress from Shakespearean characters to Goethe's *Faust*. Something was created through Shakespeare—it had to be created especially in his time—in which people could only be represented as human types in a way that shows a direct unfolding of their inner powers of soul. The progress in Goethe's *Faust* is that Goethe did not cast the individual characters as individual types—like Hamlet, Lear, Macbeth and so forth in Shakespeare—but rather Faust as the human being of our age. Faust can be put into a literary work only once; what Shakespeare had to give could be brought to us in many human types. One must keep an eye on the complexity of human spiritual life in evolution—in each period, precisely that must happen which expresses itself as what is characteristic of that period.

When we attempt today to properly find a soul mood, to properly find a deep feeling from the connection of the human soul with the higher hierarchies, it is truly, as we encounter in spiritual science, in a certain sense the fulfillment of expectations, expectations that held such a place in the development of humanity, that one can say: Such representative spirits as Herman Grimm expressed in their way the deepest yearning for something they were waiting for, which must be put in the same way we describe today the higher hierarchies and their relationship to the human being. You see, on the deepest level—properly at the most soulful, one might say with all the power of the soul—a spirit like Herman Grimm could express this. And precisely in his case it once again becomes apparent, even as we open his books, how in his personality the expectation is bound to spiritual science, which, however, as he briefly encountered it, he could not understand. It was necessary for something to intervene like what occurred after the death of Christian Morgenstern.

I met once with Herman Grimm on the occasion of his visit to the Goethe-Schiller Archive in Weimar.† Then he spoke about how he conceived the evolution of humanity: that for him history was not an accounting of what is usually laid out in history; for him history was the evolution of spiritual forces. However, he could only rise to the point of calling it a history of the imaginative work of humanity. It did not dawn on him that there are imaginations in the development of humanity that unconsciously flow into humanity and transform themselves into human activity, that there are inspirations and intuitions in history. It was for him "the imaginative work of the peoples." When he wished to find the rising from the physical world into the spiritual he could not get to the point of resolving the purely external, the factual aspect of maya, which he called "the imaginative work of the peoples," through what must reveal itself in the human spirit. One will in fact understand only later what it meant for the nineteenth century when Herman Grimm said,[†] "What can interest us particularly about the transmission of the history of Julius Caesar? Julius Caesar," in Herman Grimm's opinion, "is of much more interest to me as he is presented by Shakespeare. That is more real, more historical than everything laid out in history." Over and over again, he referred to how he enjoyed reading Tacitus, because he was a person who knew how to make what he had to describe alive from within his soul, and to transform it into the spiritual. From such ideas such a marvelous thought emerged as the one Herman Grimm wrote down during the nineties, in his book about Homer—a thought that really stands there so properly as an expectation that it should come as advance tidings of the hierarchies: "The human race as a totality acknowledges itself as subjected to an invisible court of law as if reigning in the clouds. Humanity may not stand up against this court, which it regards as a misfortune and to whose judiciary procedure it seeks to adapt its inner discord." A wonderful image of the court of justice reigning in the clouds, under which the peoples know they are subjected! Does there not live therein all yearning for the hierarchies, for the knowledge of what the hierarchies are for humanity?

In this way spirits arose in the recent development of the spirit who in their historical vision had a kind of transformative power, so that here too such spirits stand as before the portals of what spiritual science wills. Through spiritual science humanity will first learn a proper conception of the fact that Herman Grimm actually contributed something to the development of the world through speaking as he did of Michelangelo, Raphael, Tacitus, Shakespeare, Voltaire, and Homer, and will feel these thoughts about the real development of the world in their hearts as well. And what Herman Grimm said about Christ is once again an anticipation of what spiritual science says about Christ. In this way you have a sample of what really matters a great deal to me when we look at the emergence of spiritual science in the life of today: to represent how spiritual science comes as a fulfillment of much that has been expected. In 1895 the book was published in which the court of law reigning in the clouds was mentioned. We feel an intimate connection with that, if we may speak of a succession of levels of the hierarchies; an image that reproduces the inner truth of the matter is translated into the spiritual.

And the beginnings of this inner transformative quality have already shown themselves. For just as Herman Grimm, for example, has spoken about Michelangelo, Raphael, Homer, Tacitus, Shakespeare, and Voltaire at the time of the Franco-Prussian War of 1870, so the way he was able to make the works of Emerson come alive in the fifties of the last century shows us something of the transformative power for which the serious part of humanity strives, and which can now find its fulfillment in spiritual science. And spiritual science must provide exactly what can become most personal for each human being, so that human feeling becomes the broadest, the very broadest—but for all that, also the most intensive.

I really want to say that particularly in such a representative spirit as Herman Grimm—in relation to whom I believe I can bring increasingly more and more the effect of our friend Christian Morgenstern in the spiritual world—the striving for the spiritual reveals itself, and it is important not to pass over these facts. Herman Grimm was a four-year-old child when Goethe died; he was seventy-three when he died on June 16, 1901. He lived his life in the second half of the nineteenth century in such a way that he had to be unified in his personality with everything that flowed into humanity from Goethe as impulses of beauty.

In a wonderful way we see particularly in Herman Grimm this tendency of humanity toward the spiritual, this formation of an organ for the understanding of the spiritual. And when I think of the cultural value of our eurythmy, I must look again and again at how in the case of Herman Grimm everything in the outer gesture was one, and harmony was present, which tends not to emerge particularly in materialistic life when one is not so inclined to see where the spiritual passes into the physical. It is enough to drive you up the wall when you see how all the modern sports—such as soccer, and so forth—mechanize human beings and add nothing to them of what is spiritual, as much as one imagines they do. Everything one strives for in sports is indeed a mockery of the spiritual, as well intentioned as it is. Conversely, a figure like Herman Grimm, with whom everything external is in harmony with the spiritual, appears as something unified: the way he walked, even the fact that he always wore a top hat, belongs to the wholeness of his personality; the way in which he moved his hands, how he spoke, the way he sojourned in Bolzano when he was writing his book on Homer, how he could only work on the Homer book as he awaited spring in Bolzano. Everything is so beautifully harmonious: how he worked on the Homer book, how he went out in Bolzano at the day's waning and in the park contemplated the wonderful statue of Walther von der Vogelweide, how he knew how to describe it, right into the gestures, how he was able to describe the wonderful marble that comes from quarries close to Bolzano, and how he could connect everything he created, everything he did, to the cultural life, in the midst of which he stood.

I have confidence in my ability to judge some things, as I was for a time close to a workshop of German intellectual life. I was in Weimar from 1889 to 1897 at the Goethean Institute, with which Herman Grimm was also connected. There, especially, one could feel how Goethe was the king of intellectual, cultural life and Herman Grimm was his representative, accredited by the spiritual powers. One could feel how Herman Grimm tried to encompass everything that had to do with Goethe in a spiritual harmony of gestures. His striving was to take Goethe in a spiritual way, to recognize Goethe—who had passed on but was living on in the impulses he had established—as living and weaving in the cultural life, in the midst of which Grimm felt himself to be. It was the beginning of the feeling we have today that the dead are as intimately connected with us as before they passed through the portal of death, and that they live with us, as it were, but only in a different form. His striving was to gather together all individual phases, all individual moments of life in one gesture, in one spiritual gesture.

Perhaps many things back then would have led me to what is to be achieved in spiritual science, but I believe most certainly that I would not have been led to what our eurythmy offers if I had not back then stood so close to that cultural life; if I had not recognized, as well, that the striving existed to summon something that is spiritual and which is at the same time experienced in the external world—is really there in the external world. Naturally, it is all a great karmic connection, and no accident. The way Herman Grimm wanted to take life is something like an inner eurythmy, just as he had the wonderful transformative ability as a very young man to introduce Emerson into German culture in such a way as would happen in no other country. He drew attention to the fact that Emerson should be read more because he showed the best side of Americanism, and he resurrected Voltaire, Michelangelo, Raphael, and also Goethe, about whom he gave those wonderful lectures at the beginning of the 1870s at Berlin University. The scholars were not entirely happy with the lectures, but in every thought, in every word, in every sentence Goethe was alive. And in his book *Goethe*, Herman Grimm really wanted to give something to life in every aspect. That Goethe—who had been physically dead since 1832, who was almost forgotten—came back to life precisely through Herman Grimm in the 1870s was a singular occurrence.

But now, because I spoke of the unified gesture, I want to refer to how Herman Grimm always made an effort to see all things in a larger context, how he was able in this respect to become the schoolmaster for all who were seeking the transition from the spiritual life of the nineteenth century to the spiritual life of Anthroposophy. Goethe is something universal for humanity: Hermann Grimm draws attention in his *Contributions to German Cultural History* to how Goethe immediately became universal on Earth after he entered the spiritual world through the portal of death. Grimm cites a beautiful passage from a lecture of Carlyle of 1838:

> The appearance of such a man at any given era is, in my opinion, the greatest thing that can happen in it—a man who has the soul to think, and be the moral guide of his own nation and of the whole world. All people that live under his influence gather themselves round him, and therefore, although many writers made their appearance in Germany after him, Goethe was the man to whom they looked for inspiration: they took from him the color they assume. I can have little to say of him in these limits. I can say of him the same as I said of Shakespeare: there has been no such man as himself since Shakespeare. He was not like Shakespeare, yet in some respects he came near to Shakespeare—in his clearness, tolerance, and humane depth. He, too, was a devout man.

Such a statement refers at the same time to the universal, to what cuts into all human relations, to what makes the spiritual hero appear as if he does not reign only in the clouds, but in such a way that he really reaches into spiritual affairs. Something was contributed about Goethe in the entire consciousness of Herman Grimm, who was really suited to take Goethe's spirit in such a universal way that Goethe could appear to him like the spiritual emperor, the emperor of spiritual-cultural life. In Herman Grimm self-confidence and the free personality, the whole free sovereignty of the personality, express themselves in the world in a manner different than we are accustomed to. One may truly say that something is alive in Herman Grimm that allowed him to take external matters as they are and, on the other hand, allowed him always to support himself on what he had in him of the spiritual life; and he judged all worldly affairs out of the certainty of this spiritual life.

So a time comes when Herman Grimm, in his distinguished, quiet way, could catch sight of the loftiest moment in spiritual life: when a monarch of the external world pays homage to the spiritual emperor. That is also a gesture of this world of unspeakable significance.

I know that many have taken exception to that, but one must take things in their deeper context. Many have taken exception to the fact that Herman Grimm mentions something that happened to him on Christmas Eve 1876. It is significant because it leads to a point in modern times when a person stands there who feels it is natural when a monarch of the external world pays homage to the spiritual emperor. So it appears to me to be terribly characteristic of the modern spiritual life when Herman Grimm tells in his *Contribution to German Cultural History,* how on Christmas Eve 1876 the following letter from the German Kaiser Wilhelm I was delivered to him:

> Perusing your book, *Goethe,* of which you presented me copy on the twentieth of the previous month, has furnished me with very pleasant impressions. You have succeeded in sensitively adding to the luminous picture of the great poet yet many a trait, as warm as life, and in gaining new points of view for the understanding of the relations between the external events of his life and his works. While I consider myself convinced that this intelligent gift offered to the admirers of the poet directly before Christmas will be recognized as a valuable enrichment of Goethe literature, I thank you most cordially for the pleasure, which I have personally drawn from the book.
>
> Berlin, December 24, 1876
> Wilhelm

Herman Grimm says beautiful words about receiving this letter, for a spirit like him took pleasure from the relationship between spiritual and worldly life. And he saw Goethe and his time in this light as well; he sought to climb or strive up to something that escapes many people. And so it could happen that Herman Grimm, in connection with this letter, gave a beautiful, a memorable description of the confluence of spiritual life with that of the external world of the nineteenth century. He says: "From Weimar outward"—Weimar was for Herman Grimm the foremost capital of German spiritual life; I know it and have often taken pleasure in it—"the basic outlines of the spiritual development of Germany were drawn so firmly that Goethe's views remained the natural standard. And, as in the pressure of national political need Shakespeare rose anew beside him, the latter was like only a dependent province of the Goethean empire. For Schlegel had, so to speak, translated Shakespeare into Goethe's German at Goethe's behest, and Goethe and Shakespeare were united into a commonly effective power, etc. etc." And now follow the beautiful words:

> And that is how the Kaiser conceived of Goethe. Goethe was not only the great poet, the great thinker of his time; rather the brilliance of historical princely loftiness connected itself with his person. I remind you of the closing of the text cited above, where the Kaiser thinks of his personal enjoyment, which he drew from the book. What did this consist of? Hardly of anything owing to its literary quality. I would not have knowledge that the Kaiser would ever have mentioned Goethe in conversation, but he had, as I heard told, passages from the book read to him. I perceive in this the activity of a feeling in him that could not merely be defined by an interest in Goethe. Goethe was a departed power that possessed a claim on the participation of the German emperor. Something like those endowed with the highest Italian order, "les cousins du roi."

Herman Grimm understands how to show the way in which spiritual life holds everything, and he himself is such a representative spirit. He says further:

> One did not remember primarily his victories, his political successes, rather what was peaceful in the Kaiser. His gentleness. His balanced justice. It is wonderful how in the judgment of the peoples, even in the cases of warlike princes and holders of power, in the end what receives the most light is what they did for peaceful development. As in the cases of Frederick the Great and Napoleon, the admiring regard for their administrative activity already outweighs their warlike deeds.

Thus we see the spiritual life of the modern age present itself in a unified gesture with the outer life. Herman Grimm knew that he lived in times of expectation, as he expresses beautifully in the following statement:

> Goethe's age, along with the century to which it gives its name, is in the process of going under. We are excited about the past not merely because it is past. No matter how many ways people go at their seeking and their digging, no matter how emphatically the excavation reports of archaeologists speak of the importance of their most recent discoveries: the Goethean gaze rests no longer on how the marble rummaged out of the earth was transformed into spirit. And also the public who believed in the mysterious value of the thoughts that slumbered in these discoveries is lacking.
>
> The Age of Goethe is over! But Goethe himself? Did the century named after him know all the Goethean thoughts? Here we stand before a new historical knowledge.
>
> The radiance of Goethe while he was still alive had illuminated the German nation as the war against Napoleon I was completed and the liberated people began to set themselves up in their own house, in the honest belief that the victorious spirit must suffice for that. As long as the people who had been a part of it lived, an untouchable confidence in the power of higher spiritual work reigned. The years of humiliation that followed the wars of liberation could not shake it. This spirit was still alive in authoritative circles, when I gave my lectures on Goethe twenty years ago. Already, however, the people who no longer expected any advantage from science in the traditional sense were gaining the upper hand. Science, as we of the older generation understand the concept, rested on unlimited recognition of what was transmitted in the Greek and Latin languages.

Now, it is important that one understands more and more how the age of expectation is approaching, which finds in Herman Grimm a last representative spirit.

The twentieth century will perhaps discover that Goethe already knew in advance what it will eventually achieve for itself, and even what it still strives for. One will mark the passages of his works where that is expressed. The span of time that separates the successive generations from Goethe will stretch out ever more broadly. However, what does a century more or less matter for the relationship of a further developing humanity with Homer or Shakespeare? Their power to penetrate into souls is constantly growing. Goethe will one day accompany them as a star for humanity.

Everything in this man strives for spirit, for the transformation into spirit. In this way he has the expectation, and so brings us the genuine confidence that what we are offering has not arisen out of superficial arbitrariness, but rather is what humanity needs, what it has been waiting for. That is terribly important. Moreover, the universal in spiritual science is already living in this expectation. For that reason, I may refer once again to what Herman Grimm says in his book on Homer:

> Human beings as a totality recognize themselves as subjected to an invisible law court, as if it reigned in the heavens, before which they may not stand the test and which they consider as a misfortune, and to whose judicial processes they seek to adapt their discord. With anxious striving they seek justice for themselves here. What an effort the French make to present the war they intend against Germany as a moral claim that should be recognized by the other nations, even by the Germans themselves. I feel that Homer's goal was to conceive the battle of the people before Troy as if this movement lying in the most extreme antiquity had included many nations that had a common moral consciousness and were struggling with each other for the leading position. They resemble the nations of our own time in this. Neither external accidental force nor accidental protection of divine powers is decisive, but rather the justification that character bestows was decisive in the *Iliad*.

A beautiful passage, a splendid passage!

> The solidarity of the moral convictions of all people is the church that binds us all. We seek more passionately than ever a visible expression of this community. All truly serious efforts of the masses know only this one goal. The separation of the nations is here already nonexistent. We feel that in relation to an ethical worldview no national difference is valid. We all would sacrifice ourselves for our Fatherland; we are, however, far from yearning for or bringing on the moment when this could come about through war. The assurance that the most sacred wish of us all is to keep the peace is no lie. "Peace on Earth and good will to men" permeates us.

Thus spoke Herman Grimm in central Europe in the year 1895.

My dear friends, humanity has already striven to bring life into harmony with the spiritual worlds; it strove to find a society like ours. And there were efforts that adopted the correct position to all peoples of the Earth and toward the peace of humanity, which were expressed in the attitude that Homer also wanted to express, according to Herman Grimm's view of the Greek peoples: that they prefer peace to war. And in this way humanity was to learn that among many people what I have described in the case of Herman Grimm lived as an attitude bound intimately with the soul: there was the aspiration to receive life as if from one mold, and the outbreak of this war, which was really not desired by this attitude, came as a surprise.

And that the offshoots of our spiritual movement should arise from the whole of our spiritual life should indeed be a fulfillment of expectation. So it is with our eurythmy, which should not be confused with any of the exercises—physical, sportive, gymnastic, or dance-like—that emerged from the materialistic age; rather it was pulled out of our spiritual endeavors, so that people can learn especially in this sphere how the spirit works in the most direct and intimate experience. I have already shown from diverse viewpoints how we arrived at this eurythmy. The aspiration existed to give something to humanity that shows the spirit of evolution in an external sense as well. We could only do this when it was clearly understood that we, in our direct life experience, also live in a world of forms, and that our steps forward are a penetration into the world of movement. The world of forms rules our physical body, the world of movement rules our etheric body. The movements born in the etheric body must now be found. The human being must be led to bring to expression in gestures, in movements of the physical body, what is natural for the etheric body.

You will have seen in the preceding lectures about esoteric reading and esoteric hearing that some element of regular movement lies in the universe, in cosmic becoming. This carries itself over to the human etheric body. Our materialistic culture of the present, from which spirits like Herman Grimm yearned to escape, has led to the situation that we have no understanding at all for the fact that human beings can only move themselves in external forms when they are not possessed by such "dumb" (forgive the trivial expression) movements as in sport, in modern gymnastics, or in playing soccer; but rather pursue in themselves the movements born in a natural way in the etheric body and begin to carry those movements into the movements of the physical body, so that the etheric body lives on in the movements of the physical body. That is attempted in eurythmy. It will emerge that in their movements human beings are really an intermediary link between the cosmic letters, the cosmic sounds, and what we ourselves use in the human sounds and letters in our poetry.

Most assuredly a new art will arise in eurythmy, an art for everybody. We might wish that humanity would be seized by an understanding of it, so that it would be practiced by children from the smallest, who have already experienced the most intimate joy from it, to the largest, and on up to people seventy, eighty, and ninety years old. It is always good when a person learns to transfer what is natural and inborn in the etheric body into physical movements. It is pretty obvious in spiritual life that what one can say in poetry can find its interpretation in the movements our eurythmy brings.

A pedagogical, an artistic, and a hygienic principle are simultaneously expressed in eurythmy. It is a pedagogical principle in that human beings who grow up with eurythmy, who do movements in the spirit of eurythmy from the earliest years of childhood on, carry out movements that have the effect that the gods feel themselves properly connected with the Earth. Hence eurythmy is properly a means of producing a connection between the divine hierarchies and the growing child.

For esotericists it is immediately clear that a materialistic culture brings about a terrible discrepancy between what is born in a person and what the head and the heart must often learn. I do not wish to criticize this, but only refer to a fact. There is really nothing in the world up until now more unnatural than that children growing up today, from approximately the sixth or seventh year on, have to learn what they simply must learn. I am not saying they should not learn it, for obviously they must—it is a part of external social necessity. However, for souls it is in many ways as if one wanted to induce a natural development of the human body by breaking the hands and legs of children in the sixth or seventh year. That is what is done, more or less, when children are forced to learn letters, since for human beings, learning to read and write are the most unnatural activities there are. We must force them into it, although the greatest disharmony exists between the art of reading and writing and the direction the soul would naturally take. It is wretched to observe, but it is a necessity; it doesn't help to close oneself off from it. Almost anything would be more intelligent than teaching reading and writing at this age. Even instructing children to make figures out of simple filth from the street would be much more intelligent. The only thing we can do is to attempt to make the atrophied etheric body—for it is atrophied under modern necessities—move in the eurythmic movements of the physical body, as the gods wish. That is what eurythmy should offer in a pedagogical connection.

It is not surprising that many people complain today about this or that hurting when nothing is wrong with them. Humans today are attempting nothing more than to do what the Greeks did—to produce a harmony between the external movements of the physical body and those of the etheric body—and it can be very comical. When we tell ourselves that what the Greeks did in the Olympic Games was very intelligent, and so decide "We'll do that too," it is really very funny. It is the same as if, for example, a twenty-five-year-old were not happy to study at a university and preferred doing what a five- or ten-year-old does. Simply to bring Greek custom over into our time, is the most ridiculous thing one can do: it is a sin against trust in the development of humanity. If we seek today what the Greeks sought in their way at the Olympic Games, then eurythmy must live its way into humanity. We must attempt to effect health from within the soul by not allowing the etheric body to atrophy, by letting the physical body do the movements demanded by the etheric body. That is the hygienic side of eurythmy.

The artistic meaning of eurythmy will finally occur to people when they recognize that human beings are not only the creator of this or that, but must become an artistic medium or means; they will become that by practicing the artistic with their own body. And that they do through eurythmy.

Eurythmy is not something arbitrary that has arisen from approximately the same mentality as other endeavors of the present day. It asks which movements are the best pedagogically and hygienically for present-day people in respect to the etheric body. Which movements best lead human beings to the understanding of what is truly artistic and best insert them into a full life? For this reason I believe that eurythmy will soon become popular in our circles and will be accepted as something that can help a great deal. You certainly cannot teach your children Anthroposophy straight off, but if they practice eurythmy, they will grow up to meet life in an entirely different way than if they did not practice eurythmy.

I have in many respects already spoken of the relationship of the great space of the round building out there to what is within the small space. Someone could ask how the forms of the small space proceed from those of the large space, and the answer is to try to have the forms of the great space of the building danced according to the laws of eurythmy; then the forms of the small space will emerge from it. Try to imagine that a person brings together in eurythmic movements everything that is expressed in the forms of the great round building, and dances this into the small space, and radiates out from there what is danced; then the twelvefold nature of the columns and the cupola of the small space would grow out of it by themselves.

And then I hope that something else would dance eurythmically in the building: the Word! It will have good acoustics. In brief, one can define eurythmy as the fulfillment of what the human etheric body demands from the human being according to its natural laws. Hence eurythmy really offers something that belongs to our spiritual life as well, and something that is thought out from its totality.

Perhaps you will take what I have wanted to say with all of this as an answer to a question put to us by many of our Swiss friends. What I have thus defined you can, in reality, become acquainted with through the desired courses.

PART II

HOW TO ACHIEVE EXISTENCE IN THE WORLD OF IDEAS

6

The Human Organization, Memory, and Inner Reading

DORNACH, DECEMBER 12, 1914

I spoke here a while ago of what we call esoteric reading and esoteric hearing. Today and tomorrow I will add to those discussions and, in doing so, will develop several important ideas about our building.[†]

If we look at external scientific observation today, insofar as it is relevant to the life of the soul, we find many difficulties with it as soon as we attempt to get a satisfactory overview of the pertinent concepts. One difficulty, which is truly not a small one, results when we look at the external science's observation of human memory.

Now, I would have to adduce a great deal if I wanted to give an account of what external psychology, or doctrine of the soul, can say about the memory of human beings. That would not lead us very far, but I do want to make you aware of where the difficulty lies for external psychology when it comes to understanding memory and its characteristics.

It is true, is it not, that human memory shows itself to us in such a way that we can call back into consciousness—at a later time—thoughts, concepts, and ideas that we have received at any time in the past? This spiritual fact is therefore obvious. Today, for example, we can have any kind of perception or experience, and, after a certain time, without standing in front of what originally elicited the perception or experience, we can make the conception or experience of the original fact live once again from within—out of ourselves.

It appears, then, as if the human soul in some way stores up in itself everything it receives from without. Thus, when we become acquainted with someone, we have an impression of that person, which we transform into a concept and store as a conceptual image in our subconscious. When we need it, we call it back again.

From this point of view it might seem obvious that our soul, insofar as it develops the power of our memory, is, let us say, like a box in which we can put away and store all concepts and experiences, taking them out again when we need to call them up into consciousness. All possible experiences would be stored in the cupboard of the soul, and it would be possible to call them up once again from there. Indeed, when we read books today discussing memory, we get the impression that the authors often believe the soul is really such a storage cupboard for all possible experiences. Just think, you walk around with your soul and carry with you a cupboard for all your impressions and experiences.

But here we must admit immediately that a difficulty presents itself. Attempts have been made to bridge over this difficulty with all sorts of scientific concepts, but nothing particularly satisfying has emerged. Indeed, this difficulty can be overcome finally only by acquiring a deeper insight into the fourfold articulation of the human being; into the physical body, the etheric body, the astral body, and the "I." To attain real knowledge of the nature of human memory, we must study the human etheric and astral bodies.

Let us begin by forming, through a comparison, a concept of what the astral body of the human being actually is. Isn't it true that in everyday waking life we do not experience ourselves in the astral body any more than we experience ourselves in the etheric body? From waking up until going to sleep, we experience ourselves in our "I" and thus all experiences are I-experiences. We do not experience ourselves in the astral body—which is in fact infinitely wiser than the I-person. It is capable of much more than the I-person is. This astral body can read—really read—what I have described for you as esoteric writing.

So, in addition to many other concepts that can give us an understanding of the astral body, it is also a reader of esoteric writing. On the other hand, the etheric body is, among many other things, something like a tablet, upon which esoteric writing is engraved through the processes of the world.

While we live—and we are always living, whether in waking and sleeping between birth and death, or between death and a new life—processes are constantly occurring in the universe; events unfold in the cosmos. The essential lives in the cosmos, and all of it replicates itself, inscribes itself, in the etheric body. The human etheric body in fact truly replicates the whole cosmos. There is nothing in the cosmos that does not imprint an image of itself in the etheric body of the human being and mirror itself in the imagination. And the human astral body constantly reads what the world inscribes in the etheric body. This process proceeds in the human subconscious, where the human astral body reads what the world inscribes in the human etheric body.

Even in our conscious, waking life, when we encounter an event or an object that makes an impression on us, we form a concept of it. The astral body is first occupied with this formation of the concept. It is in active movement while we are forming a concept of an object or of the impression of an external event. What we form in this way as a concept, what we have as an experience in the soul, is also inscribed in our etheric body. Just as the world with its events is constantly inscribing itself in our etheric body, so we also inscribe in our etheric body what we ourselves experience in our soul. There it remains inscribed. Thus, when we remember something, a complicated process takes place. Our astral body reads what has been inscribed in our etheric body, and the result of this reading is that an idea forces its way up to the surface, which we call memory.

In this way memory can be traced back to a way of reading our astral body in the etheric body. And as soon as we know this, we can no longer entertain the simplistic idea that the soul is a storage cupboard for what we have experienced; rather we will understand that, in fact, when it has experienced something, the astral body transforms itself over and over into a few habits and then impresses these into the etheric body. (I say literally "habits"; tomorrow, we will understand this word better.) Just as our writing system has few letters, our astral body has few—very few—habits. And just as we communicate the whole infinite fullness of what human beings have to say about themselves and the world with a few letters, through different written combinations, so what memory stores is formed through the combinations of a few habits.

When we know that the process is a kind of reading, we will no longer believe that each individual experience must be inscribed; rather a few habits of the astral body are combined and then fixed in the etheric body. Just as when we hear a new word we are able to set it down with the old letters, we can set down each new experience in the etheric body with a few habits of the astral body. This reality stems from the fact that our etheric and especially our astral bodies are linked with the entire cosmos. We must not take what an older wisdom teaching has lifted out of the cosmos so simply as something lifted out by chance; rather it has a deep meaning and importance.

If we consider the twelve signs of the complete zodiac, we can say that in fact our astral body is in living connection with those twelve signs. They signify for the astral body twelve particular habits, twelve particular ways, of being in movement. And, as we have often discussed, our astral body is likewise also connected with the seven planets. These also determine certain habits in the astral body (again, I say literally "habits"). Through these habits, which are ignited in our astral body by the planets of our solar system, something arises in the astral body that is similar to the vowels; and through the habits similarly stimulated by the influence of the zodiac, something arises in the astral body that is similar to the consonants.

Let us assume that our astral body, at some particular moment in life, is connected with the powers that flow from the sign of Aries. There are always such moments, because we are always connected with the world. Because our astral body stands in connection with or under the influence of what flows out of the sign of Aries, the possibility develops in the astral body to close itself off, to give itself a boundary. And conversely, when the astral body is rather under the influence of Libra, a movement develops in it that leaves it more open to the whole world.

In this way a different particular tendency toward movement develops under the influence of each of the signs of the zodiac. Under the influence of this or that sign, the astral body stretches its upper part especially loftily upward; under the influence of one of the other signs, it extends its lower part. Twelve such particular ways of movement give twelve corresponding habits, and seven further particular habits are given under the influence of the planets. The habits under the influence of the planets are more inner movements, through which the inner parts move or bring themselves into a relationship with one another. So, basically, our astral body has been planted through the cosmos with 12 + 7 = 19 habits.

Just as with our alphabet, through combinations of the signs for the vowels and consonants, we can indicate everything we bring to light with our wisdom and wish to express, so too our astral body forms everything it has to form through the combinations of these nineteen habits. When a person approaches us with a face that regards us benevolently or with hostility in a particular way, our astral body makes particular movements that are combined from these nineteen habits. The movements are inscribed in the etheric body, and then, at a later time, the astral body can re-read what is inscribed there. That is the foundation of memory! As soon as we go beyond what the senses and the intellect bind to the senses, we come immediately to the relationship of human beings to the cosmos. But the physical body conceals this relationship of the human being to the cosmos.

We therefore possess a continuous inner reading; and if we could go back, even historically, to the origins of writing, we would find that in fact this inner reading of human beings is imitated in the oldest human logographic systems. It is not true that writing systems arose somehow by chance. The original symbols for the consonants were imitations of the signs of the zodiac, and the original signs for the vowels were imitations of the images of the planets. External reading was nothing other than an imitation in the outer world of what human beings possessed as inner reading.

This is connected to the mentality of earlier times regarding literature. Because it was drawn from cosmic secrets, literature was regarded as something especially holy. We know that, in ancient

Egyptian culture, for example, when the scribes made mistakes, they exposed themselves under the strict laws of the country, according to the magnitude of the error, to the most painful punishments; indeed, even sometimes, if the error were great enough, to the death penalty. To write down what people could know of the holy secrets was regarded as something infinitely high and holy, because people still had a feeling of the connection of the written sign and all the holy secrets of human nature to the divine.

The important thing, as we gradually absorb spiritual science, is to receive once again the feeling of the sacred in the hidden aspects of human nature. This feeling is much more important than the mere theoretical absorption of spiritual-scientific things. Along with this feeling, however, comes the fact that when, in the course of their development human beings gave up all connection with the holiness of writing, they felt that something dreadful was happening in the history of humanity. Take a book from the early Middle Ages in your hands and try to transport yourself into the situation in which such a book came into being—how a monk wrote for years, indeed decades in this book, how he painted one single letter for a long, long time. Then people knew that writing had so great a value that they had to consider it holy. They knew that through writing they stood in a relationship with the good gods, and that what they entrusted to writing was to a certain extent drawn into the outer world from what came from the good gods.

But you certainly know that a contemporary sign of human development is that everything that comes from the good gods can be shifted in the world into ahrimanic or luciferic directions. The entirely ordinary printer's art developed into the thing from which human beings primarily get their wisdom today. We get our information about what people think or do not think about the world and its secrets by leaning our heads over papers, on which are wretched signs, signs that are now only imitations of the old written signs. The art of writing has been shifted from its true place. The nature of writing and communication has entered a new stage in which writing has lost any aura of the sacred; one could say that the ahrimanic stage of communication through writing has been entered. Ancient written signs in symbolism, even in imitation, were the drawing out into the outer world of hidden secrets corresponding to the nature of beings of the spiritual world who were progressing in a good sense. What we have today, especially in printed texts, but in a broader sense also in written texts, has a decidedly ahrimanic character. And people felt that this was so. Thus, they attributed the printer's art to the dark powers, called it a "black art," and indeed even attributed its invention to the devil.

Nonetheless, the invention of the printer's art has a deeper significance, which we see in the way Goethe brings what Faust experiences in a certain phase of his life into relation with the printer's art. The ahrimanic period of communication appeared when the printer's art arrived. We know indeed that we must rightly learn not to cross ourselves before precisely all the things that are called Ahrimanic. However, we also know that we should call things by their proper names and must understand them. We may not, as spiritual scientists, be among those who say that the art of printing is Ahrimanic and that we must therefore eliminate it. That we will not do, because we understand that the Ahrimanic is also necessary in the development of the world, that it also belongs to the progress of the world. However, we must see things as they are. We must not reinterpret things in order to make ourselves feel more comfortable by attempting to live in the world without Ahriman or Lucifer. Perhaps it is more pleasant not to know that Ahriman is actually staring out at us from every modern book, but it is necessary for those who see the world in its true light to put up with this situation and not to transform it into something else. Learning to understand the world is the duty of those who feel themselves drawn to spiritual science.

In our time we see an external natural science that would prefer to transform everything into a sort of mechanical movement of the smallest particles of matter. I have often spoken about the worldview that makes an external science out of our world. It tells us that colors—red, yellow, green, violet, blue—are nothing but oscillations in reality, that color is only something the eye calls forth. Red results from so and so many oscillations, yellow from so and so many oscillations, blue from so many, and violet from so many. We could say that modern observers tend to delete what they perceive in the world from their world picture, and put a material whirl in its place.

One of the last great spirits who resisted what we can call a swirling dance of material particles, especially in the field of color theory, was Goethe. And, because the modern world has constantly stepped closer and closer to this materialistic conception—this obliteration of what is around us as a complex world—we have not been able to understand what Goethe really wanted to say in his theory of color. As spiritual science permeates humanity, it will once again bring some order into this area, and Goethe's color theory will come to be justly appreciated. Goethe no doubt saw it as a kind of petty madness (in his idiosyncratic expressions he would perhaps have even said "great madness") to think that the colors flowing through the world are nothing more than what the eye calls forth from a whirl of oscillations, from an oscillating cosmos.

This oscillating cosmos (I have often called it a fantasy of recent natural science) was simply not present for Goethe; for him it was one of Mephistopheles' seductions. Goethe, with his alert senses, was given over to the fullness of what was flowing with colors in this world; he lived in the streams of color. To hypothesize the awful vibrations of modern physics in place of this flowing sea of color would have seemed to him as the most barren, gray theory.

Why? Because Goethe had a healthy human nature in the most profound sense, developed on all sides, and was always striving to place himself in the correct relationship to the world. A healthy nature, such as Goethe's, also sleeps well. This statement appears to be very trivial, but it contains a significant piece of wisdom, for sleeping well actually means a great deal for the spiritual researcher. In sleep, human beings are outside their physical and etheric bodies, present in their "I" and their astral body—so that they are then really within the experiences that bring the astral body in relation, for example, with the entire starry cosmos. The cosmos illuminates everything in the astral body, which in turn can assert itself on the influences of the signs of the zodiac and the planets. Just as in a waking state human beings live with the outer world, so in the sleeping state they live with the world of the stars. But we do not know very much about our life with the world of the stars.

It is important to understand why we do not know much about this life together with the stars. Why, actually, don't we know?

It is true, is it not, that we do not see a landscape when it is covered with fog? The fog flows over the landscape and the elements of the landscape—the rivers, mountains, plains, and so on—do not appear to us when they are permeated with fog. In the same way, when they are asleep, human beings are permeated by a fog—a spiritual fog. What does this spiritual fog consist of? It is a fog of desires. It is composed of desires, and these desires are formed of the yearning for the physical body. When human beings are outside of the physical and the etheric body, hence in the time between falling asleep and awakening, they constantly have the desire for the physical body: they would like to return to the physical body. They are drawn out of the physical body by the powers of the cosmos, and only when those powers let them go again do they slide back into the physical body when they wake up. Then their desire for the physical body is satisfied once again.

In the case of a person like Goethe, healthy sleep is present because the desire for the physical body is less than with many other people, and hence the influences from the cosmos during sleep are greater than with other people. A person like Goethe is more sensitive to the influences of the cosmos during sleep, and that constitutes his healthy sleep. The desire for the physical body is indeed present, but healthier than with other people. And why is it healthier? It is healthier precisely because while awake Goethe was given over in such a healthy way to the impressions of the outer world: because, for example, he was not content to put something theoretical like oscillations in the place of colors, but instead observed the colors themselves in their full-blooded reality. When a person like Goethe walks through nature and, although he is full of all kinds of wisdom, looks at the content directly as color—sees the green as green, the violet as violet, and the relation of green to violet or to yellow—it is different from when a dry theoretician walks through the field and does not see the colors, but rather speculates about how many billion or million oscillations correspond to green or red or yellow.

Why does such a dried-out theoretician walk through the world in this way? He is not devoted to the world of color because he is too strongly devoted to the physical body, even when it is primarily his own physical brain. All gray theories arise from an overly strong devotion to the physical body during daytime wakefulness. We would not have all the materialistic theories today if people were not so strongly devoted to the physical body. The more people expressly and selflessly give themselves over to the content of the world during wakeful life, the more they have the possibility of being devoted to the influences of the extraterrestrial cosmos during sleep, and of bringing back the healthy aftereffects of these impressions into daytime life. Then they will not, like desiccated physicists, assume there to be swirls of atoms behind the streaming colors, but rather spirit, elemental spirituality, the real effectiveness of the spirit.

To know that the living spiritual world is behind the impressions of the senses is an aftereffect of healthy sleep. But when people during daytime wakefulness cannot be selflessly given over to what streams outside in the world, and instead form dreadful theories about it that are actually phantasms, then they receive while sleeping a stronger, overpowering impulse toward the physical body. Their consciousness is not only dimmed toward the impressions of sleep, but also the intensity and strength of these impressions themselves is diminished.

The more spiritual science takes hold of human spiritual life, the more such bodies of wisdom as Goethean physics will take hold of people, as opposed to the gray theories that now pursue their mischief in external science. The acceptance of spiritual science by humanity has many connections. It will have tremendous meaning when the general consciousness is permeated with the truth that by night you are a human being within the extraterrestrial universe in a spiritual way, and by day you dive under into your physical and etheric bodies. One will learn to perceive and feel so much in connection with this knowledge.

So, moving on to something more spiritual, what we call living with the spirit of a people—with the soul of the people among whom we count ourselves—must also be present when we dive under into the human physical and etheric bodies. Living together with the soul of the people is present from awakening until going to sleep, for what the soul of a people is, what it develops in forces and activities, is poured into the physical and etheric bodies: into the physical body more factors associated with ethnicity or culture, and into the etheric body more factors having to do with the people. It is poured into those sheathes, which we enter when we awaken. In this way, we are actually with our own folk soul constantly in the exchange of forces. The science belonging to humanity at large has nothing to do with the configurations and differentiations poured into people through the folk souls; and this knowledge must be gained from the aspect of human nature that can make itself free and independent from the physical, as a person is independent from it in sleep. This science necessarily belongs to humanity in general, because it is attained with the parts of human nature that are independent from the physical and etheric bodies.

To assume that a person who can really look into and gain knowledge of the spiritual world could be bound by national prejudices is simply an inappropriate way to consider the secrets of initiation. Although life in sleep in the previously mentioned cases is entirely different than it is in the waking state, they are related to each other in a way that is connected with the relationship of human beings to the nature of the soul and the culture of a people. From going to sleep until awakening, individuals are not connected with the forces that emerge directly from the soul of their people, for those forces can be sent only into the physical and etheric bodies. Therefore, those who have brought these forces to the conscious inner experience of their "I" and astral body are, while experiencing them, outside their physical and etheric bodies; they are having this experience outside the physical and etheric bodies. Nonetheless, they are, not outside the world. As soon as human beings slip into their physical body, and with that also into their etheric body, they are together specifically with the spirit of their people, and when they slip out of the physical and etheric bodies, as in sleep or initiation, they are outside the spirit of their own people, which does its work in the physical and etheric bodies. They are outside, but not entirely outside, the encircling dance of the folk souls, which are spiritual beings after all. And when human beings are outside the physical and etheric bodies in the spiritual world, they are really outside of one individual folk soul, which in the present has a specific meaning for them in particular; they are outside their own folk soul, the one that affects their physical and the etheric bodies. Because they are in their folk soul's company, or come into it in the waking state, the interest in it disappears in sleep and during initiation. The peculiar fact thus emerges that in sleep and during initiation individual human beings are substantially together with the souls of other peoples, but not with their own.

If you imagine yourself then in the encircling dance of contemporary folk souls, you are, as a human being, together with your own folk soul when you perceive in the physical body and when you are awake; conversely, when you are in a state of sleep or a state of initiation, you are together with all other folk souls, only not with your own. That is an objective truth.

Now, you can get an idea from this of how senseless it would be if people who can consciously be together with other folk souls were to misjudge those folk souls, or to burden them with sympathy or antipathy. That would be as if one did not want to recognize folk souls. Only for those who have not progressed as far as initiation does it make sense to harbor sympathy or antipathy for this or that folk soul, because they indeed do not know that they are actually together with the other souls for the sleeping half of their life. But there is a difference. While we are connected with our own folk soul in waking life, we are connected to the other folk souls in sleeping life, and hence connected not with the effects that proceed from only one, but rather with the common effect of the other folk souls, with what the others carry out as an encircling dance, working together in harmony.

Therefore, you can imagine life both with just one of the folk souls, and life with the other folk souls. The former is life in the

waking state, the other life in sleep. During sleep or during initiation, one is together with the common work of the other folk souls. We cannot be with our own folk soul exclusively unless we constantly stay awake. It is quite impossible for us, because we would have to stay awake all the time. The difference is that we exchanges forces with our own folk soul in a waking state, while in a sleeping state the exchange is not with our own but with the totality, with the encircling dance of the other folk souls.

However, there is a way to be together with a particular folk soul even in sleep, to be more influenced by the powers coming from one soul and not from the totality of the folk souls. For in sleep one is usually banned, in a way, from this one folk soul. The method consists of especially hating the folk soul in the waking state. By hating a folk soul during the waking state, you tear it out of the encircling dance of the other folk souls and ban it, fettering yourself to its particular characteristics. To express myself in a trivial way, to really hate the soul of a people in a waking state means to condemn oneself to be obliged to sleep with the spirit of that nation. That is an esoteric truth, if also a disturbing one; it is nothing to laugh about. You must keep an eye on this if you wish to gain an understanding from a certain angle of how spiritual science, while it spreads over the world, must influence the attitude of people, must permeate all sense and feeling.

I have purposely couched what I have to say about the relationship of human beings to the folk soul in an expression that makes you laugh. I had to do that because as an esotericist one very often tries to help out with regard to what is most disturbing, most tragic. One does not say it in its full tragic weight, for that would depress people, but rather says it in such a way that it helps people to take it in like any other scientific concept.

For that reason, the fact must not be ignored that spiritual science shows us in a quite thorough way how far we are willing to accept the world as *maya*. For as soon as we penetrate spiritual science with the deepest seriousness, it becomes serious; it and everything it ought to be for human beings becomes deeply serious. Today, most people still have something against spiritual science because they cannot understand with their intellect what spiritual science really makes of the human being. People today do not understand the basic nerve of spiritual science, and not only because they cannot understand it with their intellect; there is something much deeper. When we penetrate deeper into the wisdoms of spiritual science, it makes demands on our mind and on our will. It shows us the human being in a light in which we usually are not willing to take ourselves. It is not just our intellect that would rather turn to maya than to reality, but the will also.

If I may speak in a trivial way once again, it is extremely uncomfortable to live with the deeper wisdom of spiritual science, because life must receive another face under the influence of spiritual science. The moment one knows what it means when Capesius and Strader† stand opposite one another on the stage of life in their spiritual forms and exchange words that in truth bring about tumult and noise in the most elemental forces of the world, the moment one knows what is going on in the world, in the entire cosmos, when a person experiences this or that in the soul, then the whole seriousness of spiritual science reveals itself, and one finally understands how people want not only to live with a full understanding of maya, but also actually to live simply with the will in maya. We need only to develop this or that sympathy or this or that aversion, and what we do because of that aversion becomes the reason we are driven as sleeping or dead human beings into the region of this or that being in the cosmos, and bring about this or that event in place of another. For through our communion with this or that being in the cosmos, cosmic events happen in their turn.

Such statements are intended to evoke a feeling of how spiritual science really does not wish to speak only to people's intellect, but rather to the entire human being: it wishes to take hold of the entire soul. This is because our life is today at a stage in which the signs of the times show us clearly how we are to take hold of life, if it is to go on; they point out that wave which contains spiritual secrets and does not leave us in the maya, but leads us into true reality. Those are the things we must consider if we wish to come to a deeper understanding of our spiritual-scientific will. We will speak further of such things tomorrow and lead into something that is related to the fundamental idea of our building [the first Goetheanum].

7

Microcosm and Macrocosm: Human Gestures and the Life of the World

DORNACH, DECEMBER 13, 1914

Yesterday, I pointed out that much will depend on how at least the main concepts, the main ideas of the spiritual-scientific knowledge of general spiritual culture will be embodied. I attempted to think through, more or less, how it would be if human thinking accepted, properly accepted, the principle ideas of the physical body, of the etheric body, of the astral body, and of the "I," and made these ideas really fruitful for the most diverse areas of life and science.

Today, I want to refer to another example. What we distinguish as physical body, etheric body, astral body, and "I" are members of the human soul—we could also say of human soul life—which, in a much higher region of course, behave toward one another as the individual color nuances of our scale of colors behave in a much lower region. And just as there can be little real knowledge of the inner nature of light and its inner relations to the rest of the world without conceiving this division of color nuances, there can be little true knowledge of the soul without having an idea of such members of the soul as "I," astral body, etheric body, and physical body. However, the individual colors do not simply stand side by side, but follow a gradual transition into one another, so that one cannot always say precisely where one stops and another begins; and it is the same with the members of the soul: they follow a gradual transition, one into another, and only our understanding separates them.

Now it is important, for example, to take a good look at the transition between the "I" and the astral body. What we call the "I" of a human being really fades into the astral body more or less as the red nuance of the color spectrum fades into the orange nuance. Here we should refresh ourselves about what we are actually speaking about when we speak about the human "I." We must understand very clearly that the true essence of the "I" is outside everything we can observe as the human body. The "I" is in fact experienced only in inner experiences. As everybody knows, the etheric and astral bodies are not at all experienced directly, while the physical body is experienced through external observation, through external perception; and the "I" in its manifold experiences is experienced only in an interior way. For experience in the physical plane, this is absolutely the case. The astral and etheric bodies stand in the middle, between the physical body and the "I," and are not directly experienced by people on the physical plane. The etheric body cannot be observed directly from outside without previous esoteric training, nor can the astral body, which contains everything we often call subconscious or unconscious spiritual experience.

The "I" is divided into the most diverse experiences of consciousness. We will pick out one such experience of consciousness, or better said, a conscious kind of experience. Conscious life is very diverse, but we will pick out a very simple, elementary kind of experience: the style and manner of the experience of taste. Just as the "I" experiences sight, hearing, smell, and ideation, it also has experiences of taste, or interaction with the external physical world. I mean the perfectly ordinary experiences of taste relating to food, not those one calls artistic.

What we experience when we have the sensation of taste is an experience of the "I," insofar as the taste experience occurs consciously for us. Therefore, when we bring food into our mouths and have an experience of taste, this taste experience is an experience of our "I." The diverse experiences of taste are in fact diverse experiences of the "I."

Now, in the case of taste experiences, we can study the transition from the "I" to the astral body in an interesting way. It is not difficult to establish that taste experiences die off to a certain extent when the food has passed a certain distance. Taste experiences die off then for conscious life; but this is only so in appearance. In reality, expressed in a gross sense, the taste experience of the mouth passes over into the taste experiences of the entire organism; the whole organism is basically permeated by taste experiences during the course of the food's penetration into our body, in the course of digestion and so on; and what we consciously taste is only a small part of the general tasting that our entire body experiences.

Not only the nerve organs of our mouth taste, but our whole digestive canal tastes, and with the transition of the food into the organism, into the blood and so forth, the whole organism tastes again what the digestive organisms have prepared for it. One could say the entire organism is permeated with experiences of taste. In fact, this organism is permeated and inhabited by experiences of taste in such a way that we can speak of differentiated tastes. Each organ has its particular, specific experience of taste; the stomach has its particular taste experience; liver, lungs, and heart have their special taste experiences. Taste in general is differentiated into tastes by organ.

Here we see how the sphere of "I"-experiences dives under into the sphere of astral experiences. For these differentiated tastes of the organs are subconscious; they do not come into a person's consciousness, but nonetheless they are infinitely important. For the normal development of taste experience rests entirely on the normal development of the tastes of the organs. In fact, aging consists partly in the fact that the astral body gradually becomes dulled in relation to the habit of taste. Understand me well: the astral body becomes dull in relation to the habit of tasting. I use the word "habit," however, in the sense I used it yesterday. Gradually over time, taste gets duller. When, however, the stimulus that finds its expression in the fact of taste is no longer exercised on the astral body, and consequently likewise on the etheric and physical bodies, then the possibility no longer exists for the astral body to penetrate the life experiences of the etheric and physical bodies through experiences of taste. A good part of what we call aging lies in the fact that the astral body becomes dull to taste; when an individual human organ loses the fresh capability of taste, this means it is not permeated by its astral body in the corresponding way, and diseases of the organ arise.

Now, particular perspectives result from this premise: in the first place the perspective, which is important in a pedagogical and hygienic way, that it is not insignificant to stress having a well-developed instinct for taste. I have dealt with this once before when I spoke about the upbringing of children.† It is important to understand that in eating, one should develop a lively relationship to different foods, that whether you eat salad or spinach is not a matter of indifference, that you should have a lively relationship to the differentiations in the plant world between salad and spinach. For what you experience in tasting salad and spinach are living connections of the macrocosm to the microcosm, and these living connections carry on in the subconscious taste-experience of the astral body, which goes through all the organs. People who become vegetarians, for example, should not connect it with a false asceticism and use their vegetarianism to dull themselves as much as possible to a friendly relationship to the essence of nature. Rather, they develop the ability to taste fine distinctions in the individual kinds of food. You can do this particularly well as a vegetarian, because then you become able to taste the fine, cultivated distinctions between the individual plants and what you prepare as a dish from them; of course, if you are not a vegetarian, you have more brutal distinctions among meat dishes. When we dull ourselves in this respect, we run the danger of extending this dullness from the conscious part of astral taste experiences into the subconscious part of taste experience. With that, we frustrate the living effects that radiate from the astral body into the lower parts of our organism. And it is a discomforting sight to go into many a vegetarian restaurant and see how people pile up a mountain of all possible mixed-up food and stuff it into their mouths without understanding, yet think themselves especially lofty in relation to what the ordinary person enjoys as a friendly relationship with the natural environment in the experiences of the palate.

That is one thing. When the understanding of the external experience of eating is permeated with the understanding of the astral body and its way of working, a healthy way of eating will truly develop;

and we will use it, because unconscious instinctual life will gradually disappear in the human race and must be replaced with a conscious relationship to the cosmic environment.

On the other hand, another perspective emerges in that there really is a definite relationship between the entire plant world, which is spread out over the world, and the human organism, the microcosm. And this relationship is expressed in the tasting specific to an organ. It is really true and no mere symbol when I say that any plant that grows outside has a taste only for a very specific human organ; for the others it has none. A particular organ allows itself to be aroused by the forces of this plant, but not another. If you just study these relationships, you will gain something very important.

I have told you on various occasions that the plant consists, when we consider its form, of a physical body and an etheric body; but when it grows upward, it stretches, in a manner of speaking, its blossoming into the surrounding astrality; and, if we look over a bed of plants, we find astrality spread over the plants—astrality that belongs to the plants.

Not every plant has its special astrality, but it is nonetheless true that the general astrality that is spread out over this Earth, as the air is physically spread out, tends toward specificity. What sinks down, so to speak, from the astral body of the Earth in a particular bloom, let us say the bloom of the lily, expresses itself quite differently than what sinks down to the clover. In this way, overall astrality tends to make itself specific.

This kinship, this relationship that exists between the astrality of the Earth and the whole spread-out carpet of plants also exists inwardly between the human astral body and its individual organs. In this relation, too, the human being is entirely a microcosm. But an unhealthy relationship can arise between the human astral body and its individual organs when individual organs lose their living feeling for taste, and grow dull. The relationship between the general astrality of the Earth and the entire covering of plants is essentially a healthy one, and if we find the relations between individual plants and human organs, we can also find the possibility of stimulating organs once again and making them healthy from the inside out through the introduction of the materials of individual plants. For if we bring the materials of a particular plant into the human organism, we bring along with them the kinship the plants have to the general astrality of the Earth. So when this kinship to the astrality of the Earth is dulled in individual organs of the human organism, it can be stimulated once again, and in the human astral body as well, by introducing the forces of the relevant plants into the human organism.

You can see the possibility of laying out a system of plants that corresponds in a certain way to human organization and at the same time presents a rational system of certain medicines for particular diseases of the organs. We would, in this case, go beyond the purely empirical, experimental investigation, and would truly be able, through making parallels of the tastes of the human organs with the forces of the plant world, to achieve a rationalization of plant therapy as a result.

All these points of view come together in an uncommonly fruitful way when one is really willing to commit to making Anthroposophy or spiritual science fruitful for life. And just imagine what wonderfully stimulating tasks for present-day life grow out of spiritual knowledge after the couple of experiments that it was possible to perform yesterday or today! We might only wish that humanity were not too lazy in the immediate future to devote itself to permeating science with what spiritual science can offer in each case.

Certainly it is infinitely important to communicate the central teachings of spiritual science to humanity, for if these central teachings are not communicated the foundation for further construction will be missing. However, instead of these central teachings being accepted in this way, many feel tempted to say the same thing over and over again in all sorts of new, badly written repetitions of what is already obvious. For once, we should pay attention to finishing the construction of the individual chapters of these central teachings and really introducing spiritual-scientific teachings into science and life. I mention this because within our movement are a good number of people, and among them a few stand out, who find it more convenient to pass on and repeat over and over again what is already clearly stated in the literature, instead of getting down to introducing spiritual-scientific knowledge into the fields that are particularly close to them.

If you consider this, you will see nuances in what has been emphasized over and over: spiritual science must become an all-permeating mentality of human life. If today we experience in such a painful way how human thought, human judgment, and human action have led to a point that demands infinite sacrifice and, on the other hand, shows how human judgment and human feeling has ended up at a dead end, then that should be accepted as a significant sign of the times, a sign that a new enlivenment of the soul forces is necessary for humanity. We should regard that as the principle issue: that a new enlivenment of the essence of the soul is now necessary.

What will bring along a more worthy time, in which we can lead ourselves out of the chaotic events of the present day,[†] is less the laying out of this or that agenda, as was favored in the sad epoch recently gone by for us, than letting oneself be caught up in a lively way by spiritual-scientific knowledge. The less we believe that anything like what we have to ward off today was present in any real area of European humanity, the more we will believe that we have a new future to expect and to hope for, a future of increasingly spiritual attitudes, and the more we will be on the mark.

That an intuitive consciousness was always present in what spiritual science must bring to clear consciousness has often been touched upon, especially here in this place, and also supported with external proofs. Over and over again we must be reminded of how spiritual science is in a certain sense something radically new in our time, but nonetheless well prepared in all recent spiritual life, so that wherever vigorous spiritual life is living, presentiments have appeared—not just of spiritual-scientific knowledge, but of the decisive significance of spiritual-scientific knowledge.

The following is an interesting example. A European spirit, a thinker, once attempted to reflect on what influences had been especially significant for his inner life. He mentioned three relatively more recent spirits who had great influence on his life: Emerson, who has also been characterized in these lectures, Ruysbroeck, and the German mystic Novalis.† These three spirits had a special influence on this Central European spirit, as he himself discussed, and he attempted to gain a certain standard for what must enter human spiritual life if it would really experience the necessary new fertilization. And this spirit then says something extremely surprising. He says that when you view, for example, Shakespeare or Sophocles in a certain way, you find that human conflicts are presented there, but in the end if a spirit were to come down from another planet, where experiences are entirely different, that spirit would not be able to arouse any special interest in what transpires about Ophelia, Wallenstein, or Mary Stuart. That can interest people on Earth, but a spirit from another planet would demand that human beings tell it something that does not interest only earthly beings, but rather interests beings who belong to the wider extent of the cosmos. And in the opinion of the person in question, there are not many souls who have something to say that could offer anything to a spirit who comes down onto Earth. And among these souls the thinker in question counts the poet Novalis. He finds the soul experiences in Novalis's poems so fine, so intimate, so much drawn out of what can only interest human beings—living not only in the time-bound, but also existing and acting in the eternal—that a being from another planet could also take an interest in Novalis. I want to read you the words he wrote when he became acquainted with Novalis, or became acquainted with what experiences of the soul Novalis had to offer. The words are very beautiful, so beautiful that

I want to read what the thinker in question has to say specifically in reference to Novalis's experiences.

> But, if he [the extraterrestrial visitor] sought other proofs, they would lead him to those whose works almost touch silence. Such authors would open the door to those domains where [the human soul] is loved for itself, without concern for the little gestures of its body. Together, they would climb to those high, lonely plateaus where consciousness is heightened and where all those who are concerned about themselves wander painstakingly around that monstrous ring which links the world of appearances to our higher worlds. Such proofs would go with him to the limits of the human being, for it is at the point where human beings seem on the verge of ending that they probably begin; and their essential, inexhaustible parts exist only in the invisible, where they must observe themselves ceaselessly. It is only at these heights that there exist thoughts that the soul can possess, ideas which resemble it and are as imperious as itself. There humanity has reigned for a moment, and these dimly lit peaks are perhaps the only gleams that suggest the Earth in these spiritual spaces. Their reflections truly have the color of our souls. We feel that the passions of the spirit and of the heart, to the eyes of an alien intelligence, would resemble the plaints of church-bells; but in their works, the people of whom I speak have left the little village of the passions, and they have said things which can interest those who are not of the earthly parish.[†]

Those are truly beautiful, magnificent words! The thinker in question believes that he experienced this with Novalis—beautiful, magnificent words that characterize how humanity must really come to something that is directly connected to the eternal, that leads us out of merely earthly experiences into the experiences of the cosmos. The words I have read to you were spoken by Maurice Maeterlinck[†] about Novalis, a while ago, in any case not in the last few months! But you can see from it that everywhere among people who can reflect—in the times in which they can think—a true, real consciousness is present from within the spiritual world, which the development of humankind must really accept.

I will offer still another example. In spiritual science today we speak entirely consciously of how through initiation one can achieve an experience of oneself in the "I" and the astral body separated from the physical and etheric bodies, a conscious experience of oneself that otherwise occurs in sleep. In this case, however, spiritual science is at the same time in the position of giving necessary information about the experience of death, for what the spiritual scientist experiences outside the body with reference to the physical and etheric bodies is indeed the same thing the soul experiences after death while it looks back on the physical body and the fate of the etheric body. So the spiritual scientist speaks in a special way about the viewing of the physical body and the etheric body dissolving into the world process from the point of view the soul attains to when it has gone through the portals of death. It means something infinite for the further development of all human consciousness and for the entire life of human spiritual culture that such ideas can pass over into the life of spiritual culture, and that people will come to know them more and more: ideas such as, that when the soul has gone through the portal of death it looks in retrospect at its whole past life and what is happening to the physical body in just the way you look back in your memory at your experiences in ordinary life between birth and death. When it becomes second nature to us, or obvious, that the soul looks back at the experiences in the body just as one now looks back at experiences of earlier times in the life between birth and death, something tremendous will have been achieved. And you will understand from different things I have discussed with you how necessary it is for all of humanity that such a consciousness be attained as fast as possible.

Now let us just see—if we look to an intuitive understanding—whether these ideas, which are given so entirely consciously and in such clear outlines in elementary spiritual science, were not always entirely strange to the human race before spiritual science arose. Fichte gave a number of speeches in which he attempted to transform the educational system of his people—a transformation like the one Pestalozzi summoned up, only more universal. In these lectures,

Fichte said that certainly many people could not keep pace with the idea that one could in a way form anew and re-enliven the human race with such ideas. Such people hang on to the old things they can imagine, and Fichte sought for a comparison to express clearly what they have learned and what they cling to. This comparison is quite remarkable:

> Time [he means all the people of time, who cannot imagine that something new can come out of something old] appears to be like a shade, which stands over its corpse, from which a Lord of Diseases has just driven it out, and moans and cannot tear its gaze away from the sheath it formerly loved so much, and in despair tries by all means to get back into the shelter of plagues. Although the enlivening breezes of the other world, in which the deceased has entered, have already taken her up within them and surround her with warm breaths of love, although secret voices of her sisters are already greeting her with joy [by this he means the other spiritual beings that surround us], and welcoming her, although within her [her soul] is aroused and expands in all directions to develop the grander form into which she should grow; but still she has no feeling for these breezes or hearing for these voices or, if she did have them, she has already risen up in pain over her loss, in which she believes she has lost herself.†

Is it not as if a person coming from spiritual science is taking the comparison from spiritual science of looking at one's corpse after death? Fichte said that in 1808. We see from it how everything tends in the direction of spiritual science, and how spiritual science arises in the best spirits as a presage, but, as this example shows, a presage that expresses itself in very specific forms.

You will understand from what you are accustomed to hearing from me how such words are intended. But, could not an entirely particular feeling arise in the souls of people when they read something like that, which was expressed in 1808? Could not a very particular feeling be arising in the souls that take seriously matters of the culture of humanity? Could not these souls also be feeling that after having such intuitions they need to hold on to them and finally make some real progress toward a spiritual-scientific knowledge of the world? And then could not such souls perhaps feel shame for humanity, because if only such feelings were to appear in a good number of souls, it would be great good fortune for the development of humanity. But I think that many souls will still for a long time to come choose the easier path, and accept what pleases them in such speeches as Fichte's, but not read the things that do not please them. And if one draws their attention to it, they will say, "All right, it is permissible for great spirits to be oddballs every now and then in certain respects." And then they make comparisons that are really not taken from any kind of reality.

It will be possible for all life to be permeated with the emotions spiritual science excites in human souls through its ideas. And really our building came into being and will display the details it will contain for no other purpose than to indicate as insistently as possible how life can be permeated with spiritual-scientific ideas. It is not intended that in this building a sin should be committed against a naive life and feeling of the human being. Those who emphasize over and over that artistic creation must take its course in the most unconscious possible way believe that they are not committing this sin against themselves or others, and in truth it is more comfortable when artistic creation takes place unconsciously than when it is raised into knowledge. For knowledge, when it becomes knowledge of the cosmos, is just as naive as the primitive unconscious, which, for people's convenience, is so frequently in life put into phrases like those I have just mentioned about what is necessary in art.

Just refresh yourself about the following, which you can conclude from many discussions, and you will also receive the impression that important impulses for artistic particulars can and must be given from spiritual science. If we look at a person in the light of the spiritual science of today, we certainly know that this individual has not taken form in the one-sided way presented by today's natural science; rather, this person needed a Saturn, Sun, and Moon development to become what he or she has become. And we know also when we look at the external physical human form, that whole generations of beings of the higher hierarchies have worked through long stretches of time, and that their activity was specialized in the way we have described in the Saturn, Sun, Moon, and Earth developments.

We know that what appears today as a finished part of the human being—for example, the head—first had to go through the Sun, Moon, and the whole previous Earth development to become what it is today; that it had to evolve and be transformed: that it was first present during the Sun development; that it reappeared during the Moon development and was transformed; and that it was once again transformed during the Earth development. If we consider then how the human being must actually be studied, we will begin to feel the complexity of this human organization and its relation with the macrocosm, and then gradually learn to know it.

Today, I wanted only to suggest something that will soon be accomplished. I mention it because it will lead to a concluding thought, which we will expand on in the next few days. We have, for example, members in our organism that in their configuration today still bear very clearly the original impulses of the ancient Saturn development, which are however transformed and reshaped so that we cannot directly recognize them in their present form without studying the Akashic Chronicle. Represented schematically, the bones surrounding the spinal column were first established during the ancient Saturn development, still in the element of warmth, and have been constantly transformed during the following developments. The bones attached as the rib cage were then articulated in the time of the Moon development and are less transformed, because their first beginnings do not lie so far back [see drawing a, p. 115†].

Other organs were added on in an upward position, first during the Sun development, and then transformed. What we today call the human skull, the human head, was established during the Sun development and then transformed many times over. However, if only what the Sun development gave the human being in regard to the skull had occurred, then human beings would have to carry the head in a way they cannot carry it—in fact, as if it were always directed upward. Hence, during the Earth development, through the influence of the Sun, a ninety-degree turn intervened, so that what before had to be directed upward is now directed as follows. Instead of drawing the Sun arrow for the Earth development in this direction, ↑ we must draw it in this direction for the Earth development: → [see drawing b, p. 115].

As part of the normal development the human form has worked through under the influence of the cosmos, the form of the head has been turned from being directed upward to being directed forward.

Now, when the spirits who have remained behind in the Moon development interpenetrate and permeate the human being, they bring along the striving to direct the head upward. People inclined to carry their noses in the air in an unpleasant way, as we say, are seduced by such luciferic spirits. That has its background in fact: it is a physiognomic cosmic truth, and we entirely hit the mark when we say that those who carry their noses in the air have Lucifer sitting on the back of their necks. That is entirely true, and it will be infinitely important to know these cosmic relations.

If we consider the exterior limbs, the arms and legs, the legs belong directly to Earth development, are entirely subject to the Earth. If the arms, however, had merely followed the Earth development in their normal development, human beings would only be able to let their arms drop downward. Since we can also raise the arms upward, we direct them arbitrarily toward the Moon development; that is, we give them a luciferic character each time we raise them. For this reason, those who have refined feelings feel each movement of the arms forward and upward as something that has a luciferic character. Let us keep our sights on that and think now of a person who bows the head and raises a hand at the same time, but in a way that holds both of these movements in one human gesture: the person lets the head sink and raises an arm. Sinking the head is an activity opposing the luciferic character of the head. Raising the arms brings the Luciferic into the arms. However, now it is like this: while you allow Lucifer to flow into the arms and support the sunken head by the forehead on the arm, you redeem the luciferic power that flows through the arm, through the opposing effect of the Christ power in the head. In a way, you redeem Lucifer in the arm through Christ in the head [see drawing c, p. 115].

b

a

c

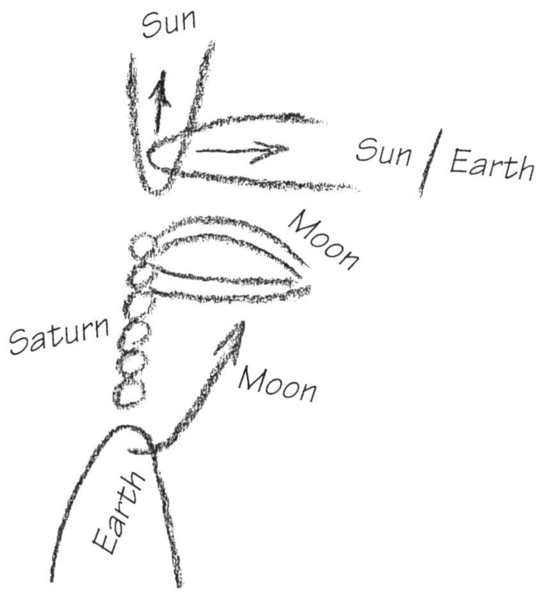

If you paint the human form in the right way, you express it in this gesture: the head resting on the arm. The person makes a gesture that expresses, "Lucifer is redeemed through Christ!" Add to it something like a bending of the knee, and you sharpen the gesture. Raise both arms upward and press back the power of the raising, as happens when you fold the hands (raise the arms with folded hands), and then try to marshal the Christ power against the luciferic upward-flowing power with the folded hands, while you in a way disable them. Human gestures become the expression for the whole life of the world, for the spiritual life of the world. We must feel how the arrangement of the human form can be immersed in art through such knowledge of the secrets of the cosmos!

We can also ask what happened when the luciferic upward-orienting of the head was turned forward in the Earth development through the Sun's influence, and human beings stood on the Earth with their heads turned forward? They became Earth beings through that! That which is not a being of the Earth can therefore not have legs and feet in the human sense. Human beings do not receive the head, and also the face, from the Earth, but rather from the cosmos; but the head arises in this form because it turns toward the Earth. If we consider other genii, other spirits, we cannot make them with human legs. To give legs to spirits that do not belong to earthly existence is simply wrong, as we can really understand from spiritual-scientific knowledge. And the art in our building should always acknowledge a debt to these feelings that come from spiritual-scientific knowledge.

You see that this knowledge can really give a new impulse to artistic form. If spiritual science becomes no longer conceived as a colorless theory, but rather as something that will enter the human being as feeling and sense, then we will understand that it can have a fructifying effect on all efforts of the development of human culture. A small beginning in this direction will be made in our building.

8

Human Beings as Illuminators of the Cherubim, Heaters of the Seraphim

DORNACH, DECEMBER 19, 1914

Today I want to present an observation that, although perhaps it falls outside the sequence of observations we have cultivated here, will be useful for the understanding of the whole.

How human beings can receive into their knowing and their world of ideas what is real in the world, is an old, old question. For us, the question is not so burning as it is for people who are not in our spiritual-scientific movement, because we actually know that the possibility exists for us to live our way up into the spiritual worlds and, by penetrating into the spiritual worlds, gain certainty about true Being, about a true reality behind the external reality lying before us on the physical plane. Only starting now, and continuing on into the future, will humanity as a whole be able to pull itself up to such a viewpoint of out-of-body knowledge. Thus the question of how one can receive knowledge, Being, and reality in the world of ideas will for a long time continue to have an infinitely great significance.

For us to be somewhat informed about this question is important, because we must attempt to seek an understanding with those who still stand outside our spiritual movement. We must be able to provide information about the riddles and questions that those who have not yet approached this spiritual movement feel when they hear one or the other result of spiritual science. The question I am thinking of is precisely the deepest, the most tragic question humanity has asked itself thus far. For, however deeply philosophical and other scientific knowledge has been cultivated, in the end the question comes from a human disposition of the heart and works on the whole human mentality and mood.

Human beings—let us start with this—wake up in the morning from a world that must remain unknown and puzzling if they are not familiar with Anthroposophy. They wake up and they think about the world they enter with awakening. In these thoughts they want to acquire what one can call a worldview. Those who really approach these things through feeling with their whole soul, in this case feel something of the weakness of intellectual life, of conceptual life. They feel, one could say, that they really are condemned to live within themselves in concepts, above the processes of the exterior world, and that they have to make these concepts for themselves. And they find as always that these concepts remain to a certain extent only concepts, and are not powerful enough to encompass real inner being.

People feel this weakness of conceptual life especially when they ponder the concepts of memory. We bring up from periods of our past what we have lived through factually and experientially. We bring up some memory and conceive of it as behind us, perhaps a long time ago. And here we must always recognize that we have the remembered experience only as an idea, and an idea does not have the power to conjure up reality anew.

That is one place where we get a really true sense of how powerless human beings are, in a way, when they are faced with full-blooded, unedited reality in their conceptual life. Another is when we enter the world of creative fantasy. In that world we call up before our soul images of the beautiful, of what satisfies us. But we can sense that we are not in a position, in relation to what we conjure up in our fantasy, to push our way into true being. More materialistically inclined people start out from the feelings one can have about this world of fantastic images. They say, "If you people make up ideas about a higher spiritual world, about God and the spirit world, what guarantees that these ideas are anything more than fantasy images?

What guarantees for you that with these ideas, however wonderful the rapture they create for you may be, you get through to a world of true reality?" What lies at the basis of these feelings about the powerlessness of conception, of the formation of ideas, has led to the thousand-year-old philosophical struggle about how human beings can get through to a reality with their concepts and ideas.

There are enough philosophical directives in this area—even if we ignore the extreme skepticism that believes a satisfactory answer to this question, a satisfactory solution to the riddle of human mental life, has not yet been found. Certainly, people can walk past these world riddles with a certain intellectual comfort. But those who stroll by consciously, who live consciously with these questions, will feel that dissatisfaction in the face of this world riddle makes waves in their astral body and elicits certain moods in relation to the world: melancholic moods. Moods can set in through which one helps oneself with cynicism. However, such a sidestepping of the world riddles can certainly not lead to a real satisfaction in one's inner soul life.

We face the necessity of approaching these world riddles just as we must approach many other things. We must look into the essence of human nature and ask: Where does this riddle come from, why does it exist? That it can be felt in a vastly tragic way has been shown by certain philosophers, who were actually in despair about the solution of the riddle, and spoke of a divinity that leads humanity astray in the chaos of worldly appearances; a divinity which has so disposed human nature that it cannot arrive at a satisfactory conception of the world.

Let us remember something that has been discussed several times in different connections, but which can be particularly useful in relation to these world riddles. I have often spoken of what our thought, sense, and conceptual life actually is. I have said that it is basically a kind of *reflection*. It is in fact the case that, with the human being, we have to do with what I want to indicate here approximately in this way:

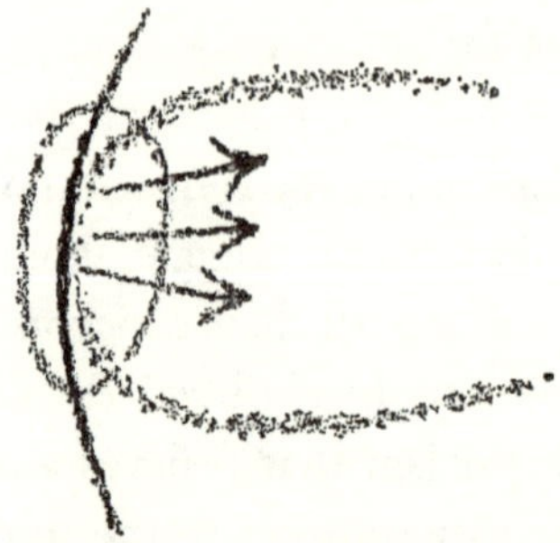

This is the physical body. Outside it, outside the physical person, the soul-spiritual nature of the human being lives, as it were, poured out into the endless universe. But during the day, in daytime waking life, this same soul-spiritual being extends itself into the soul-physical entity. And thereby a reflection arises. And this reflection is actually what we sense as the content of our daytime wakeful life. Really, our body is like a mirror, and just as we do not see the mirror, but what is reflected in it, what we see when a person is awake is fundamentally not what is happening in the body, but rather what is reflected in the body of the outer physical world.

However, insofar as we are inside the body in waking daily consciousness, our "I"—what we are as soul beings—is in fact basically also present in this world of mirror images. For the world all around us is maya; it is a sum of mirror images. Our waking "I" is inside this sum of mirror images, and, as beings on the physical plane, we are basically nothing other than a reflection among reflections.

Let me make this clear and ask: insofar as we are on the physical plane, what remains of our whole life of concepts if we extinguish daytime consciousness? The "I" goes out with it. And if the "I" is not reflected, as in deep dreamless sleep, it too is extinguished. And if we awaken and have the world of reflections before us, our "I" is also inside this world of reflections, so that we, insofar as we are living on the physical plane, can have nothing of ourselves other than a reflection.

We pass through the world as beings on the physical plane and have nothing of ourselves other than a reflection. We live in the world, but as far as we are conscious of ourselves, we do not have the living reality before us, but rather the reflection of this living reality. We live as a reflection among reflections; and what we learn to recognize through spiritual science—that we live as a reflection among reflections, as maya among the parts of the great maya—is sensed by people when they feel the powerlessness of all spiritual experience in the face of full-blooded reality. We do not say to ourselves in ordinary life that we are a reflection among reflections, but we feel it. We feel it above all when we feel, "How can I reach full-blooded being with this mere reflection?"

Let us be clear what is there. Imagine you have before you a reflective wall; it reflects back what is spread about the room—for example, a table. However, what you see is not the table, but rather the reflection of the table. Imagine you wanted to go into the reflection, take the table out, and put something in its place. You would not be able to do that, because you cannot put a plate or soup bowl on the reflected table. It is just as impossible to put a plate or a soup bowl on the reflected table as it is to derive the essence of the soul's immortality from what human beings experience on the physical plane and have around themselves in a waking state between birth and death. For the real soul is immortal. It is not its reflection, which we experience on the physical plane. Think about that.

Human beings yearn to know what is constantly hidden from them and which, while they are on the physical plane, shows them only a reflection. The philosophies of all ages have striven to draw reality out from the reflections; they have sought to prove immortality from reflections. They have taken on the duty, symbolically speaking, of fetching the table out of the reflection, putting it in the room, and placing plates and bowls upon it.

When we read philosophies that are fecundated by spiritual science, they appear to us as futile efforts of this sort. If you go through my book *The Riddles of Philosophy*, you will find the story of how, since the beginning of humanity's philosophical struggle, philosophy has made an effort to take the table out of the mirror and put plates and soup bowls on it. Therefore it is necessary now that we have a spiritual-scientific movement to add a concluding chapter,† showing that what was there before must be completed by spiritual science—which is involved not with reflections, but with realities. Now, you could ask if we need to read that sort of book, since for what purpose should we occupy ourselves with the futile struggle of humanity. Why should we take philosophy into consideration at all, since it concerns itself only with a futile effort of humanity?

But that is not how things are, not how things are at all! What we do when we immerse ourselves in what, from a certain point of view, is otherwise a futile struggle, is nonetheless something infinitely important, something that can be replaced with nothing else. Philosophy will perhaps always remain unfruitful as far as knowledge of the immortal nature of the soul, the spiritual world, and of the divine is concerned, but it will not remain unfruitful for the unfolding of certain human powers and the further development of certain human abilities. Just because philosophy as such proves unsuitable to reach the things I have mentioned—because it remains to a certain extent dull in relation to them—it strengthens the human soul all the more. And if it cannot deliver knowledge, it still—because it is a concentrated life of thought—prepares the soul to make itself suitable to penetrate the spiritual world. What we gain through the practice of philosophy raises us into the spiritual world more than anything else. Precisely because no powers for the attainment of real knowledge are wasted, all powers are applied to the uplifting of human abilities. However, we must accept from this observation that experience on the physical plane, because it is an experience in images, has something unreal, something untrue, and that we fundamentally, while we live our way into the philosophical world, live through something unreal on a soul-spiritual level. But does the fact that we experience the soul-spiritual on the physical plane as something unreal have a meaning then? Can we find some wisdom of the world order in it? We must ask ourselves such a question; and to answer this question, we must place some of the insights of spiritual science before us.

When through meditation and concentration, individuals have made a little progress by strengthening their soul-spiritual experience, they can pass over into an experience that is, in a way, a waking sleep, a state of living within the spiritual world. The first experience they then have—when they are at the point of approaching initiation—will be an experience of moments when, as if glittering and flickering, and as if in a dream, the spiritual world penetrates their consciousness. This is something that they really know afterward, when they realize they have experienced something of the spiritual world. Usually pupils of initiation pay too little attention to this experience; otherwise they would have an easier time making progress.

If human beings did not lose consciousness in sleep, they would live in the spiritual world during the whole period from going to sleep to waking up. Then they would really be in a world of the objective weaving of thoughts the whole time. Those who follow *How to Know Higher Worlds* carefully, arrive relatively soon at the realization that on awakening they are breaking the surface, as if they had been swimming under the sea and now rise up to the air; they break the surface, as if they had woven with their soul experience in a world of pure thoughts. That is how it is—as if you are still left to sort out the last shreds of this experience upon awakening.

This experience can make a great impression, although it is usually immediately lost and very hard to fix in the memory. But it is important for those who wish to make progress to ponder precisely those moments of awakening, for then the awareness arises that before they had awakened they were with their astral body inside a weaving objective world of thought, and that when they dove down into the physical body, they collided with their physical embodiment, which then reflects back what they had lived through during the whole night, so that initially it glitters in the soul. This consciousness can come into being and should be heeded, and it is exceptionally important that it come into being. When you have such a consciousness, you begin to know why it is difficult to actually receive the thoughts that you live through during sleep and during initiation into the physical world, into physical thinking, because you live with your thoughts in an entirely different way outside the body than within it.

To make that clear to ourselves, we want to look at the moment of awakening and the state of being awake. When you awaken, you plunge with your soul-spiritual nature into your physical embodiment. That you live on there in the weaving of thoughts is not surprising, for you have lived inside the weaving of thoughts throughout the whole night in sleep. What happens is as follows.

Imagine (I will draw it schematically) that you are diving from outside down into the physical body—I will draw it only in respect to the head.

While you are not yet within it, but still there on the outside, you are there in a wonderful world of weaving thoughts, in which the spirits of the next higher hierarchy are developing their activity. Before you awaken, you are with your soul-spiritual experience in the world of the angels, the archangels, the archai, and so forth. Just as in the physical world you are among animals, plants, and minerals, you are with the higher hierarchies, inside them, during sleep. And this being inside them, this working of the higher hierarchies on your soul being, occurs especially with the powers of thought, which rule there. And now you dive down into your physical body. While you are diving down into the physical body, you concentrate your thoughts so that they are restricted to the small fragment of space that your head encloses. So you must draw together in a very concentrated way what is spread out. What happens then is that the life of thoughts withdraws inside, dives down into the nervous system: the life of thoughts is shifted, in fact, through the senses into the nervous system. And what happens then? Then physical substance is seized continuously by thought experience. And stuffing a thought into the physical has to a certain extent a killing effect; while you grasp a thought in your physical body, you are actually killing something in your nervous system. "Slaying" is even a correct word for it.

We think something. After a certain time we realize what is there inside us. As many nerve corpses are now within us as the number of thoughts we harbored. What remains behind when we have thought something is really nothing but corpses; so when we go to sleep in the evening, we must turn our physical body over to itself so that it can get rid of the thought corpses we have created during the day through our thoughts.

Must these thought corpses be there? Yes, they must be there, for they are actually the imprints of thinking; and if we could not form these thought corpses, we would have thoughts just as unconsciously by day as in the night. During the night, we are inside the thoughts weaving in the spiritual world. No physical body then stands at our disposal into which we can impress thought corpses. During the night, thoughts go away immediately and dissolve in the life of all thoughts. That is the difference. We can hold onto thoughts during the day because they turn into corpses, which we bury in the physical body. Then the life of thought becomes hardened, and this hardening brings it about that we can consciously pursue a life of thoughts.

That is exactly the process. There you have once again something of the way in which we can show how materialism misses the target. Materialists believe they must seek the cause of thinking in what goes on inside, in the corpse process. But what is accomplished there is in reality a process of secretion of thought, a corpse process; and the nervous system is there so that the process of secretion can be produced through the activity of thought. Bodily physiology investigates what thinking leaves behind, what it cannot use, what it rejects. However, something takes form through physiology during waking daytime life that we can call the dying out of thinking in the physical body. The thought forces one develops will be used to produce, so to speak, copies, impressions of themselves. Then the thought forces go into these copies. During the night, when we live in a general sea of spiritual existence, they do not go into copies of this sort. This is because we can form no copies in normal life without initiation: the thoughts dissolve into this general sea. When we want to take hold of them in the morning, they are in fact dissolved; then not even memory can hold them.

When we conceive the process very exactly, we can say that some sort of thought process is developing. While it penetrates our body, it produces products of separation in the nerves. However, before it produces the separation products, it reflects itself. Before it passes over into the body and physical activity, it first reflects itself. What this activity calls forth is reflection.

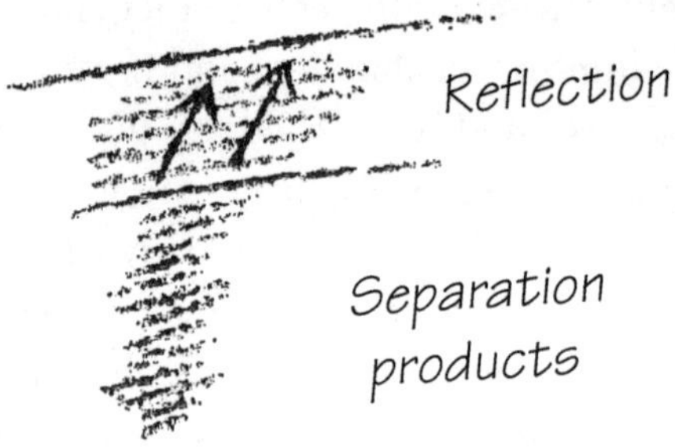

Imagine, you are looking at an object through your eyes, or hear a noise or notes sounding together in harmony through your ears. The harmony is outside; it penetrates into the ear. A process arises in the auditory nerves: corpse formation and separation. And what you hear is the sound that is cast back, actually an inner echo.

In this way we are in our everyday lives entirely in a world of reflections, and our own existence is woven into this world of reflections. We would conceive our true being if we could feel ourselves swimming outside our bodies in spiritual existence—if we could feel that now one of the angels is taking hold of us, that in what we are now weaving in, we are going up into the realm of the angels, we are passing over into the realm of the archangels, into the realm of the primal forces, and so forth. Then we would feel ourselves born into the realm of the higher entities. We would feel the immortality of souls and know it is true that these beings carry events in the world from world epoch to world epoch, that they are carrying us from world epoch to world epoch. But human beings do not perceive this in ordinary life. We dive down into the physical body and the experience of our own self in true being dies off during life in the physical body. Only the world of reflections remains.

We must therefore cast light deep into the process of cognition and wish that an awareness of the nature of this process would really take hold of the present age. For knowledge that the world is a sum of reflections and that real being lies behind it is already an ascent to where humanity should really be led by spiritual science. We can therefore say no more or less than this. People enter the physical plane, and when they do so they are in fact transported from the world of reality into a world of unreality, into a world of mere images. And we must feel the entire weight of this knowledge when we perceive and imagine.

So we can say that when the spiritual beings delivered us into the physical plane, they fetched us out of the world of true reality and transported us into a world of unreality. And we actually recognize this first as a fact from the context of the spiritual world, although not yet of the world plane. We recognize it as a fact of the world plane when we ask the question, "Why are we, insofar as we are beings of the real physical plane, transferred into a world of unreal images?"

Why? Let us assume that we have not been moved to the physical plane, so that we have before us not images, but realities. What does that actually mean? That would mean that when we stand perceiving and facing the physical plane and hear, for example, a relationship of sounds, the effect of the relationship of sounds would go into our ear and into our auditory nerves and effect a transformation there. If we were simply designed to enjoy what occurs in the auditory nerves and not to have the ability to project it up into our ideas, then we would be inside reality; we would not have images, but realities. That is, however, not the case. We are really cast out of the world of realities and transferred into a world of images, into a world of unrealities. If we were really in a world of realities, then we could never have the possibility of giving reality to a world ourselves, for in a world of reality we cannot bestow reality ourselves. An object I take in my hand from without is something. It is not only an image; the object is something. As little as I can move the table I see in the mirror, just as little can I do anything real with the world that is given to me only in images. But when it is a matter of creating realities ourselves, it is actually correct that we live in a world of images; for although the images have no reality, we can bestow reality upon them. Do we actually do that?

Yes, we do that; in one area of our life we do that. We do that when we act morally. The moment moral impulses make their way through our soul life, we create something and put it into the world—something that would not be there without us. When we form a concept of the world, we have only images; when we act morally, we put realities into the world. We would never arrive at the point of living morally in a world that came to meet us as already self-sufficiently real. For in that case we would, in respect to what we wanted to do morally, run up against the world everywhere.

Consider the animals. Animals experience the world entirely differently than people. They do not experience it as a world of images, but rather as a world of true realities. For that reason, animals cannot develop morals. Human beings can develop morals because they can themselves introduce moral impulses into the world; a world which is otherwise only one of reflections. What human beings make flow into the world as moral impulses, flows into the world as a reality coming out from them into the world. The gods have set us out on the physical plane and turned our spiritual experience into a world of unreality, so that we arrive at the position of introducing moral impulses into unreality as reality. There you have creation *ex nihilo*, creation out of nothing through ideas, which are in fact only images, only unrealities.

If we once again observe a person sleeping, we can say that insofar as that person is outside the physical and etheric bodies, he or she is experiencing the world of weaving thoughts, into which the beings of the higher hierarchies have been woven. However, something else penetrates and flows through this world. What is it? The beings of the higher hierarchies are not merely entities of thought. They are real beings. They have substance, and what they have as substance we experience now, not in our thought, but in our will; particularly in the will when it is ruled by love. In our will, when we introduce moral impulses into the world, which otherwise is a world of images for us, we bring down the substance of the higher beings into our worlds. What we really do out of moral impulses is nothing other than bringing down the substance of the beings of the higher hierarchies into our world.

Our thoughts, when we are living with our soul-spiritual nature in the physical body after awakening, are mirrored in a part of our body. They are products of the sedimentation, so to speak, of waking thought-life formed in the nervous system. The nature of moral impulses—which basically come from the nature of the higher hierarchies—enters into our whole body, penetrates our entire being, our entire organism and not just the nervous system. Thus, the human being can be presented to a certain extent as a twofold entity: as the human being of nerves, and beside it the entire remaining physical human being, into which streams everything that lives on in moral impulses. However, when we are submerged in our physical body, we come out of the world of spiritual realities. While we are submerged in our physical body, emerging from the world of thought, thoughts flutter and glitter as they reflect images, forming thought corpses in the nervous system. Thoughts live in us, but they are not living beings in us; they are reflected, and what we perceive is a kind of reading of thought corpses. But these thoughts that reflect themselves are living things, and that has great significance in the world order. When someone stands before you, and you look at them and become aware that they perceive and think—that what is within them as a weaving of thoughts goes into their nervous system, reflects itself in every perceivable thing, in sounds and colors—what is going on with the spiritual light that is going into that person, making impressions on the nervous system? What is going on with the impressions that arise there? Look, there come the cherubim; they collect the light and use it for the further world order—and all of us are lights set out in the world order. While we think, perceive, and form concepts, we are the lights of the cherubim in the world order. Just as a light illuminates the space here in the physical world, so are we the lights in the spiritual world for the cherubim. While we are thinking, light appears in us; the light of thoughts radiates from us, and that illuminates the world in which the cherubim live.

When we carry into our body from the world of the hierarchies the substances from which moral impulses are born and these penetrate our whole organization, will impulses, actions follow. Everything we do happens because will impulses are active in us. Then what is going on in the external world through us, insofar as it is a moral action, is collected by the seraphim, and this moral activity is the source of warmth for the entire world order. Under the influence of people who act immorally, the seraphim freeze; that is, they receive no warmth with which they can heat the whole cosmic world. Under the influence of moral action, the seraphim obtain the forces through which the cosmic world order is preserved, just as the physical world order is preserved through physical warmth.

You see, now the worldview that spiritual science gives us is becoming very real. It brings us to the awareness that when you think, when you form concepts, you are the ignited light of the cherubim. When you act, when you do something, when you unfold your will, then you are the source of warmth, the source of fire of the seraphim. When we walk through the world, we are conscious that we are not useless good-for-nothings, but exist inside the world order for the benefit of the entire world order, and we are conscious that we also have it within our power to make the world a source of darkness. For if we want to be dull and blunt and not to think, then we increase the darkness, and the result is that the cherubim have no light. If we are bad and immoral, we increase the cold in the whole world order, and the seraphim have no warmth.

Spiritual science does not give us mere theories, as external science does if it is not practical science that leads to technical application. Spiritual science gives us something through which we learn to know what we as human beings are within the entire world order. What follows then from spiritual science is the essential, what is important. It is an exalted feeling of responsibility in respect to being human. We feel what duties we human beings have toward the cosmos. We feel that we can be either human beings in the proper sense or in the improper sense; that we can make our own contribution either to darkness and cold or to light and warmth in the cosmos.

We would like to bring spiritual science into the world especially with the practical goal that it takes hold of people's hearts. For we can be certain that then spiritual science will really be in a position to produce a new attitude of soul and thereby an entirely new form of human experience on Earth and in the entire universe, so that experience not only delivers knowledge, but also becomes a source of true, genuine life forces. We wish that spiritual science be taken up, properly and deeply, by those who feel drawn to it! For spiritual science is still taken all too frequently as something external; as if, like some other body of knowledge, it should satisfy curiosity or, let us say, a greed for knowledge. However, the seriousness with which spiritual science is introduced into the world must grow. This is what our time needs so badly: not merely the belief in the spiritual world, but also the possibility to position oneself in relation to the spiritual world so that the human soul is really inclined toward the spiritual world. And just as an infant sucks nourishment from its mother's breast, so the human soul can suck the stuff of life for a new form of Earth experience—by knowing oneself within the spiritual order—from what spiritual science can open up for it.

Only when the relationship of the human being to spiritual science is suffused with this magical breath of sense and feeling will one understand spiritual science in its truest, most intimate form as a seed of life. This seed must take root especially among those who participate in a common task of spiritual-scientific endeavors.

Why should this building of ours be any different, then, from what we are participating in—especially those who are working on it—namely, a confluence of the attitudes that spiritual science awakens! That is tremendously important and significant. If the building is put up in this frame of mind, then it will not be only a dry structure with its forms; it will also be something those who have worked on it have built in loving creativity, in true collaborative creativity. What these people have made to flow into the building, what they have left behind in this building—be it even the slightest activity, even an activity with only a loose connection with the building—is directed in love for what the building should be. And if it flows out of the human attitude that seeks to mount up into the cosmic order, then this building will be something that is not merely a dead thing, but rather a living thing, a truly living thing.

That is indeed the secret of our thought corpses—that we can for a certain time still bring them back to life over and over again. The other side, that of memory, I discussed last time: that what thoughts have produced in us as thought corpses, as human corpses, remain behind on Earth and can be brought back to life through soul forces applied later. And when a memory rises to the surface, that which is only a thought corpse radiates in us for a while, alive once again.

Let us work on making our building in the human order something similar, so that those who come to look at it are unconsciously transported into that sphere of love with which it was constructed! For then it will be not merely a context of dead forms, but something that, when people look at it, becomes enlivened like the thought corpses of memory. And it will be true then for all eternity that, through the way we have worked on it, this building will be something that can become enlivened over and over again by those who encounter it.

While we allow these thoughts to work on our soul, we gain a living relation to this building of ours; a living relationship which humanity truly needs while it lives its way from the present into the future. For much will not be allowed to remain a dead corpse; it will be obliged to live, but will only be able to live because a new attitude arises which must come as a result of spiritual science and of spiritual knowledge.

9

The Separation of Art, Science, and Religion

DORNACH, DECEMBER 20, 1914

With the different observations I recently set forth, I attempted less to communicate individual concepts and ideas as to characterize a particular manner of positioning oneself toward the world. For we must always keep in view that the most important thing that will emerge from spiritual science is not conceptual or ideational, but rather the whole attitude or mood of the soul that human beings developing into the future will be able to gain through spiritual science.

Today, remnants of old mentalities and old soul moods adhere to all who come to Anthroposophy. This is especially the case with a certain modern soul mood, which arose relatively recently—three, four, or five centuries ago—in the search for solutions to natural phenomena. This mood emerged from so-called scientific observation of the world, and is regarded in most circles as the only valid one. But we know that scientific concepts and ideas have penetrated only a small part of humanity on Earth, for modern education basically makes sure that the scientific mentality spreads out much more widely than science itself. And since this scientific type of soul mood has taken hold only recently, it is naturally difficult for the mood of the spiritual-scientific worldview to establish itself in the midst of what has taken hold for only such a short time, and which must develop among the majority of people only as a transitional phase.

The mood of the scientific worldview leads necessarily bit by bit into a kind of materialism, for it can indeed be nothing other than one-sided. It is gained in a one-sided way through what we can call the head-experiences of the human being, and it strives to exclude where possible from its worldview all concepts not in agreement with this human head mood—everything that is not thought, cogitated, or obtained through experiment or observation with the help of thought or cognition. The mood of this worldview has also, one could say, maintained its one-sidedness in relation to human cognition, considering the impulses that have to a great extent moved into the human soul. Thus we can feel how difficult it will be to unfold through spiritual science a more comprehensive soul mood in relation to the world, one that derives from the whole human being.

When today people who stand so properly in the scientific worldview pick up a book such as, for example, *An Outline of Esoteric Science*, they obviously see its content as a kind of nonsense of a burned-out brain, since they can gain no special resonances from it because of their one-sided brain- and head-centered disposition. Now, there is something that reveals itself in a phenomenon—naturally in many, but especially strikingly in one phenomenon: that the spiritual-scientific worldview sees in a radically opposite way than the natural scientific worldview. I want to emphasize this point first.

When we study the human being from a spiritual-scientific perspective, it becomes apparent as we go further back into primeval times—into, as we say, for instance, the Moon development of our planetary existence—that precisely what appears significant to the human being of today, for the earthly development of the human being, really was not yet present in the ancient Moon development. In the ancient Moon development, what was in essence present—I say, *in essence*—was what relates more or less exactly with the development of the modern human brain. And what the human being has outside the head—outside of what primarily belongs to the skull, to the head—the rest of his corporeality, in essence is the product of the Earth, a product of earthly organization—once again, I say *in essence.*

We could also say it this way: when we follow human beings back to the ancient Moon development, we gradually see, the further back we go, that the external limbs, by virtue of which we are today terrestrial human beings, crumple together, and what then remains is the head, which has obviously been reshaped through the Earth development, but which remains in its essentials as it was if one goes back to the Moon development. The rest has organized itself around it, joined itself onto it. I explained all of this more precisely in the lectures I gave in 1911 on esoteric physiology, which I hope will appear in the Prague cycle.† Therefore, in essence, we arrive at the knowledge that the human being began with what is present today, compressed and concentrated in its skull organization; and the rest has joined itself onto it. We must therefore say that, drawn schematically,† we would have human beings in their Moon development, and in their Earth development, in such a way that the rest of their organization joins itself onto this.

Compare what I have just said to the one-sided view that the natural scientific worldview has brought to things. It begins in a one-sided way (obviously all these things are based on something justifiable) by saying that the human being has evolved upward, from the lower animal levels to its present completeness. What, then, do we see in the lower animal levels? We see in them in a stunted form exactly what was developed for human beings as they arrived at the brain and head development. We see what the human head contains. In animals the limbs, which have been added on in the case of human beings, are particularly well developed, and what was already particularly well developed in human beings in the ancient Moon development as the head, which then concentrated itself, is in animals still crumpled together, stunted. But that is all the natural scientific worldview sees. We can say the natural scientific worldview actually puts the cart before the horse, for it makes what has just joined itself onto the human being into a point of departure, and what was with the human being before it had any such organs as the animals now have into something that is supposed to have itself developed out of these forms.

Considered logically, this means nothing less than something like the following example. One first looks at a child and then at the father, and finds that the father is taller than the child. One now assumes as a consequence of logical deduction that the taller, as it develops, could only have developed from the smaller, and not the other way around. That is the kind of conclusion science makes, in fact. The one-sidedness of the modern scientific way of thinking will one day make a grotesque impression on what will be humanity's new consciousness. One will know that the one-sidedly conceived Darwinian theory is logically nothing other than the assertion that the child gave birth to its father.

Now you can conceive of what efforts will still be necessary before humanity relearns such things as they are now interpreted, and relearns everything that goes with them in order really to relearn. Natural science has succeeded in founding a worldview that turns the world onto its head, and from now on the necessity will approach humanity to turn the world back on its legs. But over only three or four hundred years, humanity has gotten quite accustomed to looking at the topsy-turvy position as the correct one.

Our duty is not to acquire mere theoretical concepts about this or that thing in the world, but rather to appropriate feelings and sensitivities for the duties that lie before us within the spiritual-scientific movement. We must be clear how very different the consequences or results that come from the spiritual-scientific concept of the world have to be from what surrounds us everywhere today. Otherwise we will repeatedly fall into the mistake of not noticing the radical difference between the two views, and of wanting to make careless, thoughtless compromises. We should be aware that we cannot graft things onto earlier worldviews, but that, out of a completely new worldview, we should develop what can become more and more apparent as the right thing out of spiritual science. Only with this consciousness will we succeed in putting our soul into our task, and we must become accustomed to the fact that many questions that appear to be outside the circle of the spiritual-scientific point of view can be grasped only when we enter into what spiritual science can call forth in our soul.

Let us consider yet another thing, which can be obvious for us in regard to the place where we now are standing—where we have put up our building. I have emphasized on several earlier occasions how art, science, and religion are three branches of human spiritual life springing from one root. If we go back into the time of the primal mysteries, we find that they were arranged such that we cannot say they were art or religion or science; rather they were all those together. Science, religion, and art were a unity, organically bound to one another, in the ancient Mysteries.

What people now attempt to remind themselves with impotent concepts and ideas, human beings saw in the Mysteries in a living representation, a living vision. They witnessed what today we can only think. We will not approach art in the future as we contemplate works of art today. In the future we will not approach a work of art by looking at it and then believing we can understand it first with thought; rather we will understand it in direct vision, experiencing it in the soul. That experiencing from within what was beheld—is how human beings initiated into the Mysteries would grasp cognitively what was seen. What they grasped in knowledge in this way—understanding in viewing, cognitively viewing—was at the same time a beautiful object, appearing in forms and colors, speaking in sounds and words: it was art at the same time. Science and art were one.

Today only art, separated from what science should give us, gives us an idea of how one is intimately unified with the object in direct external unification; and only those who want to drag into art the barbarity of symbolism, of making symbols, commit a sin against this directly experienced understanding of artwork. For the moment you begin to interpret a work of art, you leave what we can call the experiential understanding of works of art. It is fundamentally a barbarity to behave, let us say, toward "Hamlet" in such a way that the individual characters are interpreted as the principles of the theosophical worldview or the like. May I never have the experience that a person interprets the individual forms of our building symbolically in this way, for direct *understanding-experience* is what it is all about!

So, in the ancient Mysteries, scientific or cognitive experience of the world was simultaneously an artistic experience of the world, and at the same time this scientific and artistic experience of the world was also a religious feeling of the world. For what was experienced in directly living contemplation, in experiential understanding, and understanding-experience, was at the same time what people could revere, what they could raise their entire soul to with religious fervor. Religion, art, and science were one. Because of the hereditary human sin of weakness, to use the religious expression, it was necessary for the separation of science, art, and religion to emerge. What was originally one had to split, so that a religious current, an artistic current, and a scientific current arose. What the entire human soul grasped as an organism—all that was woven of scientific, religious, and artistic content—had to be distributed among the individual powers of the soul. Science thus came to be given to human beings for the intellect, for thinking, so that when they experienced the world through thinking in science, their faculties of will and feeling could rest.

Human beings became weak. They sought to experience the world scientifically, one-sidedly, in thinking; they also sought to experience the world artistically in a one-sided way, so that the other powers of the soul could sleep; and also one-sidedly, and for the same reason, they sought to experience the world in religion. Human beings would not be able to construct what they can think through in such completeness as they do today, if they had not constructed a one-sided scientific current; they would not have been able to reach what has been achieved artistically if art had not separated itself; and religious fervor would not have reached the height it had to achieve if it had not separated itself from the soul forces devoted to science and art.

But now, in regard to this separation, we have reached a crisis, and the crisis expresses itself very, very clearly. What is it about? Especially in recent decades, humanity has had increasingly to experience just how this crisis expresses itself. Science, art, and religion have separated themselves so widely that they cannot understand one another, because they no longer have any mutual relations among themselves. Gradually, we have come to see how religion, science, and art broke off "diplomatic relations." We see how such relations were still present in the heyday of the Italian Renaissance, when an intimate bond was still woven between religion and art in the creations of Raphael, Michelangelo, and Leonardo. But the more we proceed into more recent times, the more we can see how a mutual lack of understanding has gradually formed between science, art, and religion. We must unfortunately admit that we can see the extent to which in recent decades religion has become even hostile to art; we see how it has cast art out, how some religious currents attempt to reach the height of religious feeling by throwing out representational images and making churches as sober and empty of art as possible. We see, further, how another religious current has come to the point of still having artwork, but for the most part these are no longer truly works of art; for the artwork we still find in churches during the last decades for the most part are not called on to awaken the artistic, aesthetic sense, but rather to exterminate it utterly. And, on the other hand, we can see how art has increasingly shaken off its connection to the comprehension of divine spiritual existence, for everything has gone over to naturalism, and artists increasingly want to show only what can be exemplified in external nature.

Obviously, if it wants only to be naturalistic, art must break off its "diplomatic relations" with religion, for what religion must honor can have no model in external nature. And how little science has been able to maintain any of these relations, we can trace in its slow approach to the breaking-off of all relations. Yes, we see that slowly coming on.

Leonardo da Vinci was an excellent artist of the sixteenth century, who was active in the most varied fields as anatomist and technician. Whoever looks over his scientific works feels everywhere how they are permeated with an artistic sense. We see, however, how this sense has increasingly evaporated in modern times, how inartistic it has become, and how people today appear to believe that the greatest science consists particularly in being inartistic. It has become dogma, especially for a particular orientation of modern thought, that Goethe was such a dreadful physicist because artistic sense would not allow him to become a proper physicist.

There has come to be a lack of understanding between the three currents. That, however, is the sign of a crisis. For when what had originally grown from one root has split apart so drastically in its mutual relations that the sap of life no longer comes from the common root, a crisis must come. The one-sided development of these currents must lead to a general withering away. In recent times we have brought the incomprehension of what is in fact a common organism, an interrelated organism in human nature that has split itself up in its outer development, entirely to a state of crisis. We are living in crises. We can define them by saying that human nature demands the organic unification of what had to go their separate ways for a time in the external world. Those who do not go through the development of the world in a dulled, sleeping state can perceive such a state of crisis in many fields of life today, and they can observe much in the causes of this crisis, which cannot remain the same as it is in its contemporary development. Such people will gain knowledge of what has to happen in order to overcome the crisis.

We have indicated a crisis in the lapse of mutual understanding of science, art, and religion. Another crisis is going through the world, noticed by few, but terrible in its effect; a crisis derived from the lack of understanding between two currents. One of these was once whispered through the world in infinitely deep sayings that were engraved into the human heart: "My kingdom is not of this world,"† and "You are from beneath; I am from above."† In other words, the root of the human being is in the spiritual world.

The second current, which developed more and more into a dangerous opposition with what is expressed in the above words, is the saying "L'état c'est moi!"—"I am the state!"† My kingdom, the kingdom of my "I," is entirely bound to this world. The proper solution lies in the synthesis of the two sentences, in the universally conceived Christianity expressed in the words, "Render unto Caesar the things that are Caesar's, and unto God the things that are God's." In Christianity, when it is correctly understood, there is no false turning away from the world. Also absent in it is the one-sidedness that can live out its life in dependence on the material furnishings of worldly existence.

When we express such things, we truly touch the deepest duties of Anthroposophy, the deepest duties of us all. For Anthroposophy, in the true sense of the word, must not arise one-sidedly from the head mood of a person, but rather from the entire soul of the human being. And then the soul will find the transition into anthroposophical life, when it will be entirely seized by what spiritual science has given—not merely in its conceptual life, but wholly seized by it.

It is a fact that what became the human head in the Moon existence is during the Earth existence on its way to becoming the entire human being. During the ancient Moon development, the ancestor of the present-day human being existed. What was at that time an external organism has become the head today, and the limbs have attached themselves to it. In the coming Jupiter development, the whole organism of the present-day human being will become the head. What you are today as a whole human being will be the brain, the head of the Jupiter human being, just as the whole Moon human being has become the head of the Earth human being.

The task of true spiritual development is that the future really be anticipated. For that reason we must be conscious that there is a head culture all around us, and that it behooves us to create a human culture. Our head could not think, could reflect no ideas, no concepts, if it behaved like the rest of our organism; it could never really fulfill its duty then. Our head reflects the world, which is indeed becoming our world of perception only because the head can forget itself in its perception, properly forget itself. In their capacity of feeling human beings, thank God, are always without a head. If you attempt to sense yourself throughout, to feel yourself throughout, and ask yourself what you feel least in your organism, it is really the head that forgets itself most in normal life. And if for once it really does not forget itself, then it hurts; and we would much prefer that it not perceive anything, that we be left nicely in peace and kept without perception. Then the head brings our egotism into play. Otherwise it extinguishes itself, and, because it extinguishes itself, we can perceive the whole world around us. It is organized to extinguish itself.

Were you to forget the external periphery of the head a little less, but keep it in mind, then you would already no longer be able to perceive the external surroundings. Imagine that instead of perceiving the outside world, you could see your eye, for example; or that you could take a step backward with your perception and see the cavity of the skull—but then there would be no perception of the outside world. In the same proportion and in the moment that you succeed in turning off your entire organism—which you achieve through meditation and in initiation—in that same proportion and moment your organism becomes a proper mirror of the world; only you do not see the organism then, but rather the cosmos. Just as your head also does not see itself, but what is all around you, so the whole human being, when it becomes an organ of perception, sees the cosmos. That is the ideal that must float before us: to forget the organism as it appears to us on the physical plane, and thus to be able to use it as a reflective device for the secrets of the cosmos.

In this way we expand our head understanding to an understanding based on the entire human being, and we must learn to trace, to sense, to feel something of how Anthroposophy, the anthroposophical mood, must really take hold of the entire human being, overcoming this one-sided head mood that proceeds from modern science.

If you take as factual what I said yesterday when I described how we human beings can become conscious that we are illuminators for the cherubim and heaters for the seraphim, how we establish ourselves in thinking and willing in the world of the cherubim and seraphim, how we mean something for that world, how we are not here only for ourselves, but are rather in a lively relationship to the living and weaving of the spiritual hierarchies—if you make that into an attitude, you will trace something of how the whole human being, and not just the head, can properly become brain; how we as whole human beings can come into communication in this way with our environment. Then you will feel what is actually meant with this: to comprehend the world as a whole human being.

When we once again comprehend the world as a whole human being, we cannot think one-sidedly, but with feeling and willing will also live ourselves into the entire earthly existence. We will live ourselves into the entire experience of the world, and the inner dependence on having things not only in thoughts, but also in forms—not only in formless thoughts, but also in beautiful, expressive forms—will arise by itself. This drive, the need to express things in artistic forms, we now possess only intellectually.

And, once again: when human beings dive into the life of the whole spiritual world, their life becomes basically a prayer, and they no longer have any great need to separate out so nicely little moments for themselves in which they pray. Rather, they know: "When I think, I am the illuminator of the cherubim; when I act, when I act in willing, I am a heater of the seraphim." Human beings then know that they live inside the entire spiritual structure of the world. Thinking becomes a religious attitude for them; action becomes a moral prayer.

We see how these three prayers—art, religion, and science—which had to walk separately for a while in the world, seek each other once again from within the entire human being. Human beings brought so much from their extraterrestrial development with them at the beginning of the Earth development that they still had the living, unified feeling, the unified striving that expressed itself in ancient times in the unification of art, religion, and science. We could say that the angels were still striving within human beings. But human beings would have never become free if it had gone on like that. Human beings had to be emancipated from this ancient legacy, but we must find again in the upward course of our development what we lost in the downward course.

We have often spoken of a beautiful saying of Goethe about architecture.† He called architecture frozen music. Let us remain with this statement. We can really call architecture in its development up until now a kind of frozen music. The forms of architecture are like still melodies, like fixed harmonies and rhythms. But we have the duty, since we are within the crisis alluded to, to bring what is frozen once again into movement, into liveliness; to a certain extent to make the stilled forms once again musically alive. If you see our building, you will notice its striving to bring the old motionless architectural forms into movement, to reshape them into life, to make them musical once again. That is why we don't have a round building, but rather one single symmetrical axis, along which the motives move forward.

So we see how what the spiritual-scientific worldview intends also as art is in intimate relation with all the tasks, with all necessary impulses of our time, which we recognize in the crises of our time. To understand this, to see into it, is hugely necessary for our duty. We must gradually get a combined perspective of all particulars of our duty from this point of view.

Human beings today forget early on to use their entire organism as a kind of brain. They have the predisposition. But hardly have they developed in the first years of life from a crawling child to a human being who walks erect, before they unlearn how to have a relation to their entire organism just as they have to their brain throughout their entire life. This setting-up of oneself, this bringing of oneself into the vertical, is in fact a working of the spirit on the entire human being. It is the last remnant of what we bring along from the spiritual life before birth. In earthly life we rapidly forget it, and then we drag the entire organism, which eats and drinks and digests, as a burden through life; we drag it through life and no longer bring it into a respectable relation to the spiritual world, but rather carry it far away from the spiritual world.

The child still has the great wisdom to direct itself according to the fact that the duty of human beings lies in heights far from the world, and in that in their organism the direction is toward heights far from the world. When that stage is over, the organism—I don't want to be so impolite as the mystics of the Middle Ages who said that the organism was becoming a disgusting bag of maggots, but I will say that the organism is becoming a bag of digestion and maggots—becomes cut off from its relation to the external world.

Not even that relation to the exterior world, of which I spoke yesterday, will still be preserved. When we, for example, support our head in our hands in order to bring something important in the external organism to expression, we hardly pay attention to it. And when someone who has still kept slightly unconscious the habit of bringing the entire organism into use and not thinking only with the head, lays the hand or the index finger on the forehead or the nose, indicating thereby that he or she is now really making a distinction and a judgment, we do not notice that this is an instinctive striving to use the entire organism as a brain. It does not have to happen in this external way. Obviously spiritual science does not think to make a "fidget-widget" of the human being who thinks with his or her whole body. But consciousness must obviously expand itself spiritually to stand within the cosmos with the entire human being, to know that the cosmos can reflect itself through the entire body, just as now it is reflected only through the brain.

When consciousness is expanded in this way; when human beings really get beyond dragging along their entire organism through life, when they learn to use it, to take it in hand, then what must be prepared in our time is prepared: a totally human worldview instead of the mere cerebral worldview. This must become what Anthroposophy strives for.

Let us try it, and try in this way to raise into an attitude what otherwise remains a mere concept; then we will reach what is intended with this spiritual-scientific movement of ours. For as we rise up in development, when we live our way more and more into the whole human comprehension of the world, we will as human beings gradually find the true Christ figure. Only the cerebral worldview is to blame that the Christ figure cannot be found. The moment the cerebral view is overcome, when spiritual science will have become so strong that it reorganizes the consciousness of human beings in the ways I have characterized, what has already often been said about the view of Christ will truly come about. Then our human world will be able to reach what it can only reach by growing from within outward, and with this can lead itself over and away from much that has led straight to a crisis among the educated of the Earth—not only in human beings' views of the world, but externally in reference to peoples and nations.

We would wish that people, or at least a small part of humanity, gradually come to understand that help is really necessary. Then we will also understand that the help humanity needs can be achieved only from within souls, only from within outward, and that nothing else can be a surrogate, nothing else can help, but rather only the true and the genuine. And the true and the genuine must be won in the spirit by humankind.

PART III

THE CELEBRATION OF CHRISTMAS

10

Toward a New Understanding of the Mystery of Golgotha

DORNACH, DECEMBER 26, 1914

Above all the memory of this Christmas celebration will make an impression with sharp traits on many souls, for one can hardly think of a sharper mental contrast to our present time than the one that arises when we raise our souls to the voice that sounded out to the shepherds, presenting an eternal truth for all human exaltation in the age following Christ:

Divine revelation in the heights
And peace to human beings on Earth
Who are of good will!

Truly, no greater contrast exists than when we raise our souls to "Peace on Earth" and then consider the reality, which we find spread out over the horizon of a great part of the educated world today.

Precisely because of this contrast, the Christmas celebration we are now experiencing will be an emblem for human hearts across the Earth, which will long remain in memory. If we can indeed maintain what we have to maintain on the field of our spiritual-scientific thought—inner uprightness of heart and inner truth of soul—we truly cannot celebrate this Christmas with the same feelings as we have celebrated other Christmastides. For it must urge us to deep reflection. It must urge us most especially to reflect on what emerges from spiritual-scientific meditation as the idea of our human future, on what therefore can lead people's hearts back to times that are not like our own.

We have in the course of the years inscribed a great deal into our souls that can point us in the direction of the kind of constitution of soul that such times brought about. What is it, then, that we must feel is still so severely lacking in the present? When we call before our souls' eyes what has often formed the heart of our considerations, we see that still missing in the depths of the human soul is the recognition of the truth of what entered the world on the day we commemorate every year in this winter night of celebration.

The whole significance, the whole profundity that transpired at the time this the winter night of celebration reminds us of, is expressed—truly not in vain and with deep significance—in the saying that earthly humanity has always regarded as the most haunting of all, one might say; in the saying, "Divine revelation in the heights and peace to human beings on Earth who are of good will!"

The simplest thing is often the most difficult for human hearts to understand. As simple as this saying sounds to us, we do well to get a clearer and clearer idea that all coming times of earthly existence will be able to understand it more and more deeply, and to live their way into its important words.

The appearance of the Jesus child entering into earthly life on the holy night of Christmas has not become the most popular part of the mysterious story of the appearance of Christ Jesus on Earth in vain. With it, we can place something before the human soul that it can take up with love—something we can place even in the heart of the smallest child, insofar as that child can receive the external sense impressions, even if not with words. It is something that sinks deeply into the depths of the soul where love flows through the human being most gently, but at the same time with the strongest, most warming powers.

In truth, earthly humanity is still no further advanced than the childish conception of the secret of Jesus Christ, and will continue to wilt away in epoch after epoch until the human soul once again wins the strength through which it can absorb the entire greatness of the beginning of the Mystery of Golgotha. Therefore, this year I will not reflect on Christmas as in other years. Rather, let me bring before your souls something that can indicate how much we still lack of the depth necessary to allow the Mystery of Golgotha to glow in our souls as it should.

We have, particularly in the last year, often spoken about how actually, on the basis of our spiritual-scientific research, we must celebrate the appearance not only of one Jesus child, but of two Jesus children.† And it may be said that with what has revealed itself to us through the spiritual-scientific contemplation of this secret of the two Jesus children, a weak beginning to a new understanding of the Mystery of Golgotha has been made. Only slowly and gradually can this mystery take hold of people's minds. How it moves into human minds can come before our souls when we look, for example, at the fact that to a certain extent what Christians of today have gained in the contemplation of the Christmas child was won through a struggle, which went from east to west, through other conceptions of a divine mediator between the highest divine spiritual beings and the human soul.

We have also often looked at how, in parallel with the current of Christian life moving from east to west, another current of revelation flowed more in the north, north of the Black Sea along the Danube, upward along the Rhine into Western Europe. This cult, which we know as the cult of Mithras, disappeared in the first centuries of the Christian era. But by that time it had taken hold of just as many hearts as Christianity itself, and had made a deep impression and spread in the regions of Central and Eastern Europe. Mithras appeared to those who declared themselves his followers as just as great and sublime a divine intermediary, who had descended from the spiritual heights into earthly existence, as Christ appeared to Christians. Just as we hear how the entrance of Mithras into earthly existence was celebrated in the holy winter evening of the shortest day, so also we hear that shepherds first heard of his revelation. Sunday was dedicated to him, just like the Christian holy day.

And when we ask what is characteristic about the descent of this Mithras figure, we must say that Mithras could not be conceived as

Christ was conceived in Jesus. The consciousness was present that when one represented Mithras externally in a figure, the representation could only be an external symbolic conception, for the true Mithras was only to be seen by those who had clairvoyant vision. True, he was conceived as the mediator between the spirits of the higher hierarchies and the human soul, but he was not conceived in such a way that he incarnated in a human being. He was conceived as descending to Earth, but in his true nature—not in the image, in which everyone could see him, but in his true nature—he was visible only to initiates, to those who had clairvoyant vision. In the cult of Mithras, the idea was not yet present that a divine spiritual being, conceived as the intermediary between the spirits of the higher hierarchies and the human soul, incarnates in an earthly body; for the cult of Mithras rested on the ancient primitive clairvoyance, which was still present in a great number of people.

When we investigate the path the Mithras cult followed from east to west, we find that a great many of those who became servants of Mithras could themselves see in the intermediary circumstances between sleeping and waking—when the soul lives in dreams—and could see in spiritual reality the actual descent of Mithras from eon to eon, from stage to stage, from the spiritual worlds down to Earth. Others were carried along by these seers. Many could bear witness that such an intermediary had been given to people; but he was an intermediary belonging to the spiritual worlds.

What those in the cult of Mithras possessed was in fact an external, more or less pictorial representation of what the seers beheld. What is it really that confronts us in the Mithraic cult? We must not think that something was known about Christ only after the Mystery of Golgotha—this follows from our whole worldview. The initiates of the mysteries and their pupils even in pre-Christian times had known Christ well as the spirit who would come for humanity. The initiates referred to Him as the high Sun Spirit, and they saw Him coming down from the spiritual heights, approaching the Earth in order to set up His dwelling there. They designated Him as the Future and the Coming One. They knew Him in their spirit and saw Him making His descent.

Then came the Mystery of Golgotha. We know what it means. We know that through the Mystery of Golgotha the spirit through which the Earth has received its meaning entered into a human body. We know that since then this Christ spirit is bound with the Earth, and we also know how humanity should develop in order to behold once again in the not-too-distant future the Christ spirit who united his life with the life of earthly humanity through the Mystery of Golgotha. We are not saying anything untrue when we say that what the ancient initiates saw at the various cult sites of the spiritual is to be recognized since then as penetrating, flowing through, pulsing through, weaving through earthly life.

But the ability of clairvoyant knowledge to see into the spiritual spheres had increasingly to disappear in order for this clairvoyant knowledge to see the Christ after he had descended to Earth to those who were supposed to recognize that the Earth not only contains human love, but is also pulsed through with divine love, which will reveal itself more and more as the highest treasure to earthly human beings. So people should properly feel that they have received in their earthly house the great gift of cosmic love, the Christ, from the God whom one calls God the Father; they should properly recognize Him as the being who from then on should be bound to the deeds, and with the whole meaning of earthly evolution; they should properly recognize Him in His life, from His first breath as a child to the greatest deed that can be revealed to human hearts through the Mystery of Golgotha.

It was indeed still possible for us, in the course of recent times, to fill in through the Fifth Gospel the gap that has remained in the four other Gospels. Indeed, it has been granted to our time to become acquainted even more exactly with every step of this life of God on Earth. People should become as familiar with Christ Jesus as with one of their brothers, for such a being traveled from the wide spiritual realms into the narrow valley of Earth out of love for human beings. And because human beings should get to know Him in the most familiar, intimate acquaintance, the human mind's forces of knowledge and love had to be collected for a while in order to behold in pure human-divine closeness what transpired among people at the beginning of a new age, the Christian age. The forces in human beings had to be wholly concentrated and directed toward the life of Christ Jesus, so for a while they had to be directed away from gazing up into the spiritual spheres toward what has come into the child of Bethlehem, what has come down from the cosmic heights.

Today, however, we live in a time when our gaze must be broadened, when human progress and human salvation should really rule the Earth. Also, what Christ Jesus was in the body of Jesus of Nazareth must be broadened into the divine spiritual heights from which he descended to the life of the Earth.

The cult of Mithras was something like a final, powerful recollection of the Christ still not yet arrived on Earth, but descending. Then it was granted humanity to comprehend the Christ ever more intimately in the soul, so that this comprehension was possible even for the smallest child, but in such a way that together with it went a draining away of the old way of looking up with a clairvoyant gaze toward the heights from which Christ descended. And it is through the contemplation of these heights that we know Christ is a cosmic being, and also know what value He has for the narrow valley of Earth. Slowly and gradually this gazing upward into the cosmic expanses in which Christ can appear to human beings as a cosmic being drained away. The cult of Mithras was a powerful echo of the ancient knowledge of the superterrestrial Christ.

Then we see how, in a way, clairvoyant knowledge gradually drained away, diminished; even for those who still had clairvoyant knowledge in the old style, a draining away of the clairvoyant capabilities occurred, and with this draining away the possibility also ceased of knowing Christ entirely in His true essence, of knowing him not only in His earthly, human effect, but also in His whole heavenly glory.

More and more the possibility of seeing Christ in His heavenly glory beside His earthly existence disappeared. We see how what still lived in the cult of Mithras appears already weakened—in spite of the noble greatness that the corresponding doctrine contains—in the person whose name we have often mentioned: the founder of Manichaeism.† Mani directs us toward Jesus, but because ancient clairvoyance was still present in this spirit who founded Manichaeism, it is not the sort of reference we find in a simple, primitive, faithful soul; the understanding of the Mystery of Golgotha is not yet what it can be for the present. For Mani, Christ Jesus was a being who had not really assumed earthly human incarnation, but rather lived on Earth only in an apparent body, in an etheric body. We see the struggle in Manichaeism to understand the Mystery of Golgotha. Why did this struggle take place? Because it was still possible for the founder of Manichaeism to look into the spiritual heights to see how the spiritual being, the Christ Being, descended. However, the possibility was not yet available to really understand how this spiritual being penetrates into the earthly world, how it actually takes up residence in a human body. A struggle of the soul was first necessary before this full understanding was possible.

We see once again also that the doctrine of the Manichaeans spread from east to west, a doctrine that on the one hand still looked to the divine spirit descending, looked toward everything the old worldview still had: looked not only at the physical beings who offer themselves to human sensual eyes, but also at the beings who travel through the universe as star beings. On the other hand, the connected chain of human fate, of human life, permeated the souls of the Manichaeans with this cosmic life. The question struck deep roots in them: "How is the evil that exercises power in human life to be unified with the work of a good God?" Manichaeism looked deeply, very deeply, into the riddle of evil. However, this riddle of evil can come before the eye of our soul in its profundity when we are in a position to understand it in connection with the Mystery of Golgotha; when we permeate the Mystery of Golgotha with the riddle of evil, as Manichaeism also strove to do. Hence the struggle of the remnant of ancient clairvoyant knowledge with the problem of evil, with the riddle of evil in Manichaeism.

And in truth, precisely the people who were called to devote their souls most deeply and intensively to the understanding of the Mystery of Golgotha have struggled with what still sent its glow into more recent times from the remnants of ancient clairvoyant knowledge. We need only to think of a great teacher of the West,

Saint Augustine. Before he struggled through to the understanding of Pauline Christianity, he was devoted to the doctrine of the Manichaeans. Pauline Christianity made an even greater impression on him when he was able to perceive that the divine mediator had descended from the divine spiritual spheres from eon to eon. Even in the earliest times of his struggle, this spiritual vision illuminated for Augustine the knowledge of how Christ took up dwelling on Earth in a body of flesh, and how the riddle of evil is solved with the Mystery of Golgotha. It is striking to see how Augustine held dialogues with Faustus, the renowned bishop of the Manichaeans,† and actually only turned away from Manichaeism and to Pauline Christianity because Faustus could not make the necessary impression on him.

Then we see draining away what we can call the knowledge of the superterrestrial Christ, as He was before the Mystery of Golgotha; and basically the remnants of the ancient clairvoyant knowledge vanished completely with the emergence of the new age of the fifth post-Atlantean epoch. This ancient clairvoyant knowledge still knew the heavenly Christ beside the earthly Christ. One could obviously still also feel this heavenly Christ in the beginnings of Christianity, but to have a vision, an intelligent vision, of how He descended was only possible for the old clairvoyant knowledge. It must touch us deeply when we perceive how in the earliest times of the dissemination of Christianity, those who still took their knowledge from the ancient visionaries wanted to make Christ present to themselves: how, in order to recognize Christ, they not only looked to Bethlehem, but gazed up into the heavenly spheres in order to see how He descended from there to bring salvation to humankind.

We know that besides the Mithras cult, besides Manichaeism, Gnosis was present in the West. It, too, wanted to link, at least as far as it was Christian Gnosis, the descent of Christ from divine spheres from eon to eon with the knowledge of the earthly life of Christ Jesus. But it is striking to see how the human mind wanted to concentrate more and more on the contemplation of the merely earthly life of Christ Jesus. It is striking to see how the simple human mind, which did not have the ancient clairvoyance to show the life of Jesus, was almost afraid of the grandiose idea of the Christ descending from the heavenly heights. The first Christians were fully unconscious of the ideas that Gnosis still possessed. They were afraid of those ideas.

Still into our time a certain fear is present with those who, although deeply touched by the Mystery of Golgotha, cannot pull themselves up to that recognition of the spirit—fear that the mind can enter a state of chaos if one can see what spiritual knowledge dwells in the doctrines of the Gnostics. However, what the Gnostics can still say about the heavenly Christ beside the earthly Christ is indeed very moving for us.† And the gaze of our souls becomes in no way duller toward the earthly life of Christ Jesus if He is raised up now through new clairvoyance to the spiritual heights where the heavenly Christ is to be found and from where He has descended. Then it touches us so very deeply when Gnosis relates:

> Jesus said:
> Look there, O Father,
> How this being on Earth,
> Of all evil the goal and sacrifice,
> Far from Thy breath wanders.
> Look, it flees bitter chaos,
> Helpless, how it should find its way through.
> Therefore, send me, O Father!
> Bearing the seal, I descend,
> I stride through the host of eons,
> Every holy teaching I unfold,
> Showing then the portrait of the gods.
> And so I give you
> Of the holy path
> Deep-hidden lore:
> "Gnosis" is its name for you.

We feel that the new spiritual science must lead us once again to the point where we can, in our contemplation, weave around the Christ event the spiritual aura that, for reasons we have already explained quite often and to which we have found it necessary to allude once again today, had to be lost for humanity for a while. We must do this slowly and gradually. We must to a certain extent try to grasp what spiritual science can reveal in such a way that the human mind, which is today still far from spiritual science, is able to understand it.

For that reason an attempt has been made to put basically the entire anthroposophical wisdom about the Christ event, specifically about Christmas and its connection with the human soul, in these simple words:

In the soul's eye is reflected
The worlds' light of hope,
Wisdom devoted to the spirit
Speaks in human hearts:
The Father's eternal love
Sends the Son to Earth,
Who in grace on humans' path
Sheds the glow of heaven.†

Hopefully the time will come for evolution on Earth when one will be able to say more, much more, and in clearer words, about the secret of Golgotha—in simple words for the whole world, that can express for all of humanity what spiritual science has to say about the Mystery of Golgotha.

Indeed we see how until the end of the fourth post-Atlantean epoch, even until the beginning of the fifth, ancient clairvoyant knowledge was drawing away, so that the last remnant still granted to human souls was subject to contempt. We see this disturbingly embodied in the form that appeared in Europe, particularly in the draining away of the fourth Post-Atlantean period and much more widely than is thought: the form of the folkloric adventurer (for he has become an adventurer) who could still carry the contemporary last remnants of clairvoyant knowledge. The popular books call him "Magister Georgius Sabellicus, Faustus junior, fons necromanticorum, astrologus, magus secoundus, chiromanticus, aeromanticus, pyromanticus, in hydra arte secundus." These are the words of the complete title of that Faust in the sixteenth century† who represented the ancient clairvoyance as it was fading out entirely, who still had a view into the spiritual worlds, even if it was somewhat chaotic.

Then, in more recent times it emerged that the human soul is no longer granted, when it puts itself passively into certain situations as in ancient times, to see spiritually, but rather can only see passively the sensual and what the mind can put together from the sensual. The whole tragedy of recent spiritual vision was expressed in the simple accounts about Faust the Younger. Basically he refers to himself in his titles in such a way that we can recognize that he is the last offshoot of those who could still look into the spheres from which Christ descended. He called himself Faust the Younger, a clear allusion to the old Faust, the Manichaean bishop Faustus, the teacher of Augustine, who still possessed what Augustine yearned for; indeed, the writings of Augustine were never so widely distributed in Europe as in the time when the sagas of Faust the Younger came into being. Moreover, he called himself Magus Secundus, alluding to Magus Primus, who for those who look into these affairs, was still there as one who looked out with a clairvoyant gaze and reached up to the heavenly spheres, and whom those who only wanted to acknowledge and concentrate on the earthly life of Christ Jesus feared. In calling himself Magus Secundus, Faustus refers to the ancient Simon Magus,[†] the Magus Primus. However, he also refers to yet another man, whom we indeed know of from our spiritual-scientific observations and whose gaze was directed upward into the spiritual world. Faustus also calls himself "In hydra arte secundus," referring to Pythagoras, who in olden times was called Primus in this field of art.

We see the last flickering sunset of what was ancient clairvoyance, and we see how this ancient clairvoyance became incomprehensible to people. And what Augustine yearned for from Faustus Senior, and how he then became acquainted with the doctrine of Faustus Senior, as we are told, through an old man and physician, truly came to pass in what is presented to us so grippingly in the Faust saga. Just so, we encounter Faustus Junior in the popular saga. The old man appears there as well, and warns Faustus Junior, but he has already made his pact and handed over his legacy to Doctor Wagner.

And truly, when we look over the ages at what has been handed down as vision of a spiritual world since the fifth post-Atlantean epoch, we must say that it is the legacy handed over to Doctor Wagner. For it all hangs on how one can manage such an inheritance. In the case of Faust it is still a gazing into the spiritual worlds; in the case of Wagner it is something that only rummages around in parchments, looks back at old times, and is basically quite rightly characterized with the words, "One is desirous of treasures and is content when he finds earthworms."

That is the materialistic worldview of our recent age, and it is no wonder that in this materialistic worldview any vision of the Christ of Heaven has been lost, or that a fear of the expansion of the image on which the Earth forces should concentrate is still present today. But we also know that earthly humanity will lose all understanding of this image if it is incapable of weaving, through a new spiritual view, a new aura around the so gripping image of the Christmas Child and of His growth over thirty-three earthly years. Spiritual science will be called to sharpen the sight of human souls again for the Christ of Heaven beside the earthly Christ. Then the Christ will be recognized in such a way that for all future ages on Earth He can never be lost again for human progress and human salvation.

When wisdom presses upward again into spiritual heights where the fire of love also burns in divine spheres, then the human soul will not lose again what people can win through Christ Jesus—all that is wonderful, all that penetrates into the deepest forces of love. However, the eternal will be won as well. What additionally must be won will be won if the development of humanity proceeds in the appropriate way.

What we are able to say today is that nonetheless the modern sources of a knowledge of the spirit have truly opened, and that one does well in the symbol of the Christmas festival. Those who live themselves properly into what our spiritual-scientific knowledge still is today will find that a deep, deep humility overcomes their soul. We may only feel a presentiment of what spiritual science should become for humanity at some time in the future, for what we are able to know about it today can only do justice to what will one day be given to humanity when much, much time will have flowed by, as from the very young Jesus child to the adult Jesus Christ.

Today we have in our newly beginning spiritual science first the child. Hence the Christmas celebration is so properly our celebration, and we sense that we live today in a deep, dark winter night in respect to what can reign as human light in the development of the Earth, and that with our present knowledge we really stand before something that reveals itself to us in the deep winter darkness of the evolution of the Earth, just as the shepherds once stood before the Christ child, who first revealed Himself to them. In respect to the understanding of Christ Jesus, we can adjust ourselves as the shepherds of long ago and so properly pray that the sources of spiritual life may always flow more and more generously for human beings; properly pray that they may ever more realize divine revelation in the spiritual heights and grant the peace that this revelation can give to human souls who are truly of good will. This Christmas celebration in particular then appears to us as an emblem. We know little still of what depth of spiritual science the world will have one day. We feel a presentiment of what may be yet to come; we feel it in deep humility. However little, when we are willing to let it properly penetrate our heart, ah! What it looks like to us then!

Looking over the Europe of today, what do the nations think about one another? How do the nations, one and the other, look for the blame for what is happening! If spirit knowledge truly inscribes itself into our souls, we will understand the blame sought by one nation in another. In truth, someone has this blame, and he is really entirely international, directing his steps from nation to nation. But we speak of him only in the circles of those in whose hearts a little spiritual science has come. There we speak of Ahriman, the so properly international being, who, in alliance with Lucifer, has the true blame. You do not find him if you always direct your gaze toward the others, but only if you seek the paths of knowledge in self-knowledge. There it goes down below into the depths of chaos. Then we feel him, this Ahriman. But when we recognize him correctly and learn to understand him in the context of what the Mystery of Golgotha can be for us—the annunciation of the revelation of wisdom in the heights and of peace in the depths of the valley of Earth—then we get a sense of the whole fire of love that can radiate from the Mystery of Golgotha and does not know the boundaries that have been erected between nations and peoples.

A great deal exists in what has already appeared before our souls as spiritual science. But if we direct our attention to what has been revealed already before this chaotic present day of ours and what has now found such a deeply disturbing, sad, and tragic expression, we find how very small is the dwelling of the soul in which the new understanding of the Christmas child who came to Earth must live today. Did not this Christmas child have to appear to poor shepherds, did not he have to be born in a stall, hidden from what ruled the world in that time, and is that not once again so for the new understanding of what is connected with the Mystery of Golgotha? Is not what appears to us outside in the world infinitely far from this understanding in the world at the beginning of our time-reckoning, from what revealed itself to the shepherds when they heard: "Divine revelation in the heights and peace on Earth to people of good will!"

Let us celebrate, my dear friends, this Christmastide of the renewed Christ understanding in our hearts and in our souls; let us feel ourselves, if we want to celebrate a proper Christmas like those shepherds, far away from what fills the world now. But through what is revealed to us as shepherds, let us recognize what necessarily had to be recognized back then—let us recognize the promise of a certain future. And let us build up in our souls the trust in the fulfillment of this promise: the trust that what we feel today, like the child we wish to worship—the new Christ understanding is this child—will grow, will live, and will develop, in not such a long time, in such a way that the etherically manifesting Christ can incarnate into it, as the Christ could incarnate in the body of flesh at the time of the Mystery of Golgotha. Let us fill ourselves with the light that, through trust in this promise, can illuminate us into the innermost depths of the soul; let us warm ourselves with the warmth that can pulse through our souls! If we feel the relation to the spiritual heights in which the light of that spiritual world can appear before our intuitive souls, then alone can we be certain that it will one day brighten the world.

If we think like this, then we are making—precisely in this difficult, painful time—a real Christmas celebration. For not only is the deep, dark winter night of the season present; the result of ahrimanic darkness is there on the horizon of nations, as it has gradually come up since the beginning of the fifth post-Atlantean epoch. Just as the annunciation of Christ first came only to the shepherds and then increasingly filled the world, so the new understanding of the Mystery of Golgotha will increasingly fill the world. And times will come that will dissolve the winter darkness we live in today. They will be times of light for human beings as well.

Lets us feel ourselves like shepherds in relation to what is still a child—in relation to the new Christ understanding—and let us feel that we can pulse through, pulse through in all humility, with a new sense the saying that not only should endure within the progress of the development of the Earth, but should become increasingly more significant. Let us unite ourselves not only with the mind, but also with raised consciousness in the saying so full of promise in this Christmas season:

Divine revelation in spiritual heights,
Peace, peace, more and more
To all human souls on Earth,
Who are of good will.

11

The Birth of Christ in the Human Heart

BASEL, DECEMBER 27, 1914

The great modern mystic Angelus Silesius uttered a fine phrase: "If Christ be born in Bethlehem a thousand times and not in you, you remain in eternal perdition."† This saying has two sides. One is that in it the confession of faith is delivered: the proper, true Christmastide must be celebrated in the inner heart of people, and all external celebration of Christmas must be a stimulus to a striving for the inner fact, which then in the winter night of consecration brings up from the depths of our soul, from the darkness that reigns in the heart of the soul as the winter darkness without, the deepest powers the soul can find within itself. And these deepest powers feel themselves bound with the nature of what the human being can sense rushing through all earthly becoming, swelling through it and giving it meaning. We find in the depths of our soul something that is with the Christ, if only we go down into the depths of our soul life where we still unfold our consciousness with our intelligence devoted to the spiritual powers of the world.

And the other side of the saying consists of the promise that human beings who today have a proper sense of themselves in the becoming of the Earth can bring to their consciousness how true human existence, not being lost as a true human being, is linked to the soul's feeling itself most intimately bound with the essential substantiality of Christ Jesus. However, it has become clear to us through many reflections over the course of the years that Christ consciousness must immerse itself in the progress of the development of the Earth; that human beings, as they go from incarnation to incarnation, must come more and more deeply to the understanding of what Christ really is. And we have attempted in recent times to deepen this Christ knowledge by creating a source through which we can celebrate in a deeper sense the Christmas night of consecration, the winter night of consecration: the celebration of the birth of Jesus. How this is intended will emerge from our reflection today.

A great historian of modern times† was asked by a person interested in world events why in his books the events that unfolded in connection with the Mystery of Golgotha were eliminated, why the books never mentioned intervention of the forces and powers of Christ Jesus in the progression of human events. The great historian was asked why he explains how the popes have intervened in history, kings, armies, the exercise of administrative authority, even natural events, but one can find nothing in his writings about how the forces that were transferred into humanity through the Mystery of Golgotha have moved through human events since then. The historian grew thoughtful. Then, after some time, after he had consulted thoroughly with himself about the matter, he said: "For the observation of history I must stay with the style I have used in the past, for the Christ forces that swell and flow through world events belong to a sort of primal world into which the human soul is not able to peer. One can indeed observe what effects have emerged from the Mystery of Golgotha and from the deeds of Christ, but one cannot describe the particular quality of these Christ deeds in history."

Now this is only one of the illustrations that can be given for the fact that even for something like the observation of history, the most illustrious personalities of modern times cannot say for themselves that their souls have already celebrated the Christmas festival; the living form, the living essence of Christ Jesus had not yet appeared in the soul of this historian so that he could behold how it goes, from year to year, from week to week, indeed from hour to hour, through everything that happens in human becoming. A thorough historian today can peer into the historical process of becoming and perceive nothing of the fact that since the Mystery of Golgotha the power of Christ is present everywhere in that historical process of becoming. We can seek various causes—and find them, too—for the fact that, to a certain extent, in the souls of many people the winter festival of consecration, which is devoted to the Christmas mystery, has not yet been celebrated.

The man who showed, to a certain extent, out of the depths of his being that he so properly felt the Christian mystery—Goethe—can tell us something about it. Goethe has Wilhelm Meister,† whose entire course of development as a human being is so lovingly described, enter an estate. Wilhelm Meister is led around by the lord of the estate and then is shown the estate's picture gallery. It is a peculiar gallery; it contains in particular, one after another, the principal scenes of human development: how world history flowed among the various nations of antiquity and also among the ancient Hebrew people, from the age of paradise, from the expulsion on, right through to more recent historical periods. The historical process is displayed in important scenes, ending with the destruction of Jerusalem—and nowhere is there any picture whatsoever containing any scene from the life of Christ Jesus, although the history continues past the Mystery of Golgotha as far as the destruction of Jerusalem. Then Wilhelm asks, "Why have you nothing at all in your picture gallery about the divine man who brought so much salvation into the development of humanity? I find a gap in the course of this history; I see the temple of Jerusalem destroyed, without the entrance of the man whom shortly before they were unwilling to give a hearing." And Wilhelm received the answer: "To do what you demand would have been an error. The life of this divine man stands in no relation to the world history of His time. It was a private life, and his doctrine was a doctrine for individuals. What publicly comes in the path of the masses among the nations and their offshoots belongs to world history, to world religion, which we consider the prime. What individuals encounter within themselves belongs to the second religion, that of the wise. It was such a religion that Christ taught and practiced, as long as He went about on the Earth."

Indeed, a word that speaks deeply to our heart! In reference to the Christ fact, every person living on the Earth stands as an individual, as a direct individuality. What can be presented as popular history creeps into the affairs of individual nations, for it relates to what happens in the environs of human fate, what happens in the human sphere. What Christ brought into the world—whatever part of the Earth's development it may belong with—goes deep, deep inside into what every heart, every human soul feels and experiences insofar as it feels itself as a human being in the true sense of the word, a mere human being. We must feel again that this feeling oneself as a human being first entered the human development of the Earth with what came with the Mystery of Golgotha.

Let us go further. The lord of the estate now leads Wilhelm Meister farther and shows him another gallery, which he keeps hidden. Now they enter another room, where the events of the New Testament are displayed. Therefore, Wilhelm does not see the events of the New Testament where the worldly events are displayed from stage to stage, where one shows the exoteric, but rather in an esoteric space. Before contemplating the events of the New Testament, the soul prepares itself by withdrawing from the affairs of world history belonging to individual peoples. The soul should place itself only on the esoteric foundation of the individual human being. Then it will cross the threshold to where the pictures of the New Testament are arranged. Also, the entire New Testament is not displayed in this room, but only the scenes up to the Last Supper. Wilhelm asks, "Have you then also, as you display the life of this divine man as a picture for teaching and example, likewise raised up His sufferings, His death as an example of exalted patience?" He received a significant answer, from which is to be gleaned with what dread one can feel the holiest event that has occurred on Earth with the being who made His dwelling in a body, which we celebrate in the winter night of consecration. Wilhelm will be led into the next level of the esoteric, which will be expressed with a holy thrill as follows: "We draw a veil over these sufferings precisely because we venerate them so highly. We consider it to be a presumption worthy of damnation to expose to the sight of the Sun those instruments of martyrdom and the Holy Man suffering from them."

That is how one could feel on an esoteric level in the eighteenth century. It was good to feel that way esoterically, for we can admit entirely from our point of view that in a certain way, if the pictorial representations, particularly of the Passion, were not given by the highest, the truly most important artists, then they have served to drag the holy Mystery of Golgotha down to the human level. And we can understand the feeling that a man who deeply felt the Mystery of Golgotha in those times did not wish to see the distorted images that have been made many times of this holy mystery; he wished to draw a veil over all that, because he felt that only the most intimate, sacred forces wish to be supersensibly bound with what is connected to the secrets of the Last Supper.

But then what feeling is basically in all this? What should we feel, exactly, when we wish to comprehend such a feeling in the esoteric experience of the soul? We must comprehend that yearning was in human hearts when something of this sort was seen: the human heart yearned for a conception, a vision of the Christ Mystery greater than what one could experience back in those days. In all humility, in still much greater humility than in respect to other aspects of spiritual science, we may admit to ourselves, really admit, that the finest souls for a long, long time have thirsted yearningly for what Christ knowledge should become for us through esoteric science.

What we could know earlier only in another form will soon be seen by souls, when the time shall be fulfilled! The consciousness that such knowledge will be able to flash through the human heart, and the yearning for it, live as a life riddle in the best of souls. People aspire for a Christ discovery commensurate with the great event that happened on Golgotha, upon which one can focus one's eye, the soul's eye as well, when the veils are drawn away. I related yesterday how in a certain way Christ knowledge had to go back; how in the earliest times of the development of Christianity this Christ knowledge, still fertilized by ancient clairvoyance, was taken up, and how it later gradually subsided. And I read an ancient Gnostic couplet† that I will recite here as well, in order to refer properly to how an awareness was present in regard to the ancient atavistic clairvoyant knowledge: the Christ, whom we contemplate when we see Him coming into the world through the Christmas child, is a being of the universe who grows greater and greater the higher the spiritual spheres into which we turn our soul's gaze—for through these spheres He descends. For that reason a worn-out humanity found it necessary to draw a veil before this event, because it was still not able to point to how in the secret of the child, which every child understands in feeling, lies at the same time the highest wisdom. In this child a being was born who went through the worlds before He appeared on Earth.

Jesus said:
Look there, O Father,
How this being [the human soul] on Earth,
Of all evil the goal and sacrifice,
Far from thy breath wanders.
Look, it flees bitter chaos,
Helpless, how it should find its way through.

In the dialogue with the divine Father Being, Christ is shown as He makes his way downward through the world spheres; as He looks at the human soul wandering in chaos but yearning in His direction, to which He wants to bring salvation. And therefore Christ speaks further to the Father:

Therefore, send me, O Father!
Bearing the seal [the seal of heaven] I descend,
I stride through the host of eons ...

In the spiritual spheres the spiritual worlds are layers on top of one another, and the higher we climb, the more we find that the older worlds still live in the present; the one that was the oldest is at the same time today to be found in the highest spheres. What was once bound with the Saturn development we find today in the highest spiritual sphere, and insofar as we bring this succession of spiritual spheres together with the development of time, they are called eons.

I stride through the host of eons,
Every holy teaching I unfold,
Show then the portrait of the gods.
And so I give you
Of the holy path
Deep-hidden lore:
"Gnosis" is its name for you.

Lost to a certain degree to humanity is the consciousness of this cosmic Christ. It had to be lost, because the ancient clairvoyance had to disappear; a transitional period had to come, a spiritless eon, so to speak, so that a new kind of clairvoyant sight could come into being. It must, however, direct itself once again up into the spiritual world, must not merely characterize the being who enters the development of humanity through the winter night of consecration with external human vision, but rather must follow how this being climbs from heavenly sphere to heavenly sphere, walks down onto the Earth and gives meaning to the world; yes, gives meaning to the Earth.

Look there, O Father,
How this being on Earth,
Of all evil the goal and sacrifice,
Far from thy breath wanders.
Look, it flees bitter chaos,
Helpless, how it should find its way through.
Therefore, send me, O Father!
Bearing the seal, I descend,
I stride through the host of eons,
Every holy teaching I unfold,
Show then the portrait of the gods.
And so I give you
Of the holy path
Deep-hidden lore:
"Gnosis" is its name for you.

How does this Earth actually appear to us, insofar as it is all around us, when we consider it in its true meaning? Will you ever say, "This is a human being," when one brings you the sort of corpse whose soul is already dwelling in the spiritual world outside the corpse? Will you ever say, "This is in the full sense of the word still a human being"? Precisely the higher members of human nature are no longer in the soulless corpse. The Earth, since the middle of the Atlantean period of development, is in the same situation, however: a soulless corpse. Since the middle of the Atlantean period the Earth all around us, in spite of its beauties, has been in the process of becoming a corpse; it is becoming more and more a corpse. And when you go out and stand before a gigantic cliff, the best you can say to yourself is: "That is the skeleton the Earth has been forming since the middle of the Atlantean period!" And while you look at what covers the cliff as earth, you see the dying part of the actual Earth organism, which was alive only up until the middle of the Atlantean period. Even geology clearly understands that when we walk over the earth or direct a plow through a furrow in the earth, we walk over the corpse of the Earth or direct a plow through the corpse. Our geologists have expressed it,† and even external science itself, when it begins to think, can do no other than to recognize such things. So when we are surrounded by the Earth, we stand, basically, in relation to death and observe how our ball of the Earth is gradually dying away.

And now let us imagine that the Mystery of Golgotha did not happen, that the cosmic entity we call the Christ never entered the development of the Earth through the Jesus boys†—then nothing would have come of the Earth development; it would already have been dying by now. But the Christ Being went through the two Jesus children and then, through one of the Jesus children over a three-year period in Earth time, went through the Mystery of Golgotha, and the Earth received a new seed of life. And the Earth will not, once the time has been fulfilled, remain in the space of the universe, and the soul will not fall prey to Ahriman and Lucifer! That would have happened if the Christ had not come to Earth as a living seed, but since He has come the Earth will not fall into earthly dust, for a new life entered Earth development with the Christ seed.

Just as the Earth split off from the Sun and became a son of the Sun, now, because the Christ gave Earth development a meaning, the Earth will be permeated by this meaningful being towards a new development.

So we see into the Mystery of Golgotha through spiritual science, and we stand trembling in the present time and feel ourselves called, because we have permission to raise the veil from the territories into which sensory perception no longer reaches. But we do not wish to see there only what an age that has developed its destiny gradually in the direction of materialism must indeed see.

The possibility begins once again in our time that those who know their soul to be filled with spiritual-scientific impulses will look up to Christ as a cosmic being. Through this the eternal devotion—it must be said again and again—that we can have for the child of the consecrated Christmastide will not be diminished. Simple Christian feeling will not be decreased through it. It will rather be deepened when we can therefore feel the Christ as our dear friend Christian Morgenstern felt Him when a poem blossomed from his soul† that can appear to us as a resurrection of primal Gnostic ideas, in which at the same time the love of Christ ruled and cosmic wisdom was active. And so we celebrate a new Christmas, when in the dark night of materialism voices resound once more—not those of the ancient Gnostics, but fertilized by the same sense, which is directed toward the living cosmic Christ:

Light is love ... Sun-weaving
Love-radiance of a world
of creative beings—

which through ages unheard-of
holds us to its heart,
and which at last has given us
its highest spirit in the sheath
of a man for three
years: then He came into His

Father's legacy—now the Earth's
innermost heavenly fire:
that it, too, may once become Sun.

If Christ be born in Bethlehem a thousand times
And not in you, you remain in eternal perdition.

Let us allow the internal winter festival of consecration to move into our souls, let us allow our souls to feel how a new Christ knowledge must be born in our time. This Christ knowledge, of what sort is it then? It connects what is most intimate in the human being and in a way brings the entire being together to the simplest thing of all: it connects the life of a child, not yet the fully developed life of a human being, to the highest cosmic being and becoming. We feel, while we contemplate the Christ child, whom we commemorate in the winter night of consecration, the most powerful winter consecration standing before the sight of our soul, which reaches through all eons; and we bind all world becoming, wherever we look, with everything human, with the deepest humanity.

That is how those feel who take their feeling from our spiritual science, as the victory over all death will be won through uniting the soul with the Christ Being in our time—to which I alluded today on a deeply moving occasion for us at the grave of a friend,† torn away from us by the war. However, for so long we could not get a feel for how the loftiest cosmic is related to the most intimate human, since we could not see the story in its innermost essence in the secret of Bethlehem. That, however, will happen for those who put the mystery of the two Jesus boys before their eyes. There we have the power of the wisest person of the pre-Christian age, of Zarathustra, in one of the Jesus boys. We have in one of the Jesus boys the part of human development that flows down from the one side. We have the aura of the other brightened and illuminated through what proceeded from Buddha. We have the external physical life descended from the noblest strains of the ancient Hebrew people, and we have what makes up the soul content of the Jesus boy in the Luke Gospel leading back to the origin of the Earth. For we know that the deepest soul content of the Luke Jesus boy remained behind as the human being walked the Earth in the ancient Lemurian age, and that it was stored up by the sacred mysteries and then led down, as the Luke Jesus boy was born, to the body being born. Hence that peculiar speech of the Luke Jesus boy directly after birth, which only the mother could understand, which was like no language, and which also the Boy immediately forgot, as early consciousness emerged in him. But it was an expression of a secret directly after birth. Basically, much of what we have to lay bare about the Christ Mystery is an interpretation of what the Luke Jesus boy said immediately after his birth.

So we have understood through our spiritual science the Christ impulse entirely out of the deeper human development of ancient pre-Christian times, when to a certain extent the distinctions also cease again, the initiates speak again. When we will have finally understood everything that entered the development of humanity with the Mystery of Golgotha, we will also find the possibility of advancing the powers further in every area where there is human development, even in history. However, we must first know who Christ really was, before we can, for example, speak of Him in history as well.

When more and more souls within our spiritual movement seek the impulse to ignite the inner light that can be ignited when we descend into the deepest forces of our soul, which human beings can have today following the Mystery of Golgotha, it will be revealed that through such descent the light of Christ really is ignited in each individual soul. This light of Christ becomes a tree, the Christmas tree, which will then send forth light in all future human development so that the soul will find what it looks for in the reanimated Earth; so that it will find Christ everywhere in the reanimated Earth. This it will accomplish. Moreover, the Christ message of spiritual science can be taken so seriously that among the believers in this spiritual science, the Christmas festival will really be celebrated in each individual soul and will show the birth of the Christ knowledge that comes from Christ Himself and is therefore a true Christ birth, a birth of Christ in us. This Christ birth must, however, enter into us.

True, true is the saying:

If Christ be born in Bethlehem a thousand times
And not in you, you remain in eternal perdition.

And let us add to this very beautiful dictum of the mystic Angelus Silesius: there we want to find ourselves eternally, as we eternally seek the experience of the winter night of consecration, the birth of Christ in the depths of our soul!

REFERENCE NOTES

Page 3, "what was intended for Munich"
For the time of August 18-27, 1914, a lecture cycle titled, "Über okkultes Hören und okkultes Lesen" [Concerning inner hearing and inner reading], as well as the performance of a new, fifth Mystery Drama had been planned. Because of the outbreak of World War I, these events could not take place.

Page 4, "review of my book, *Theosophy*"
The review, written by the university lecturer, Dr. Hermann Westermann, appeared in the magazine, *Die Zukunft* [The future], Vol. XIX, No. 15, on January 1, 1911.

Page 6, "in the sixth edition"
See the closing chapter of *Theosophy* (CW 9).

Page 10, "in the final chapter of my book, *Riddles of Philosophy*"
"A Brief Outline of an Approach to Anthroposophy." This added chapter was published for the first time in 1914.

Page 13, "the building outside"
While the first Goetheanum was being built, Rudolf Steiner's lectures were held in the "schreinerei" [carpentry studio] directly beside the construction site.

Page 15, "as I described in my book, *How to Know Higher Worlds*"
(CW 10). The chapter titled "The Splitting of the Personality during Spiritual Training."

Page 31, "In many respects"
The content at the end of this lecture, taken down by four note-takers, is full of gaps, and is, therefore, incomplete.

Page 35, "in a series of lectures held in Munich"
Initiation, Eternity, and the Passing Moment (CW 138)

Page 35, "in a lecture cycle in Munich"
Initiation, Eternity, and the Passing Moment (CW 138).

Page 38, "something I experienced concerning our dear friend Christian Morgenstern"
In the lecture of May 9, 1914, in Kassel. Contained in *Unsere Toten* [Our dead] (GA 261). See also the note for page 63.

Page 39, "through the described experiences"
See the lecture of April 9, 1914, in *The Inner Nature of Man and the Life Between Death and New Birth* (CW 153).

Page 40, "*The Threshold of the Spiritual World*"
(CW 17).

Page 46, "in a public lecture"
On January 15, 1914, in Berlin. The lecture titled: "Das Böse in Lichte der Erkenntnis vom Geiste" [Evil in the light of knowledge of the spirit]. Contained in *Geisteswissenschaft als Lebensgut* [Spiritual science as a treasure for life] (GA 63).

Page 52, "in allowing the Cosmic Word to rule in the weaving of our own being"
In another record taken down, it says "to let the cosmic word sound forth."

Page 56, "into the Akashic Chronicle"
The sentence is not given in its entirety in any of the records from the note-takers. Only the following fragment exists from two people:

> "Through what you speak with another being, through the actions in common with another being, there really arise in the spiritual world ... to hear and to ... what is communicated ... what is experienced there ...."

Page 56, "*Theosophy*"
(CW 9).

Page 56, "*Outline of Esoteric Science*"
(CW 13).

Page 59, "Saint Paul says"
1Corinthians 3:19.

Page 62, "the building we are raising here"
See *Architecture as a Synthesis of the Arts* (CW 286), 8 lectures between December 12, 1911 and July 26, 1914.

Page 63, "Christian Morgenstern"
The poet Christian Morgenstern (1871-1914) first heard lectures by Rudolf Steiner in 1909 in Berlin and became a member of the Theosophical Society (as of 1923, the Anthroposophical Society) a few months afterward. The last collection he brought out was *We Found a Path.* The poetry he left behind, and which was recited, appeared in print first in 1927 with the title *Mensch Wanderer* [Human wanderer].

Page 64, "on the day of the laying of the foundation stone...Herman Grimm."
On September 20, 1914, at the commemoration for the anniversary of the laying of the foundation stone of the Dornach building (first Goetheanum). To be included in GA 250 which is yet to be published. Earlier partial editions appeared in Dornach (in 1938) with the title, "Die Sehnsucht der Seelen nach dem Geist" [The souls' yearning for the spirit].

Page 65, "Goethe's conversation with Eckermann"
On July 6,1831. In *Goethe's Conversations with Eckermann.*

Page 66, "in a Berlin lecture"
Lecture of December 15, 1910, contained in *Antworten der Geisteswissenschaft auf die großen Fragen des Daseins* [The answers of spiritual science to the biggest questions of existence] (GA 60).

Page 70, "the second essay that I ever had published"
"Goethe und Shakespeare, eine Parallele" [Goethe and Shakespeare, a parallel], appeared about 1883. The essay could, unfortunately, not be found.

Page 70, "I met once with Herman Grimm"
See the lecture of December 15, 1910 (See the note for page 66 above). (GA 60).

Page 71, "When Herman Grimm said"
The following quotes are taken from *Homers Ilias* [Homer's Iliad], Introduction to Part 2, Berlin, 1895, and from *Beiträge zur deutschen Kulturgeschichte* [Contributions to German cultural history], chapter titled, "Erinnerungen und Ausblicke" [Looking back and forward], Berlin 1897.

Page 87, "several important ideas about our building"
See *Architecture as a Synthesis of the Arts* (CW 286).

Page 100, "Capesius and Strader"
See Rudolf Steiner's *Four Mystery Dramas* (CW 14), "The Portal of Initiation," fourth scene.

Page 104, "about the upbringing of children"
See the essay, "The Education of the Child," in *The Education of the Child and Early Lectures on Education*, a collection of essays and lectures. Rudolf Steiner held lectures on this topic at various locations.

Page 107, "the chaotic events of the present day"
World War I had begun only a few months before.

Page 108, "Emerson, who has also been characterized in these lectures"
See the lecture of November 15, 1914, in *Der Zusammenhang des Menschen mit der elementarischen Welt* [The connection between the human being and the elemental world] (GA 158).

Page 108, "Ralph Waldo Emerson"
Emerson (1803-1882). American poet and philosopher. "Essays," 1841.

Page 108, "Jan van Ruysbroek"
Flemish mystic (1293-1381).

Page 109, "But if he sought other proofs...not of the earthly parish"
Quote from Maurice Maeterlinck from *Der Schatz der Armen* [The treasure of the poor]. Translated into German by Friedrich von Oppeln-Bronikowski, Jena 1898.

Page 109, "Maurice Maeterlinck"
(1862-1949). French-Belgian poet.

Page 111, "Time appears to be like a shade ...believes she has lost herself"
Quote from Johann Gottlieb Fichte out of *Reden an die deutsche Nation* [Addresses to the German nation], Reclam Edition (Leipzig, O.J.), 1807/08. First address.

Page 113, "[About the drawing]"
The drawing is given as it was sketched by note-takers. Rudolf Steiner drew it in three parts during the lecture. To make it more comprehensible, the individual parts are designated with a, b, c. This is a change from the 1967 edition of this book (in German), in which the parts were inserted into the text and the proportions were not quite correct.

Page 121, "add a concluding chapter"
"A Brief Outline of an Approach to Anthroposophy," in *Riddles of Philosophy* (CW 18). The closing chapter appeared first in the 1914 edition.

Page 135, "the Prague cycle"
An Occult Physiology (CW 128), 8 lectures in Prague, from March 20-28, 1911.

Page 135, "drawn schematically...human beings"
The sketch inserted into the 1967 German edition of the book was left out of this edition, because it was not found in any of the original records of the various note-takers or in the original stenographic record by Franz Seiler.

Page 140, "My kingdom is not of this world"
John 18:36

Page 140, "You are from beneath, I am from above"
John 8:23.

Page 140, "L'état c'est moi"
This is ascribed to the French King Ludwig XIV. He reigned from 1643-1715).

Page 143, "a beautiful saying of Goethe"
A noble philosopher spoke of architecture as a frozen music ...." In *Maxims and Reflections*. See the German edition of Goethe's Natural Scientific Writings (introduced and edited by Rudolf Steiner), volume 5: Sprüche in Prosa [Sayings in prose], the part on art. See also the annotation by Rudolf Steiner in *Nature's Open Secrets* (CW1) (Anthroposophic Press 2000), as well as Goethe's conversation with Eckermann on March 23, 1829.

Page 151, "two Jesus children"
Compare Rudolf Steiner's, *The Fifth Gospel* (CW 148).

Page 154, "Mani"
(216-277 C.E.) Original Manichean documents were found in central Egypt in 1930.

Page 156, "Faustus"
A meeting in 383 C.E. between Augustine and Faust of Milene. *Confessions*, vol. 5.

Page 157, "what the Gnostics can still say"
The original text is in the tenth chapter of Book 5 of Philosophumena [Philosophy] by the opponent of Gnosticism. Hippolytos. It was found only in the mid-nineteenth century in an Athos cloister. Published by P. Wendland in *Die griechische christlichen Schriftsteller der ersten drei Jahrhunderts* [The Greek Christian authors in the first three centuries], Vol. XXVI, Leipzig 1916. The literal translation true to the actual meaning was done by Rudolf Steiner. Compare Thomas Maurer in *Das Goetheanum*, XV, No. 7.

Page 158, "In the soul's eye is reflected"
See Rudolf Steiner's, *Truth-Wrought Words* (CW 40).

Page 158, "title of that Faust in the sixteenth century"
Abbott Johannes Trithemius told how Faust, when he was trying to avoid meeting him in Gelhausen in 1506, left a calling card for him on which stood: "conjurer of the dead, astrologer, healing magus, palm reader, interpreter of the atmosphere, fire interpreter, and medical interpreter of urine." Compare Herman Grimm's, "Die Entstehung des Volkbuches von Dr. Faust" [The origin of the folklore book of Dr. Faust], in *Fünfzehn Essays, Dritte Folge* [Fifteen essays,

third issue], Berlin 1882; as well as Karl Kiesewetter's *Faust in der Geschichte und Tradition* [Faust in history and tradition, or folklore], Leipzig 1893.

Page 159, "Simon Magus"
See Acts 8:9.

Page 164, "Angelus Silesius"
Actually Johannes Scheffler (1624-1677). *Cherubinian Wanderer.*

Page 165, "a great historian"
Leopold von Ranke (1795-1886). See Herman Grimm's *Fragmente* [Fragments], second and last parts. Berlin 1902.

Page 166, "Wilhelm Meister"
In *Wilhem Meister's Journeyman Years* by Johann Wolfgang von Geothe.

Page 168, "ancient Gnostic couplet"
See note for page 157.

Page 171, "our geologists"
For instance, Eduard Sueß (1831-1914), in *Das Antlitz der Erde* [The countenance of the Earth].

Page 171, "the Jesus boys"
See Rudolf Steiner, *The Spiritual Guidance of the Individual and Humanity* (CW 15).

Page 172, "Christian Morgenstern"
(1871-1914). Poem in *We Found a Path.*

Page 173, "a deeply moving occasion"
See Rudolf Steiner's address at the grave of Albert Faiß, in *Unsere Toten* [Our dead]. Addresses, eulogies, and meditational verses 1912-1924. (CW 261).

RUDOLF STEINER'S COLLECTED WORKS

The German Edition of Rudolf Steiner's Collected Works (the Gesamtausgabe [GA] published by Rudolf Steiner Verlag, Dornach, Switzerland) presently runs to over 354 titles, organized either by type of work (written or spoken), chronology, audience (public or other), or subject (education, art, etc.). For ease of comparison, the Collected Works in English [CW] follows the German organization exactly. A complete listing of the CWs follows with literal translations of the German titles. Other than in the case of the books published in his lifetime, titles were rarely given by Rudolf Steiner himself, and were often provided by the editors of the German editions. The titles in English are not necessarily the same as the German; and, indeed, over the past seventy-five years have frequently been different, with the same book sometimes appearing under different titles.

For ease of identification and to avoid confusion, we suggest that readers looking for a title should do so by CW number. Because the work of creating the Collected Works of Rudolf Steiner is an ongoing process, with new titles being published every year, we have not indicated in this listing which books are presently available. To find out what titles in the Collected Works are currently in print, please check our website at www.steinerbooks.org, or write to SteinerBooks 610 Main Street, Great Barrington, MA 01230:

Written Work

CW 1	Goethe: Natural-Scientific Writings, Introduction, with Footnotes and Explanations in the text by Rudolf Steiner
CW 2	Outlines of an Epistemology of the Goethean World View, with Special Consideration of Schiller
CW 3	Truth and Science
CW 4	The Philosophy of Freedom
CW 4a	Documents to "The Philosophy of Freedom"
CW 5	Friedrich Nietzsche, A Fighter against His Own Time
CW 6	Goethe's Worldview
CW 6a	Now in CW 30
CW 7	Mysticism at the Dawn of Modern Spiritual Life and Its Relationship with Modern Worldviews
CW 8	Christianity as Mystical Fact and the Mysteries of Antiquity
CW 9	Theosophy: An Introduction into Supersensible World Knowledge and Human Purpose
CW 10	How Does One Attain Knowledge of Higher Worlds?
CW 11	From the Akasha-Chronicle
CW 12	Levels of Higher Knowledge

CW 13	Occult Science in Outline
CW 14	Four Mystery Dramas
CW 15	The Spiritual Guidance of the Individual and Humanity
CW 16	A Way to Human Self-Knowledge: Eight Meditations
CW 17	The Threshold of the Spiritual World. Aphoristic Comments
CW 18	The Riddles of Philosophy in Their History, Presented as an Outline
CW 19	Contained in CW 24
CW 20	The Riddles of the Human Being: Articulated and Unarticulated in the Thinking, Views and Opinions of a Series of German and Austrian Personalities
CW 21	The Riddles of the Soul
CW 22	Goethe's Spiritual Nature and Its Revelation in "Faust" and through the "Fairy Tale of the Snake and the Lily"
CW 23	The Central Points of the Social Question in the Necessities of Life in the Present and the Future
CW 24	Essays Concerning the Threefold Division of the Social Organism and the Period 1915-1921
CW 25	Cosmology, Religion and Philosophy
CW 26	Anthroposophical Leading Thoughts
CW 27	Fundamentals for Expansion of the Art of Healing according to Spiritual-Scientific Insights
CW 28	The Course of My Life
CW 29	Collected Essays on Dramaturgy, 1889-1900
CW 30	Methodical Foundations of Anthroposophy: Collected Essays on Philosophy, Natural Science, Aesthetics and Psychology, 1884-1901
CW 31	Collected Essays on Culture and Current Events, 1887-1901
CW 32	Collected Essays on Literature, 1884-1902
CW 33	Biographies and Biographical Sketches, 1894-1905
CW 34	Lucifer-Gnosis: Foundational Essays on Anthroposophy and Reports from the Periodicals "Lucifer" and "Lucifer-Gnosis," 1903-1908
CW 35	Philosophy and Anthroposophy: Collected Essays, 1904-1923
CW 36	The Goetheanum-Idea in the Middle of the Cultural Crisis of the Present: Collected Essays from the Periodical "Das Goetheanum," 1921-1925
CW 37	Now in CWs 260a and 251
CW 38	Letters, Vol. 1: 1881-1890
CW 39	Letters, Vol. 2: 1890-1925
CW 40	Truth-Wrought Words
CW 40a	Sayings, Poems and Mantras; Supplementary Volume
CW 42	Now in CWs 264-266

Public Lectures

CW 78	Anthroposophy, Its Roots of Knowledge and Fruits for Life
CW 79	The Reality of the Higher Worlds
CW 80	Public lectures in various cities, 1922
CW 81	Renewal-Impulses for Culture and Science–Berlin College Course
CW 82	So that the Human Being Can Become a Complete Human Being
CW 83	Western and Eastern World-Contrast. Paths to Understanding It through Anthroposophy
CW 84	What Did the Goetheanum Intend and What Should Anthroposophy Do?

Lectures to the Members of the Anthroposophical Society

CW 88	Concerning the Astral World and Devachan
CW 89	Consciousness–Life–Form. Fundamental Principles of a Spiritual-Scientific Cosmology
CW 90	Participant Notes from the Lectures during the Years 1903-1905
CW 91	Participant Notes from the Lectures during the Years 1903-1905
CW 92	The Occult Truths of Ancient Myths and Sagas
CW 93	The Temple Legend and the Golden Legend
CW 93a	Fundamentals of Esotericism
CW 94	Cosmogony. Popular Occultism. The Gospel of John. The Theosophy in the Gospel of John
CW 95	At the Gates of Theosophy
CW 96	Origin-Impulses of Spiritual Science. Christian Esotericism in the Light of New Spirit-Knowledge
CW 97	The Christian Mystery
CW 98	Nature Beings and Spirit Beings – Their Effects in Our Visible World
CW 99	The Theosophy of the Rosicrucians
CW 100	Human Development and Christ-Knowledge
CW 101	Myths and Legends. Occult Signs and Symbols
CW 102	The Working into Human Beings by Spiritual Beings
CW 103	The Gospel of John
CW 104	The Apocalypse of John
CW 104a	From the Picture-Script of the Apocalypse of John
CW 105	Universe, Earth, the Human Being: Their Being and Development, as well as Their Reflection in the Connection between Egyptian Mythology and Modern Culture
CW 106	Egyptian Myths and Mysteries in Relation to the Active Spiritual Forces of the Present
CW 107	Spiritual-Scientific Knowledge of the Human Being
CW 108	Answering the Questions of Life and the World through Anthroposophy

CW 109 The Principle of Spiritual Economy in Connection with the Question of Reincarnation. An Aspect of the Spiritual Guidance of Humanity
CW 110 The Spiritual Hierarchies and Their Reflection in the Physical World. Zodiac, Planets and Cosmos
CW 111 Contained in 109
CW 112 The Gospel of John in Relation to the Three Other Gospels, Especially the Gospel of Luke
CW 113 The Orient in the Light of the Occident. The Children of Lucifer and the Brothers of Christ
CW 114 The Gospel of Luke
CW 115 Anthroposophy – Psychosophy – Pneumatosophy
CW 116 The Christ-Impulse and the Development of "I"- Consciousness
CW 117 The Deeper Secrets of the Development of Humanity in Light of the Gospels
CW 118 The Event of the Christ-Appearance in the Etheric World
CW 119 Macrocosm and Microcosm. The Large World and the Small World. Soul-Questions, Life-Questions, Spirit-Questions
CW 120 The Revelation of Karma
CW 121 The Mission of Individual Folk-Souls in Connection with Germanic-Nordic Mythology
CW 122 The Secrets of the Biblical Creation-Story. The Six-Day Work in the First Book of Moses
CW 123 The Gospel of Matthew
CW 124 Excursus in the Area of the Gospel of Mark
CW 125 Paths and Goals of the Spiritual Human Being. Life Questions in the Light of Spiritual Science
CW 126 Occult History. Esoteric Observations of the Karmic Relationships of Personalities and Events of World History
CW 127 The Mission of the New Spiritual Revelation. The Christ-Event as the Middle-Point of Earth Evolution
CW 128 An Occult Physiology
CW 129 Wonders of the World, Trials of the Soul, and Revelations of the Spirit
CW 130 Esoteric Christianity and the Spiritual Guidance of Humanity
CW 131 From Jesus to Christ
CW 132 Evolution from the View Point of the Truth
CW 133 The Earthly and the Cosmic Human Being
CW 134 The World of the Senses and the World of the Spirit
CW 135 Reincarnation and Karma and their Meaning for the Culture of the Present
CW 136 The Spiritual Beings in Celestial Bodies and the Realms of Nature

CW 137	The Human Being in the Light of Occultism, Theosophy and Philosophy
CW 138	On Initiation. On Eternity and the Passing Moment. On the Light of the Spirit and the Darkness of Life
CW 139	The Gospel of Mark
CW 140	Occult Investigation into the Life between Death and New Birth. The Living Interaction between Life and Death
CW 141	Life between Death and New Birth in Relationship to Cosmic Facts
CW 142	The Bhagavad Gita and the Letters of Paul
CW 143	Experiences of the Supersensible. Three Paths of the Soul to Christ
CW 144	The Mysteries of the East and of Christianity
CW 145	What Significance Does Occult Development of the Human Being Have for His Sheaths–Physical Body, Etheric Body, Astral Body, and Self?
CW 146	The Occult Foundations of the Bhagavad Gita
CW 147	The Secrets of the Threshold
CW 148	Out of Research in the Akasha: The Fifth Gospel
CW 149	Christ and the Spiritual World. Concerning the Search for the Holy Grail
CW 150	The World of the Spirit and Its Extension into Physical Existence; The Influence of the Dead in the World of the Living
CW 151	Human Thought and Cosmic Thought
CW 152	Preliminary Stages to the Mystery of Golgotha
CW 153	The Inner Being of the Human Being and Life Between Death and New Birth
CW 154	How does One Gain an Understanding of the Spiritual World? The Flowing in of Spiritual Impulses from out of the World of the Deceased
CW 155	Christ and the Human Soul. Concerning the Meaning of Life. Theosophical Morality. Anthroposophy and Christianity
CW 156	Occult Reading and Occult Hearing
CW 157	Human Destinies and the Destiny of Peoples
CW 157a	The Formation of Destiny and the Life after Death
CW 158	The Connection Between the Human Being and the Elemental World. Kalevala – Olaf Asteson – The Russian People – The World as the Result of the Influences of Equilibrium
CW 159	The Mystery of Death. The Nature and Significance of Middle Europe and the European Folk Spirits
CW 160	In CW 159
CW 161	Paths of Spiritual Knowledge and the Renewal of the Artistic Worldview
CW 162	Questions of Art and Life in Light of Spiritual Science

CW 163 Coincidence, Necessity and Providence. Imaginative Knowledge and the Processes after Death
CW 164 The Value of Thinking for a Knowledge That Satisfies the Human Being. The Relationship of Spiritual Science to Natural Science
CW 165 The Spiritual Unification of Humanity through the Christ-Impulse
CW 166 Necessity and Freedom in the Events of the World and in Human Action
CW 167 The Present and the Past in the Human Spirit
CW 168 The Connection between the Living and the Dead
CW 169 World-being and Selfhood
CW 170 The Riddle of the Human Being. The Spiritual Background of Human History. Cosmic and Human History, Vol. 1
CW 171 Inner Development-Impulses of Humanity. Goethe and the Crisis of the 19th Century. Cosmic and Human History, Vol. 2
CW 172 The Karma of the Vocation of the Human Being in Connection with Goethe's Life. Cosmic and Human History, Vol. 3
CW 173 Contemporary-Historical Considerations: The Karma of Untruthfulness, Part One. Cosmic and Human History, Vol. 4
CW 174 Contemporary-Historical Considerations: The Karma of Untruthfulness, Part Two. Cosmic and Human History, Vol. 5
CW 174a Middle Europe between East and West. Cosmic and Human History, Vol. 6
CW 174b The Spiritual Background of the First World War. Cosmic and Human History, Vol. 7
CW 175 Building Stones for an Understanding of the Mystery of Golgotha. Cosmic and Human Metamorphoses
CW 176 Truths of Evolution of the Individual and Humanity. The Karma of Materialism
CW 177 The Spiritual Background of the Outer World. The Fall of the Spirits of Darkness. Spiritual Beings and Their Effects, Vol. 1
CW 178 Individual Spiritual Beings and their Influence in the Soul of the Human Being. Spiritual Beings and their Effects, Vol. 2
CW 179 Spiritual Beings and Their Effects. Historical Necessity and Freedom. The Influences on Destiny from out of the World of the Dead. Spiritual Beings and Their Effects, Vol. 3
CW 180 Mystery Truths and Christmas Impulses. Ancient Myths and their Meaning. Spiritual Beings and Their Effects, Vol. 4
CW 181 Earthly Death and Cosmic Life. Anthroposophical Gifts for Life. Necessities of Consciousness for the Present and the Future.
CW 182 Death as Transformation of Life
CW 183 The Science of the Development of the Human Being
CW 184 The Polarity of Duration and Development in Human Life. The Cosmic Pre-History of Humanity

CW 185 Historical Symptomology
CW 185a Historical-Developmental Foundations for Forming a Social Judgment
CW 186 The Fundamental Social Demands of Our Time–In Changed Situations
CW 187 How Can Humanity Find the Christ Again? The Threefold Shadow-Existence of our Time and the New Christ-Light
CW 188 Goetheanism, a Transformation-Impulse and Resurrection-Thought. Science of the Human Being and Science of Sociology
CW 189 The Social Question as a Question of Consciousness. The Spiritual Background of the Social Question, Vol. 1
CW 190 Impulses of the Past and the Future in Social Occurrences. The Spiritual Background of the Social Question, Vol. 2
CW 191 Social Understanding from Spiritual-Scientific Cognition. The Spiritual Background of the Social Question, Vol. 3
CW 192 Spiritual-Scientific Treatment of Social and Pedagogical Questions
CW 193 The Inner Aspect of the Social Riddle. Luciferic Past and Ahrimanic Future
CW 194 The Mission of Michael. The Revelation of the Actual Mysteries of the Human Being
CW 195 Cosmic New Year and the New Year Idea
CW 196 Spiritual and Social Transformations in the Development of Humanity
CW 197 Polarities in the Development of Humanity: West and East Materialism and Mysticism Knowledge and Belief
CW 198 Healing Factors for the Social Organism
CW 199 Spiritual Science as Knowledge of the Foundational Impulses of Social Formation
CW 200 The New Spirituality and the Christ-Experience of the 20th Century
CW 201 The Correspondences Between Microcosm and Macrocosm. The Human Being – A Hieroglyph of the Universe. The Human Being in Relationship with the Cosmos: 1
CW 202 The Bridge between the World-Spirituality and the Physical Aspect of the Human Being. The Search for the New Isis, the Divine Sophia. The Human Being in Relationship with the Cosmos: 2
CW 203 The Responsibility of Human Beings for the Development of the World through their Spiritual Connection with the Planet Earth and the World of the Stars. The Human Being in Relationship with the Cosmos: 3
CW 204 Perspectives of the Development of Humanity. The Materialistic Knowledge-Impulse and the Task of Anthroposophy. The Human Being in Relationship with the Cosmos: 4

CW 205 Human Development, World-Soul, and World-Spirit. Part One: The Human Being as a Being of Body and Soul in Relationship to the World. The Human Being in Relationship with the Cosmos: 5

CW 206 Human Development, World-Soul, and World-Spirit. Part Two: The Human Being as a Spiritual Being in the Process of Historical Development. The Human Being in Relationship with the Cosmos: 6

CW 207 Anthroposophy as Cosmosophy. Part One: Characteristic Features of the Human Being in the Earthly and the Cosmic Realms. The Human Being in Relationship with the Cosmos: 7

CW 208 Anthroposophy as Cosmosophy. Part Two: The Forming of the Human Being as the Result of Cosmic Influence. The Human Being in Relationship with the Cosmos: 8

CW 209 Nordic and Central European Spiritual Impulses. The Festival of the Appearance of Christ. The Human Being in Relationship with the Cosmos: 9

CW 210 Old and New Methods of Initiation. Drama and Poetry in the Change of Consciousness in the Modern Age

CW 211 The Sun Mystery and the Mystery of Death and Resurrection. Exoteric and Esoteric Christianity

CW 212 Human Soul Life and Spiritual Striving in Connection with World and Earth Development

CW 213 Human Questions and World Answers

CW 214 The Mystery of the Trinity: The Human Being in Relationship to the Spiritual World in the Course of Time

CW 215 Philosophy, Cosmology, and Religion in Anthroposophy

CW 216 The Fundamental Impulses of the World-Historical Development of Humanity

CW 217 Spiritually Active Forces in the Coexistence of the Older and Younger Generations. Pedagogical Course for Youth

CW 217a Youth's Cognitive Task

CW 218 Spiritual Connections in the Forming of the Human Organism

CW 219 The Relationship of the World of the Stars to the Human Being, and of the Human Being to the World of the Stars. The Spiritual Communion of Humanity

CW 220 Living Knowledge of Nature. Intellectual Fall and Spiritual Redemption

CW 221 Earth-Knowing and Heaven-Insight

CW 222 The Imparting of Impulses to World-Historical Events through Spiritual Powers

CW 223 The Cycle of the Year as Breathing Process of the Earth and the Four Great Festival-Seasons. Anthroposophy and Human Heart (Gemüt)

CW 224	The Human Soul and its Connection with Divine-Spiritual Individualities. The Internalization of the Festivals of the Year
CW 225	Three Perspectives of Anthroposophy. Cultural Phenomena observed from a Spiritual-Scientific Perspective
CW 226	Human Being, Human Destiny, and World Development
CW 227	Initiation-Knowledge
CW 228	Science of Initiation and Knowledge of the Stars. The Human Being in the Past, the Present, and the Future from the Viewpoint of the Development of Consciousness
CW 229	The Experiencing of the Course of the Year in Four Cosmic Imaginations
CW 230	The Human Being as Harmony of the Creative, Building, and Formative World-Word
CW 231	The Supersensible Human Being, Understood Anthroposophically
CW 232	The Forming of the Mysteries
CW 233	World History Illuminated by Anthroposophy and as the Foundation for Knowledge of the Human Spirit
CW 233a	Mystery Sites of the Middle Ages: Rosicrucianism and the Modern Initiation-Principle. The Festival of Easter as Part of the History of the Mysteries of Humanity
CW 234	Anthroposophy. A Summary after 21 Years
CW 235	Esoteric Observations of Karmic Relationships in 6 Volumes, Vol. 1
CW 236	Esoteric Observations of Karmic Relationships in 6 Volumes, Vol. 2
CW 237	Esoteric Observations of Karmic Relationships in 6 Volumes, Vol. 3: The Karmic Relationships of the Anthroposophical Movement
CW 238	Esoteric Observations of Karmic Relationships in 6 Volumes, Vol. 4: The Spiritual Life of the Present in Relationship to the Anthroposophical Movement
CW 239	Esoteric Observations of Karmic Relationships in 6 Volumes, Vol. 5
CW 240	Esoteric Observations of Karmic Relationships in 6 Volumes, Vol. 6
CW 243	The Consciousness of the Initiate
CW 245	Instructions for an Esoteric Schooling
CW 250	The Building-Up of the Anthroposophical Society. From the Beginning to the Outbreak of the First World War
CW 251	The History of the Goetheanum Building-Association
CW 252	Life in the Anthroposophical Society from the First World War to the Burning of the First Goetheanum
CW 253	The Problems of Living Together in the Anthroposophical Society. On the Dornach Crisis of 1915. With Highlights on Swedenborg's Clairvoyance, the Views of Freudian Psychoanalysts, and the Concept of Love in Relation to Mysticism

CW 254 The Occult Movement in the 19th Century and Its Relationship to World Culture. Significant Points from the Exoteric Cultural Life around the Middle of the 19th Century

CW 255 Rudolf Steiner during the First World War

CW 255a Anthroposophy and the Reformation of Society. On the History of the Threefold Movement

CW 255b Anthroposophy and Its Opponents, 1919-1921

CW 256 How Can the Anthroposophical Movement Be Financed?

CW 256a Futurum, Inc. / International Laboratories, Inc.

CW 256b The Coming Day, Inc.

CW 257 Anthroposophical Community-Building

CW 258 The History of and Conditions for the Anthroposophical Movement in Relationship to the Anthroposophical Society. A Stimulus to Self-Contemplation

CW 259 The Year of Destiny 1923 in the History of the Anthroposophical Society. From the Burning of the Goetheanum to the Christmas Conference

CW 260 The Christmas Conference for the Founding of the General Anthroposophical Society

CW 260a The Constitution of the General Anthroposophical Society and the School for Spiritual Science. The Rebuilding of the Goetheanum

CW 261 Our Dead. Addresses, Words of Remembrance, and Meditative Verses, 1906-1924

CW 262 Rudolf Steiner and Marie Steiner-von Sivers: Correspondence and Documents, 1901-1925

CW 263/1 Rudolf Steiner and Edith Maryon: Correspondence: Letters, Verses, Sketches, 1912-1924

CW 264 On the History and the Contents of the First Section of the Esoteric School from 1904 to 1914. Letters, Newsletters, Documents, Lectures

CW 265 On the History and Out of the Contents of the Ritual-Knowledge Section of the Esoteric School from 1904 to 1914. Documents, and Lectures from the Years 1906 to 1914, as well as on New Approaches to Ritual-Knowledge Work in the Years 1921-1924

CW 266/1 From the Contents of the Esoteric Lessons. Volume 1: 1904-1909. Notes from Memory of Participants. Meditation texts from the notes of Rudolf Steiner

CW 266/2 From the Contents of the Esoteric Lessons. Volume 2: 1910-1912. Notes from Memory of Participants

CW 266/3 From the Contents of the Esoteric Lessons. Volume 3: 1913, 1914 and 1920-1923. Notes from Memory of Participants. Meditation texts from the notes of Rudolf Steiner

CW 267 Soul-Exercises: Vol. 1: Exercises with Word and Image Meditations for the Methodological Development of Higher Powers of Knowledge, 1904-1924
CW 268 Soul-Exercises: Vol. 2: Mantric Verses, 1903-1925
CW 269 Ritual Texts for the Celebration of the Free Christian Religious Instruction. The Collected Verses for Teachers and Students of the Waldorf School
CW 270 Esoteric Instructions for the First Class of the School for Spiritual Science at the Goetheanum 1924, 4 Volumes
CW 271 Art and Knowledge of Art. Foundations of a New Aesthetic
CW 272 Spiritual-Scientific Commentary on Goethe's "Faust" in Two Volumes. Vol. 1: Faust, the Striving Human Being
CW 273 Spiritual-Scientific Commentary on Goethe's "Faust" in Two Volumes. Vol. 2: The Faust-Problem
CW 274 Addresses for the Christmas Plays from the Old Folk Traditions
CW 275 Art in the Light of Mystery-Wisdom
CW 276 The Artistic in Its Mission in the World. The Genius of Language. The World of the Self-Revealing Radiant Appearances – Anthroposophy and Art. Anthroposophy and Poetry
CW 277 Eurythmy. The Revelation of the Speaking Soul
CW 277a The Origin and Development of Eurythmy
CW 278 Eurythmy as Visible Song
CW 279 Eurythmy as Visible Speech
CW 280 The Method and Nature of Speech Formation
CW 281 The Art of Recitation and Declamation
CW 282 Speech Formation and Dramatic Art
CW 283 The Nature of Things Musical and the Experience of Tone in the Human Being
CW284/285 Images of Occult Seals and Pillars. The Munich Congress of Whitsun 1907 and Its Consequences
CW 286 Paths to a New Style of Architecture. "And the Building Becomes Human"
CW 287 The Building at Dornach as a Symbol of Historical Becoming and an Artistic Transformation Impulse
CW 288 Style-Forms in the Living Organic
CW 289 The Building-Idea of the Goetheanum: Lectures with Slides from the Years 1920-1921
CW 290 The Building-Idea of the Goetheanum: Lectures with Slides from the Years 1920-1921
CW 291 The Nature of Colors
CW 291a Knowledge of Colors. Supplementary Volume to "The Nature of Colors"
CW 292 Art History as Image of Inner Spiritual Impulses

CW 293 General Knowledge of the Human Being as the Foundation of Pedagogy
CW 294 The Art of Education, Methodology and Didactics
CW 295 The Art of Education: Seminar Discussions and Lectures on Lesson Planning
CW 296 The Question of Education as a Social Question
CW 297 The Idea and Practice of the Waldorf School
CW 297a Education for Life: Self-Education and the Practice of Pedagogy
CW 298 Rudolf Steiner in the Waldorf School
CW 299 Spiritual-Scientific Observations on Speech
CW 300a Conferences with the Teachers of the Free Waldorf School in Stuttgart, 1919 to 1924, in 3 Volumes, Vol. 1
CW 300b Conferences with the Teachers of the Free Waldorf School in Stuttgart, 1919 to 1924, in 3 Volumes, Vol. 2
CW 300c Conferences with the Teachers of the Free Waldorf School in Stuttgart, 1919 to 1924, in 3 Volumes, Vol. 3
CW 301 The Renewal of the Pedagogical-Didactical Art through Spiritual Science
CW 302 Knowledge of the Human Being and the Forming of Class Lessons
CW 302a Education and Teaching out of a Knowledge of the Human Being
CW 303 The Healthy Development of the Human Being
CW 304 Methods of Education and Teaching Based on Anthroposophy
CW 304a Anthroposophical Knowledge of the Human Being and Pedagogy
CW 305 The Soul-Spiritual Foundational Forces of the Art of Education. Spiritual Values in Education and Social Life
CW 306 Pedagogical Praxis from the Viewpoint of a Spiritual-Scientific Knowledge of the Human Being. The Education of the Child and Young Human Beings
CW 307 The Spiritual Life of the Present and Education
CW 308 The Method of Teaching and the Life-Requirements for Teaching
CW 309 Anthroposophical Pedagogy and Its Prerequisites
CW 310 The Pedagogical Value of a Knowledge of the Human Being and the Cultural Value of Pedagogy
CW 311 The Art of Education Out of an Understanding of the Being of Humanity
CW 312 Spiritual Science and Medicine
CW 313 Spiritual-Scientific Viewpoints on Therapy
CW 314 Physiology and Therapy Based on Spiritual Science
CW 315 Curative Eurythmy
CW 316 Meditative Observations and Instructions for a Deepening of the Art of Healing
CW 317 The Curative Education Course
CW 318 The Working Together of Doctors and Pastors

CW 319	Anthroposophical Knowledge of the Human Being and Medicine
CW 320	Spiritual-Scientific Impulses for the Development of Physics 1: The First Natural-Scientific Course: Light, Color, Tone, Mass, Electricity, Magnetism
CW 321	Spiritual-Scientific Impulses for the Development of Physics 2: The Second Natural-Scientific Course: Warmth at the Border of Positive and Negative Materiality
CW 322	The Borders of the Knowledge of Nature
CW 323	The Relationship of the various Natural-Scientific Fields to Astronomy
CW 324	Nature Observation, Mathematics, and Scientific Experimentation and Results from the Viewpoint of Anthroposophy
CW 324a	The Fourth Dimension in Mathematics and Reality
CW 325	Natural Science and the World-Historical Development of Humanity since Ancient Times
CW 326	The Moment of the Coming Into Being of Natural Science in World History and Its Development Since Then
CW 327	Spiritual-Scientific Foundations for Success in Farming. The Agricultural Course
CW 328	The Social Question
CW 329	The Liberation of the Human Being as the Foundation for a New Social Form
CW 330	The Renewal of the Social Organism
CW 331	Work-Council and Socialization
CW 332	The Alliance for Threefolding and the Total Reform of Society. The Council on Culture and the Liberation of the Spiritual Life
CW 332a	The Social Future
CW 333	Freedom of Thought and Social Forces
CW 334	From the Unified State to the Threefold Social Organism
CW 335	The Crisis of the Present and the Path to Healthy Thinking
CW 336	The Great Questions of the Times and Anthroposophical Spiritual Knowledge
CW 337a	Social Ideas, Social Reality, Social Practice, Vol. 1: Question-and-Answer Evenings and Study Evenings of the Alliance for the Threefold Social Organism in Stuttgart, 1919-1920
CW 337b	Social Ideas, Social Realities, Social Practice, Vol. 2: Discussion Evenings of the Swiss Alliance for the Threefold Social Organism
CW 338	How Does One Work on Behalf of the Impulse for the Threefold Social Organism?
CW 339	Anthroposophy, Threefold Social Organism, and the Art of Public Speaking
CW 340	The National-Economics Course. The Tasks of a New Science of Economics, Volume 1

CW 341 The National-Economics Seminar. The Tasks of a New Science of Economics, Volume 2

CW 342 Lectures and Courses on Christian Religious Work, Vol. 1: Anthroposophical Foundations for a Renewed Christian Religious Working

CW 343 Lectures and Courses on Christian Religious Work, Vol. 2: Spiritual Knowledge – Religious Feeling – Cultic Doing

CW 344 Lectures and Courses on Christian Religious Work, Vol. 3: Lectures at the Founding of the Christian Community

CW 345 Lectures and Courses on Christian Religious Work, Vol. 4: Concerning the Nature of the Working Word

CW 346 Lectures and Courses on Christian Religious Work, Vol. 5: The Apocalypse and the Working of the Priest

CW 347 The Knowledge of the Nature of the Human Being According to Body, Soul and Spirit. On Earlier Conditions of the Earth

CW 348 On Health and Illness. Foundations of a Spiritual-Scientific Doctrine of the Senses

CW 349 On the Life of the Human Being and of the Earth. On the Nature of Christianity

CW 350 Rhythms in the Cosmos and in the Human Being. How Does One Come To See the Spiritual World?

CW 351 The Human Being and the World. The Influence of the Spirit in Nature. On the Nature of Bees

CW 352 Nature and the Human Being Observed Spiritual-Scientifically

CW 353 The History of Humanity and the World-Views of the Folk Cultures

CW 354 The Creation of the World and the Human Being. Life on Earth and the Influence of the Stars

SIGNIFICANT EVENTS IN THE LIFE OF RUDOLF STEINER

1829: June 23: birth of Johann Steiner (1829-1910)—Rudolf Steiner's father—in Geras, Lower Austria.

1834: May 8: birth of Franciska Blie (1834-1918)—Rudolf Steiner's mother—in Horn, Lower Austria. "My father and mother were both children of the glorious Lower Austrian forest district north of the Danube."

1860: May 16: marriage of Johann Steiner and Franciska Blie.

1861: February 25: birth of *Rudolf Joseph Lorenz Steiner* in Kraljevec, Croatia, near the border with Hungary, where Johann Steiner works as a telegrapher for the South Austria Railroad. Rudolf Steiner is baptized two days later, February 27, the date usually given as his birthday.

1862: Summer: the family moves to Mödling, Lower Austria.

1863: The family moves to Pottschach, Lower Austria, near the Styrian border, where Johann Steiner becomes stationmaster. "The view stretched to the mountains...majestic peaks in the distance and the sweet charm of nature in the immediate surroundings."

1864: November 15: birth of Rudolf Steiner's sister, Leopoldine (d. November 1, 1927). She will become a seamstress and live with her parents for the rest of her life.

1866: July 28: birth of Rudolf Steiner's deaf-mute brother, Gustav (d. May 1, 1941).

1867: Rudolf Steiner enters the village school. Following a disagreement between his father and the schoolmaster, whose wife falsely accused the boy of causing a commotion, Rudolf Steiner is taken out of school and taught at home.

1868: A critical experience. Unknown to the family, an aunt dies in a distant town. Sitting in the station waiting room, Rudolf Steiner sees her "form," which speaks to him, asking for help. "Beginning with this experience, a new soul life began in the boy, one in which not only the outer trees and mountains spoke to him, but also the worlds that lay behind them. From this moment on, the boy began to live with the spirits of nature...."

1869: The family moves to the peaceful, rural village of Neudorfl, near Wiener-Neustadt in present-day Austria, where Rudolf Steiner attends the village school. Because of the "unorthodoxy" of his writing and spelling, he has to do "extra lessons."

1870: Through a book lent to him by his tutor, he discovers geometry: "To grasp something purely in the spirit brought me inner happiness. I know that I first learned happiness through geometry." The same tutor allows him to draw, while other students still struggle with their reading and writing. "An artistic element" thus enters his education.

1871: Though his parents are not religious, Rudolf Steiner becomes a "church child," a favorite of the priest, who was "an exceptional character." "Up to the age of ten or eleven, among those I came to know, he was far and away the most significant." Among other things, he introduces Steiner to Copernican, heliocentric cosmology. As an altar boy, Rudolf Steiner serves at Masses, funerals, and Corpus Christi processions. At year's end, after an incident in which he escapes a thrashing, his father forbids him to go to church.

1872: Rudolf Steiner transfers to grammar school in Wiener-Neustadt, a five-mile walk from home, which must be done in all weathers.

1873-75: Through his teachers and on his own, Rudolf Steiner has many wonderful experiences with science and mathematics. Outside school, he teaches himself analytic geometry, trigonometry, differential equations, and calculus.

1876: Rudolf Steiner begins tutoring other students. He learns bookbinding from his father. He also teaches himself stenography.

1877: Rudolf Steiner discovers Kant's *Critique of Pure Reason*, which he reads and rereads. He also discovers and reads von Rotteck's *World History*.

1878: He studies extensively in contemporary psychology and philosophy.

1879: Rudolf Steiner graduates from high school with honors. His father is transferred to Inzersdorf, near Vienna. He uses his first visit to Vienna "to purchase a great number of philosophy books"—Kant, Fichte, Schelling, and Hegel, as well as numerous histories of philosophy. His aim: to find a path from the "I" to nature.

October 1879-1883: Rudolf Steiner attends the Technical College in Vienna—to study mathematics, chemistry, physics, mineralogy, botany, zoology, biology, geology, and mechanics—with a scholarship. He also attends lectures in history and literature, while avidly reading philosophy on his own. His two favorite professors are Karl Julius Schröer (German language and literature) and Edmund Reitlinger (physics). He also audits lectures by Robert Zimmerman on aesthetics and Franz Brentano on philosophy. During this year he begins his friendship with Moritz Zitter (1861-1921), who will help support him financially when he is in Berlin.

1880: Rudolf Steiner attends lectures on Schiller and Goethe by Karl Julius Schröer, who becomes his mentor. Also "through a remarkable combination of circumstances," he meets Felix Koguzki, an "herb gatherer" and healer, who could "see deeply into the secrets of nature." Rudolf Steiner will meet and study with this "emissary of the Master" throughout his time in Vienna.

1881: January: "... I didn't sleep a wink. I was busy with philosophical problems until about 12:30 a.m. Then, finally, I threw myself down on my couch. All my striving during the previous year had been to research whether the following statement by Schelling was true or not: *Within everyone dwells a secret, marvelous capacity to draw back from the stream of time—out of the self clothed in all that comes to us from outside—into our innermost being and there, in the immutable form of the Eternal, to look into ourselves.* I believe, and I am still quite certain of it, that I discovered this capacity in myself; I had long had an inkling of it. Now the whole of idealist philosophy stood before me in modified form. What's a sleepless night compared to that!"

Rudolf Steiner begins communicating with leading thinkers of the day, who send him books in return, which he reads eagerly.

July: "I am not one of those who dives into the day like an animal in human form. I pursue a quite specific goal, an idealistic aim—knowledge of the truth! This cannot be done offhandedly. It requires the greatest striving in the world, free of all egotism, and equally of all resignation."

August: Steiner puts down on paper for the first time thoughts for a "Philosophy of Freedom." "The striving for the absolute: this human yearning is freedom." He also seeks to outline a "peasant philosophy," describing what the worldview of a "peasant"—one who lives close to the earth and the old ways—really is.

1881-1882: Felix Koguzki, the herb gatherer, reveals himself to be the envoy of another, higher initiatory personality, who instructs Rudolf Steiner to penetrate Fichte's philosophy and to master modern scientific thinking as a preparation for right entry into the spirit. This "Master" also teaches him the double (evolutionary and involutionary) nature of time.

1882: Through the offices of Karl Julius Schröer, Rudolf Steiner is asked by Joseph Kurschner to edit Goethe's scientific works for the *Deutschen National-Literatur* edition. He writes "A Possible Critique of Atomistic Concepts" and sends it to Friedrich Theodore Vischer.

1883: Rudolf Steiner completes his college studies and begins work on the Goethe project.

1884: First volume of Goethe's *Scientific Writings* (CW 1) appears (March). He lectures on Goethe and Lessing, and Goethe's approach to science. In July, he enters the household of Ladislaus and Pauline Specht as tutor to the four Specht boys. He will live there until 1890. At this time, he meets Josef Breuer (1842-1925), the coauthor with Sigmund Freud of *Studies in Hysteria*, who is the Specht family doctor.

1885: While continuing to edit Goethe's writings, Rudolf Steiner reads deeply in contemporary philosophy (Edouard von Hartmann, Johannes Volkelt, and Richard Wahle, among others).

1886: May: Rudolf Steiner sends Kurschner the manuscript of *Outlines of Goethe's Theory of Knowledge* (CW 2), which appears in October, and which he sends out widely. He also meets the poet Marie Eugenie Delle Grazie and writes "Nature and Our Ideals" for her. He attends her salon, where he meets many priests, theologians, and philosophers, who will become his friends. Meanwhile, the director of the Goethe Archive in Weimar requests his collaboration with the *Sophien* edition of Goethe's works, particularly the writings on color.

1887: At the beginning of the year, Rudolf Steiner is very sick. As the year progresses and his health improves, he becomes increasingly "a man of letters," lecturing, writing essays, and taking part in Austrian cultural life. In August-September, the second volume of Goethe's *Scientific Writings* appears.

1888: January-July: Rudolf Steiner assumes editorship of the "German Weekly" (*Deutsche Wochenschrift*). He begins lecturing more intensively, giving, for example, a lecture titled "Goethe as Father of a New Aesthetics." He meets and becomes soul friends with Friedrich Eckstein (1861-1939), a vegetarian, philosopher of symbolism, alchemist, and musician, who will introduce him to various spiritual currents (including Theosophy) and with whom he will meditate and interpret esoteric and alchemical texts.

1889: Rudolf Steiner first reads Nietzsche (*Beyond Good and Evil*). He encounters Theosophy again and learns of Madame Blavatsky in the Theosophical circle around Marie Lang (1858-1934). Here he also meets well-known figures of Austrian life, as well as esoteric figures like the occultist Franz Hartman and Karl Leinigen-Billigen (translator of C.G. Harrison's *The Transcendental Universe*.) During this period, Steiner first reads A.P. Sinnett's *Esoteric Buddhism* and Mabel Collins's *Light on the Path*. He also begins traveling, visiting Budapest, Weimar, and Berlin (where he meets philosopher Edouard von Hartman).

1890: Rudolf Steiner finishes volume 3 of Goethe's scientific writings. He begins his doctoral dissertation, which will become *Truth and Science* (CW 3). He also meets the poet and feminist Rosa Mayreder (1858-1938), with whom he can exchange his most intimate thoughts. In September, Rudolf Steiner moves to Weimar to work in the Goethe-Schiller Archive.

1891: Volume 3 of the Kurschner edition of Goethe appears. Meanwhile, Rudolf Steiner edits Goethe's studies in mineralogy and scientific writings for the *Sophien* edition. He meets Ludwig Laistner of the Cotta Publishing Company, who asks for a book on the basic question of metaphysics. From this will result, ultimately, *The Philosophy of Freedom* (CW 4), which will be published not by Cotta but by Emil Felber. In October, Rudolf Steiner takes the oral exam for a doctorate in philosophy, mathematics, and mechanics at Rostock University, receiving his doctorate on the twenty-sixth. In November, he gives his first lecture on Goethe's "Fairy Tale" in Vienna.

1892: Rudolf Steiner continues work at the Goethe-Schiller Archive and on his *Philosophy of Freedom. Truth and Science*, his doctoral dissertation, is published. Steiner undertakes to write introductions to books on Schopenhauer and Jean Paul for Cotta. At year's end, he finds lodging with Anna Eunike, née Schulz (1853-1911), a widow with four daughters and a son. He also develops a friendship with Otto Erich Hartleben (1864-1905) with whom he shares literary interests.

1893: Rudolf Steiner begins his habit of producing many reviews and articles. In March, he gives a lecture titled "Hypnotism, with Reference to Spiritism." In September, volume 4 of the Kurschner edition is completed. In November, *The Philosophy of Freedom* appears. This year, too, he meets John Henry Mackay (1864-1933), the anarchist, and Max Stirner, a scholar and biographer.

1894: Rudolf Steiner meets Elisabeth Förster Nietzsche, the philosopher's sister, and begins to read Nietzsche in earnest, beginning with the as yet unpublished *Antichrist.* He also meets Ernst Haeckel (1834-1919). In the fall, he begins to write *Nietzsche, A Fighter against His Time* (CW 5).

1895: May, *Nietzsche, A Fighter against His Time* appears.

1896: January 22: Rudolf Steiner sees Friedrich Nietzsche for the first and only time. Moves between the Nietzsche and the Goethe-Schiller Archives, where he completes his work before year's end. He falls out with Elisabeth Förster Nietzsche, thus ending his association with the Nietzsche Archive.

1897: Rudolf Steiner finishes the manuscript of *Goethe's Worldview* (CW 6). He moves to Berlin with Anna Eunike and begins editorship of the *Magazin fur Literatur.* From now on, Steiner will write countless reviews, literary and philosophical articles, and so on. He begins lecturing at the "Free Literary Society." In September, he attends the Zionist Congress in Basel. He sides with Dreyfus in the Dreyfus affair.

1898: Rudolf Steiner is very active as an editor in the political, artistic, and theatrical life of Berlin. He becomes friendly with John Henry Mackay and poet Ludwig Jacobowski (1868-1900). He joins Jacobowski's circle of writers, artists, and scientists—"The Coming Ones" (*Die Kommenden*)—and contributes lectures to the group until 1903. He also lectures at the "League for College Pedagogy." He writes an article for Goethe's sesquicentennial, "Goethe's Secret Revelation," on the "Fairy Tale of the Green Snake and the Beautiful Lily."

1898-99: "This was a trying time for my soul as I looked at Christianity. . . I was able to progress only by contemplating, by means of spiritual perception, the evolution of Christianity . . . . Conscious knowledge of real Christianity began to dawn in me around the turn of the century. This seed continued to develop. My soul trial occurred shortly before the beginning of the twentieth century. It was decisive for my soul's development that I stood spiritually before the Mystery of Golgotha in a deep and solemn celebration of knowledge."

1899: Rudolf Steiner begins teaching and giving lectures and lecture cycles at the Workers' College, founded by Wilhelm Liebknecht (1826-1900). He will continue to do so until 1904. Writes: *Literature and Spiritual Life in the Nineteenth Century; Individualism in Philosophy; Haeckel and His Opponents; Poetry in the Present;* and begins what will become (fifteen years later). *The Riddles of Philosophy* (CW 18). He also meets many artists and writers, including Käthe Kollwitz, Stefan

Zweig, and Rainer Maria Rilke. On October 31, he marries Anna Eunike.

1900: "I thought that the turn of the century must bring humanity a new light. It seemed to me that the separation of human thinking and willing from the spirit had peaked. A turn or reversal of direction in human evolution seemed to me a necessity." Rudolf Steiner finishes *World and Life Views in the Nineteenth Century* (the second part of what will become *The Riddles of Philosophy*) and dedicates it to Ernst Haeckel. It is published in March. He continues lecturing at *Die Kommenden*, whose leadership he assumes after the death of Jacobowski. Also, he gives the Gutenberg Jubilee lecture before 7,000 typesetters and printers. In September, Rudolf Steiner is invited by Count and Countess Brockdorff to lecture in the Theosophical Library. His first lecture is on Nietzsche. His second lecture is titled "Goethe's Secret Revelation." October 6, he begins a lecture cycle on the mystics that will become *Mystics after Modernism* (CW 7). November-December: "Marie von Sivers appears in the audience...." Also in November, Steiner gives his first lecture at the Giordano Bruno Bund (where he will continue to lecture until May, 1905). He speaks on Bruno and modern Rome, focusing on the importance of the philosophy of Thomas Aquinas as monism.

1901: In continual financial straits, Rudolf Steiner's early friends Moritz Zitter and Rosa Mayreder help support him. In October, he begins the lecture cycle *Christianity as Mystical Fact* (CW 8) at the Theosophical Library. In November, he gives his first "Theosophical lecture" on Goethe's "Fairy Tale" in Hamburg at the invitation of Wilhelm Hubbe-Schleiden. He also attends a tea to celebrate the founding of the Theosophical Society at Count and Countess Brockdorff's. He gives a lecture cycle, "From Buddha to Christ," for the circle of the *Kommenden*. November 17, Marie von Sivers asks Rudolf Steiner if Theosophy does not need a Western-Christian spiritual movement (to complement Theosophy's Eastern emphasis). "The question was posed. Now, following spiritual laws, I could begin to give an answer...." In December, Rudolf Steiner writes his first article for a Theosophical publication. At year's end, the Brockdorffs and possibly Wilhelm Hubbe-Schleiden ask Rudolf Steiner to join the Theosophical Society and undertake the leadership of the German section. Rudolf Steiner agrees, on the condition that Marie von Sivers (then in Italy) work with him.

1902: Beginning in January, Rudolf Steiner attends the opening of the Workers' School in Spandau with Rosa Luxemberg (1870-1919). January 17, Rudolf Steiner joins the Theosophical Society. In April, he is asked to become general secretary of the German Section of the Theosophical Society, and works on preparations for its founding. In July, he visits London for a Theosophical congress. He meets Bertram

Keightly, G.R.S. Mead, A.P. Sinnett, and Annie Besant, among others. In September, *Christianity as Mystical Fact* appears. In October, Rudolf Steiner gives his first public lecture on Theosophy ("Monism and Theosophy") to about three hundred people at the Giordano Bruno Bund. On October 19-21, the German Section of the Theosophical Society has its first meeting; Rudolf Steiner is the general secretary, and Annie Besant attends. Steiner lectures on practical karma studies. On October 23, Annie Besant inducts Rudolf Steiner into the Esoteric School of the Theosophical Society. On October 25, Steiner begins a weekly series of lectures: "The Field of Theosophy." During this year, Rudolf Steiner also first meets Ita Wegman (1876-1943), who will become his close collaborator in his final years.

1903: Rudolf Steiner holds about 300 lectures and seminars. In May, the first issue of the periodical *Luzifer* appears. In June, Rudolf Steiner visits London for the first meeting of the Federation of the European Sections of the Theosophical Society, where he meets Colonel Olcott. He begins to write *Theosophy* (CW 9).

1904: Rudolf Steiner continues lecturing at the Workers' College and elsewhere (about 90 lectures), while lecturing intensively all over Germany among Theosophists (about a 140 lectures). In February, he meets Carl Unger (1878-1929), who will become a member of the board of the Anthroposophical Society (1913). In March, he meets Michael Bauer (1871-1929), a Christian mystic, who will also be on the board. In May, *Theosophy* appears, with the dedication: "To the spirit of Giordano Bruno." Rudolf Steiner and Marie von Sivers visit London for meetings with Annie Besant. June: Rudolf Steiner and Marie von Sivers attend the meeting of the Federation of European Sections of the Theosophical Society in Amsterdam. In July, Steiner begins the articles in *Luzifer-Gnosis* that will become *How to Know Higher Worlds* (CW 10) and *Cosmic Memory* (CW 11). In September, Annie Besant visits Germany. In December, Steiner lectures on Freemasonry. He mentions the High Grade Masonry derived from John Yarker and represented by Theodore Reuss and Karl Kellner as a blank slate "into which a good image could be placed."

1905: This year, Steiner ends his non-Theosophical lecturing activity. Supported by Marie von Sivers, his Theosophical lecturing—both in public and in the Theosophical Society—increases significantly: "The German Theosophical Movement is of exceptional importance." Steiner recommends reading, among others, Fichte, Jacob Boehme, and Angelus Silesius. He begins to introduce Christian themes into Theosophy. He also begins to work with doctors (Felix Peipers and Ludwig Noll). In July, he is in London for the Federation of European Sections, where he attends a lecture by Annie Besant: "I have seldom seen Mrs. Besant speak in so inward and heartfelt a manner...." "Through Mrs. Besant I have found the way to H.P. Blavatsky."

September to October, he gives a course of thirty-one lectures for a small group of esoteric students. In October, the annual meeting of the German Section of the Theosophical Society, which still remains very small, takes place. Rudolf Steiner reports membership has risen from 121 to 377 members. In November, seeking to establish esoteric "continuity," Rudolf Steiner and Marie von Sivers participate in a "Memphis-Misraim" Masonic ceremony. They pay forty-five marks for membership. "Yesterday, you saw how little remains of former esoteric institutions." "We are dealing only with a 'framework'... for the present, nothing lies behind it. The occult powers have completely withdrawn."

1906: Expansion of Theosophical work. Rudolf Steiner gives about 245 lectures, only 44 of which take place in Berlin. Cycles are given in Paris, Leipzig, Stuttgart, and Munich. Esoteric work also intensifies. Rudolf Steiner begins writing *An Outline of Esoteric Science* (CW 13). In January, Rudolf Steiner receives permission (a patent) from the Great Orient of the Scottish A & A Thirty-Three Degree Rite of the Order of the Ancient Freemasons of the Memphis-Misraim Rite to direct a chapter under the name "Mystica Aeterna." This will become the "Cognitive Cultic Section" (also called "Misraim Service") of the Esoteric School. (See: *From the History and Contents of the Cognitive Cultic Section* (CW 264). During this time, Steiner also meets Albert Schweitzer. In May, he is in Paris, where he visits Edouard Schuré. Many Russians attend his lectures (including Konstantin Balmont, Dimitri Mereszkovski, Zinaida Hippius, and Maximilian Woloshin). He attends the General Meeting of the European Federation of the Theosophical Society, at which Col. Olcott is present for the last time. He spends the year's end in Venice and Rome, where he writes and works on his translation of H.P. Blavatsky's *Key to Theosophy*.

1907: Further expansion of the German Theosophical Movement according to the Rosicrucian directive to "introduce spirit into the world"—in education, in social questions, in art, and in science. In February, Col. Olcott dies in Adyar. Before he dies, Olcott indicates that "the Masters" wish Annie Besant to succeed him: much politicking ensues. Rudolf Steiner supports Besant's candidacy. April-May: preparations for the Congress of the Federation of European Sections of the Theosophical Society—the great, watershed Whitsun "Munich Congress," attended by Annie Besant and others. Steiner decides to separate Eastern and Western (Christian-Rosicrucian) esoteric schools. He takes his esoteric school out of the Theosophical Society (Besant and Rudolf Steiner are "in harmony" on this). Steiner makes his first lecture tours to Austria and Hungary. That summer, he is in Italy. In September, he visits Edouard Schuré, who will write the introduction to the French edition of *Christianity as Mystical Fact* in Barr, Alsace. Rudolf Steiner writes the autobiographical statement known as the "Barr Document." In *Luzifer–Gnosis*, "The Education of the Child" appears.

1908: The movement grows (membership: 1150). Lecturing expands. Steiner makes his first extended lecture tour to Holland and Scandinavia, as well as visits to Naples and Sicily. Themes: St. John's Gospel, the Apocalypse, Egypt, science, philosophy, and logic. *Luzifer-Gnosis* ceases publication. In Berlin, Marie von Sivers (with Johanna Mücke (1864-1949) forms the *Philosophisch-Theosophisch* (after 1915 *Philosophisch-Anthroposophisch*) *Verlag* to publish Steiner's work. Steiner gives lecture cycles titled *The Gospel of St. John* (CW 103) and *The Apocalypse* (104).

1909: *An Outline of Esoteric Science* appears. Lecturing and travel continues. Rudolf Steiner's spiritual research expands to include the polarity of Lucifer and Ahriman; the work of great individualities in history; the Maitreya Buddha and the Bodhisattvas; spiritual economy (CW 109); the work of the spiritual hierarchies in heaven and on Earth (CW 110). He also deepens and intensifies his research into the Gospels, giving lectures on the Gospel of St. Luke (CW 114) with the first mention of two Jesus children. Meets and becomes friends with Christian Morgenstern (1871-1914). In April, he lays the foundation stone for the Malsch model—the building that will lead to the first Goetheanum. In May, the International Congress of the Federation of European Sections of the Theosophical Society takes place in Budapest. Rudolf Steiner receives the Subba Row medal for *How to Know Higher Worlds*. During this time, Charles W. Leadbeater discovers Jiddu Krishnamurti (1895-1986) and proclaims him the future "world teacher," the bearer of the Maitreya Buddha and the "reappearing Christ." In October, Steiner delivers seminal lectures on "anthroposophy," which he will try, unsuccessfully, to rework over the next years into the unfinished work, *Anthroposophy (A Fragment)* (CW 45).

1910: New themes: *The Reappearance of Christ in the Etheric* (CW 118); *The Fifth Gospel; The Mission of Folk Souls* (CW 121); *Occult History* (CW 126); the evolving development of etheric cognitive capacities. Rudolf Steiner continues his Gospel research with *The Gospel of St. Matthew* (CW 123). In January, his father dies. In April, he takes a month-long trip to Italy, including Rome, Monte Cassino, and Sicily. He also visits Scandinavia again. July-August, he writes the first mystery drama, *The Portal of Initiation* (CW 14). In November, he gives "psychosophy" lectures. In December, he submits "On the Psychological Foundations and Epistemological Framework of Theosophy" to the International Philosophical Congress in Bologna.

1911: The crisis in the Theosophical Society deepens. In January, "The Order of the Rising Sun," which will soon become "The Order of the Star in the East," is founded for the coming world teacher, Krishnamurti. At the same time, Marie von Sivers, Rudolf Steiner's coworker, falls ill. Fewer lectures are given, but important new ground is broken. In Prague, in March, Steiner meets Franz Kafka (1883-1924) and Hugo Bergmann (1883-1975). In April, he delivers his paper to the

Philosophical Congress. He writes the second mystery drama, *The Soul's Probation* (CW 14). Also, while Marie von Sivers is convalescing, Rudolf Steiner begins work on *Calendar 1912/1913*, which will contain the "Calendar of the Soul" meditations. On March 19, Anna (Eunike) Steiner dies. In September, Rudolf Steiner visits Einsiedeln, birthplace of Paracelsus. In December, Friedrich Rittelmeyer, future founder of the Christian Community, meets Rudolf Steiner. The *Johannes-Bauverein*, the "building committee," which would lead to the first Goetheanum (first planned for Munich), is also founded, and a preliminary committee for the founding of an independent association is created that, in the following year, will become the Anthroposophical Society. Important lecture cycles include *Occult Physiology* (CW 128); *Wonders of the World* (CW 129); *From Jesus to Christ* (CW 131). Other themes: esoteric Christianity; Christian Rosenkreutz; the spiritual guidance of humanity; the sense world and the world of the spirit.

1912: Despite the ongoing, now increasing crisis in the Theosophical Society, much is accomplished: *Calendar 1912/1913* is published; eurythmy is created; both the third mystery drama, *The Guardian of the Threshold* (CW 14) and *A Way of Self-Knowledge* (CW 16) are written. New (or renewed) themes included life between death and rebirth and karma and reincarnation. Other lecture cycles: *Spiritual Beings in the Heavenly Bodies and the Kingdoms of Nature* (CW 136); *The Human Being in the Light of Occultism, Theosophy, and Philosophy* (CW 137); *The Gospel of St. Mark* (CW 139); and *The Bhagavad Gita and the Epistles of Paul* (CW 142). On May 8, Rudolf Steiner celebrates White Lotus Day, H.P. Blavatsky's death day, which he had faithfully observed for the past decade, for the last time. In August, Rudolf Steiner suggests the "independent association" be called the "Anthroposophical Society." In September, the first eurythmy course takes place. In October, Rudolf Steiner declines recognition of a Theosophical Society lodge dedicated to the Star of the East and decides to expel all Theosophical Society members belonging to the order. Also, with Marie von Sivers, he first visits Dornach, near Basel, Switzerland, and they stand on the hill where the Goetheanum will be. In November, a Theosophical Society lodge is opened by direct mandate from Adyar (Annie Besant). In December, a meeting of the German section occurs at which it is decided that belonging to the Order of the Star of the East is incompatible with membership in the Theosophical Society. December 28: informal founding of the Anthroposophical Society in Berlin.

1913: Expulsion of the German section from the Theosophical Society. February 2-3: Foundation meeting of the Anthroposophical Society. Board members include: Marie von Sivers, Michael Bauer, and Carl Unger. September 20: Laying of the foundation stone for the *Johannes Bau* (Goetheanum) in Dornach. Building begins immediately. The third mystery drama, *The Soul's Awakening* (CW 14), is completed.

Also: *The Threshold of the Spiritual World* (CW 147). Lecture cycles include: *The Bhagavad Gita and the Epistles of Paul* and *The Esoteric Meaning of the Bhagavad Gita* (CW 146), which the Russian philosopher Nikolai Berdyaev attends; *The Mysteries of the East and of Christianity* (CW 144); *The Effects of Esoteric Development* (CW 145); and *The Fifth Gospel* (CW 148). In May, Rudolf Steiner is in London and Paris, where anthroposophical work continues.

1914: Building continues on the *Johannes Bau* (Goetheanum) in Dornach, with artists and coworkers from seventeen nations. The general assembly of the Anthroposophical Society takes place. In May, Rudolf Steiner visits Paris, as well as Chartres Cathedral. June 28: assassination in Sarajevo ("Now the catastrophe has happened!"). August 1: War is declared. Rudolf Steiner returns to Germany from Dornach—he will travel back and forth. He writes the last chapter of *The Riddles of Philosophy*. Lecture cycles include: *Human and Cosmic Thought* (CW 151); *Inner Being of Humanity between Death and a New Birth* (CW 153); *Occult Reading and Occult Hearing* (CW 156). December 24: marriage of Rudolf Steiner and Marie von Sivers.

1915: Building continues. Life after death becomes a major theme, also art. Writes: *Thoughts during a Time of War* (CW 24). Lectures include: *The Secret of Death* (CW 159); *The Uniting of Humanity through the Christ Impulse* (CW 165).

1916: Rudolf Steiner begins work with Edith Maryon (1872-1924) on the sculpture "The Representative of Humanity" ("The Group"—Christ, Lucifer, and Ahriman). He also works with the alchemist Alexander von Bernus on the quarterly *Das Reich*. He writes *The Riddle of Humanity* (CW 20). Lectures include: *Necessity and Freedom in World History and Human Action* (CW 166); *Past and Present in the Human Spirit* (CW 167); *The Karma of Vocation* (CW 172); *The Karma of Untruthfulness* (CW 173).

1917: Russian Revolution. The U.S. enters the war. Building continues. Rudolf Steiner delineates the idea of the "threefold nature of the human being" (in a public lecture March 15) and the "threefold nature of the social organism" (hammered out in May-June with the help of Otto von Lerchenfeld and Ludwig Polzer-Hoditz in the form of two documents titled *Memoranda*, which were distributed in high places). August-September: Rudolf Steiner writes *The Riddles of the Soul* (CW 20). Also: commentary on "The Chemical Wedding of Christian Rosenkreutz" for Alexander Bernus (*Das Reich*). Lectures include: *The Karma of Materialism* (CW 176); *The Spiritual Background of the Outer World: The Fall of the Spirits of Darkness* (CW 177).

1918: March 18: peace treaty of Brest-Litovsk—"Now everything will truly enter chaos! What is needed is cultural renewal." June: Rudolf Steiner visits Karlstein (Grail) Castle outside Prague. Lecture cycle: *From Symptom to Reality in Modern History* (CW 185). In mid-November,

Emil Molt, of the Waldorf-Astoria Cigarette Company, has the idea of founding a school for his workers' children.

1919: Focus on the threefold social organism: tireless travel, countless lectures, meetings, and publications. At the same time, a new public stage of Anthroposophy emerges as cultural renewal begins. The coming years will see initiatives in pedagogy, medicine, pharmacology, and agriculture. January 27: threefold meeting: " We must first of all, with the money we have, found free schools that can bring people what they need." February: first public eurythmy performance in Zurich. Also: "Appeal to the German People" (CW 24), circulated March 6 as a newspaper insert. In April, *Toward Social Renewal* (CW 23)—"perhaps the most widely read of all books on politics appearing since the war"—appears. Rudolf Steiner is asked to undertake the "direction and leadership" of the school founded by the Waldorf-Astoria Company. Rudolf Steiner begins to talk about the "renewal" of education. May 30: a building is selected and purchased for the future Waldorf School. August-September, Rudolf Steiner gives a lecture course for Waldorf teachers, *The Foundations of Human Experience (Study of Man)* (CW 293). September 7: Opening of the first Waldorf School. December (into January): first science course, the *Light Course* (CW 320).

1920: The Waldorf School flourishes. New threefold initiatives. Founding of limited companies *Der Kommenden Tag* and *Futurum A.G.* to infuse spiritual values into the economic realm. Rudolf Steiner also focuses on the sciences. Lectures: *Introducing Anthroposophical Medicine* (CW 312); *The Warmth Course* (CW 321); *The Boundaries of Natural Science* (CW 322); *The Redemption of Thinking* (CW 74). February: Johannes Werner Klein—later a cofounder of the Christian Community—asks Rudolf Steiner about the possibility of a "religious renewal," a "Johannine church." In March, Rudolf Steiner gives the first course for doctors and medical students. In April, a divinity student asks Rudolf Steiner a second time about the possibility of religious renewal. September 27-October 16: anthroposophical "university course." December: lectures titled *The Search for the New Isis* (CW 202).

1921: Rudolf Steiner continues his intensive work on cultural renewal, including the uphill battle for the threefold social order. "University" arts, scientific, theological, and medical courses include: *The Astronomy Course* (CW 323); *Observation, Mathematics, and Scientific Experiment* (CW 324); the *Second Medical Course* (CW 313); *Color*. In June and September-October, Rudolf Steiner also gives the first two "priests' courses" (CW 342 and 343). The "youth movement" gains momentum. Magazines are founded: *Die Drei* (January), and—under the editorship of Albert Steffen (1884-1963)—the weekly, *Das Goetheanum* (August). In February-March, Rudolf Steiner takes his first trip outside Germany since the war (Holland). On April 7, Steiner receives a letter regarding "religious renewal," and May 22-23, he agrees to address the question in a practical way. In June, the Klinical-Therapeutic Institute opens in Arlesheim under the direction of Dr. Ita Wegman. In August, the Chemical-Pharmaceutical Laboratory opens in Arlesheim (Oskar Schmiedel and Ita Wegman, directors). The Clinical Therapeutic Institute is inaugurated in Stuttgart (Dr. Ludwig Noll, director); also the Research Laboratory in Dornach (Ehrenfried Pfeiffer and Gunther Wachsmuth, directors). In November-December, Rudolf Steiner visits Norway.

1922: The first half of the year involves very active public lecturing (thousands attend); in the second half, Rudolf Steiner begins to withdraw and turn toward the Society—"The Society is asleep." It is "too weak" to do what is asked of it. The businesses—*Die Kommenden Tag* and *Futura A.G.*—fail. In January, with the help of an agent, Steiner undertakes a twelve-city German tour, accompanied by eurythmy performances. In two weeks he speaks to more than 2,000 people. In April, he gives a "university course" in The Hague. He also visits England. In June, he is in Vienna for the East-West Congress. In August-September, he is back in England for the Oxford Conference on Education. Returning to Dornach, he gives the lectures *Philosophy, Cosmology, and Religion* (CW 215), and gives the third priest's course (CW 344). On September 16, The Christian Community is founded. In October-November, Steiner is in Holland and England. He also speaks to the youth: *The Youth Course* (CW 217). In December, Steiner gives lectures titled *The Origins of Natural Science* (CW 326), and *Humanity and the World of Stars: The Spiritual Communion of Humanity* (CW 219). December 31: Fire at the Goetheanum, which is destroyed.

1923: Despite the fire, Rudolf Steiner continues his work unabated. A very hard year. Internal dispersion, dissension, and apathy abound. There is conflict—between old and new visions—within the society. A wake-up call is needed, and Rudolf Steiner responds with renewed lecturing vitality. His focus: the spiritual context of human life; initiation science; the course of the year; and community building. As a foundation for an artistic school, he creates a series of pastel sketches. Lecture cycles: *The Anthroposophical Movement; Initiation Science* (CW 227) (in England at the Penmaenmawr Summer School); *The Four Seasons and the Archangels* (CW 229); *Harmony of the Creative Word* (CW 230); *The Supersensible Human* (CW 231), given in Holland for the founding of the Dutch society. On November 10, in response to the failed Hitler-Ludendorf putsch in Munich, Steiner closes his Berlin residence and moves the *Philosophisch-Anthroposophisch Verlag* (Press) to Dornach. On December 9, Steiner begins the serialization of his *Autobiography: The Course of My Life* (CW 28) in *Das Goetheanum*. It will continue to appear weekly, without a break, until his death. Late December-early January: Rudolf Steiner refounds the Anthroposophical Society (about 12,000 members internationally) and takes over its leadership. The new board members are: Marie Steiner, Ita Wegman, Albert Steffen, Elizabeth Vreede, and Guenther Wachsmuth. (See *The Christmas Meeting for the Founding of the General Anthroposophical Society* (CW 260). Accompanying lectures: *Mystery Knowledge and Mystery Centers* (CW 232); *World History in the Light of Anthroposophy* (CW 233). December 25: the Foundation Stone is laid (in the hearts of members) in the form of the "Foundation Stone Meditation."

1924: January 1: having founded the Anthroposophical Society and taken over its leadership, Rudolf Steiner has the task of "reforming" it. The process begins with a weekly newssheet ("What's Happening in the Anthroposophical Society") in which Rudolf Steiner's "Letters to Members" and "Anthroposophical Leading Thoughts" appear (CW 26). The next step is the creation of a new esoteric class, the "first class" of the "University of Spiritual Science" (which was to have been followed, had Rudolf Steiner lived longer, by two more advanced classes). Then comes a new language for Anthroposophy—practical, phenomenological, and direct; and Rudolf Steiner creates the model for the second Goetheanum. He begins the series of extensive "karma" lectures (CW 235-40); and finally, responding to needs, he creates two new initiatives: biodynamic agriculture and curative education. After the middle of the year, rumors begin to circulate regarding Steiner's health. Lectures: January-February, *Anthroposophy* (CW 234); February: *Tone Eurythmy* (CW 278); June: *The Agriculture Course* (CW 327); June-July: Speech [?] Eurythmy (CW 279); *Curative Education* (CW 317); August: (England, "Second International Summer School"), *Initiation Consciousness: True and False Paths in Spiritual Investigation* (CW 243); September: *Pastoral Medicine* (CW 318). On September 26, for the first time, Rudolf Steiner cancels a lecture. On September 28, he gives his last lecture. On September 29, he withdraws to his studio in the carpenter's shop; now he is definitively ill. Cared for by Ita Wegman, he continues working, however, and writing the weekly installments of his *Autobiography* and *Letters to the Members/Leading Thoughts* (CW 26).

1925: Rudolf Steiner, while continuing to work, continues to weaken. He finishes *Extending Practical Medicine* (CW 27) with Ita Wegman. On March 30, around ten in the morning, Rudolf Steiner dies.

INDEX

INNER READING
AND
INNER HEARING

RUDOLF STEINER (1913)

INNER READING
AND
INNER HEARING

& How to Achieve Existence in the World of Ideas

Two Lectures Cycles, Followed by Two Christmas Lectures
Dornach, October 3–7 and December 12–20, 1914
Dornach, December 26 and Basel, December 27, 1914

TRANSLATED BY MICHAEL MILLER
INTRODUCTION BY CHRISTOPHER BAMFORD

RUDOLF STEINER

SteinerBooks

CW 156

SteinerBooks
Anthropsophic Press

610 Main Street
Great Barrington, Massachusetts 01230
www.steinerbooks.org

Translation by Michael Miller

This book is volume 156 in the Collected Works (CW) of Rudolf Steiner, published by SteinerBooks, 2008. It is a translation of *Okkultes Lesen und okkultes Horën* published by Rudolf Steiner Verlag, Dornach, Switzerland, 2003.

The drawings in the text were done by Hedwig Frey and Lenore Uhlig, based on the stenographer's sketches of Rudolf Steiner's blackboard drawings.

Library of Congress Cataloging-in-Publication Data

Steiner, Rudolf, 1861-1925.
[Okkultes Lesen und okkultes Horkn. English]
Inner reading and inner hearing ; and, How to achieve existence in the world of ideas : two lecture cycles, followed by two Christmas lectures, Dornach, October 3-7 and December 12-26, 1914 and Basel, December 27, 1914 / Rudolf Steiner ; translated by Michael Miller ; introduction by Christopher Bamford.
p. cm. – (The collected works of rudolf steiner ; v. 156)
Includes bibliographical references and index.
ISBN 978-0-88010-619-1
1. Anthroposophy. I. Steiner, Rudolf, 1861-1925. How to achieve existence in the world of ideas. II. Title. III. Title: How to achieve existence in the world of ideas.
BP595.S8656513 2008
299'.935–dc22

2008038737

Printed in the United States

CONTENTS

3.

The Vowels and Consonants of the Spiritual World

DORNACH, OCTOBER 5, 1914

Experience of the cosmic vowels. Standing at the portal of death. Human thoughts and ideas as shadow pictures of real imaginations. The beings of the hierarchy of angels. About practicing loving interest in the world and its manifestations. The animal world as the physiognomy of nature; the plant world as the facial expression; the mineral world as the gesture of nature. The capability to change into other beings. The evil misuse of higher spiritual forces.

4.

Inner Mobility of Thought

DORNACH, OCTOBER 6, 1914

Space and time relationships upon gaining spiritual ideas or imaginations of the being of the angels, archangels, archai. Experience of the Cosmic Word. Reflections of the seven cosmic vowels in the etheric body and the twelve cosmic consonants in the physical body. Perception in the spiritual world between death and new birth. Concerning the correct reading of spiritual-scientific books. The future organ of thinking during the Jupiter and Venus periods.

5.

Times of Expectation

DORNACH, OCTOBER 7, 1914

Christian Morgenstern's connection with the spiritual-scientific Movement. Christian Morgenstern's soul after death as spiritual guide for souls that had felt on Earth the yearning for the spiritual. Johann von Goethe, Hermann Grimm, and Christian Morgenstern and their relationship to the supersensible worlds. Hermann Grimm as representative of the nineteenth-century yearning for the spiritual: the age of expectation. Spiritual science as fulfillment of this expectation. The nature of eurythmy. The pedagogical, hygienic, and artistic aspects of eurythmy.

PART II
How to Achieve Existence in the World of Ideas

6.
The Human Organization, Memory, and Inner Reading

DORNACH, DECEMBER 12, 1914

About the nature of human memory. The astral body as reader of the esoteric script. The sacred art of writing in ancient times. The origin of the art of printing books. Goethe's relation to color. The significance of judgments out of the folk nature, of sympathy and antipathy for a particular folk soul.

pages 87–100

7.
Microcosm and Macrocosm: Human Gestures and the Life of the World

DORNACH, DECEMBER 13, 1914

The transition of the "I" into the astral body, from conscious to subconscious experience. Possibilities of a plant therapy. Ideas in Maeterlinck's book, *Der Schatz der Armen* [The treasure of the poor] and Fichte's *Reden an die deutsche Nation* [Addresses to the German nation] as examples of the striving for the re-enlivening of human spiritual development. Spiritual-scientific impulses for artistic creating. The building of the human form under the influence of the cosmos.

pages 101–116

8.
Human Beings as Illuminators of the Cherubim, Heaters of the Seraphim

DORNACH, DECEMBER 19, 1914

How can human beings enter into reality with their concepts and ideas? Perception of the world in mirror image. Spiritual science adds a concluding chapter to *Riddles of Philosophy*. Development of specific capacities by working through philosophy thoroughly. The objective thought world; the world of the hierarchies. The dying of thoughts in the physical body. The world of images and the world of realities. How can we bring reality to the world of images? Moral impulses of human beings and their significance for the hierarchies.

pages 117–132

9.

The Separation of Art, Science, and Religion

DORNACH, DECEMBER 20, 1914

The transformation of a one-sided head culture into a whole-human view of the world as the task of spiritual science. Separation and re-uniting of art, science, and religion. Artistic experience. The transformation of the human organism in the coming Jupiter evolution. The building-forms of the [first] Goetheanum.

pages 133–145

PART III

THE CELEBRATION OF CHRISTMAS

10.

Toward a New Understanding of the Mystery of Golgotha

DORNACH, DECEMBER 26, 1914

The Christmas festival of the renewed understanding of Christ. The descent of Christ out of the spiritual heights. The various views of a divine mediator in the Mithras service, in Manichaeism, and in Gnosis. Augustine and Faust, the renewed understanding of Christ.

pages 149–163

INTRODUCTION

Christopher Bamford

If one reads them carefully, despite their vast quantity—the figure usually given is around 6,000—Rudolf Steiner's lectures rarely fail to astonish and surprise; and always for unique reasons. No matter how many lectures one has read, one always finds new insights, either because the research is new or because Steiner's mood or disposition in relation to his audience shades his remarks in a way that brings out previously hidden nuances or perspectives not available elsewhere. Such is the case with the three short lecture cycles printed here. The year is 1914; the months October and December: a fate-filled moment both for Anthroposophy and Western civilization.

The year before (1913) had seen the expulsion of the German Section from the Theosophical Society and the establishment of the Anthroposophical Society. This finally gave Rudolf Steiner the untrammeled freedom to form his own spiritual movement without the constraints that working within the Adyar-based Theosophical Movement had inevitably imposed. On February 3, the first constitutive General Meeting of the new Society took place and by the middle of the year, it numbered over 3,000 members, active in 85 working groups. That same month, a second, equally epoch-making event occurred when it was finally decided that the "Building," which in 1918 would be renamed the Goetheanum, but was then still known as the "Johannesbau" or "John Building" after John the Evangelist, would be located in Dornach, Switzerland, rather than in Munich, Germany, as had been previously considered. This decision, long in coming, was made on May 18, and on September 20 the Foundation Stone was laid. By November construction was underway. Clearly, the spiritual world was seeking to found something, as may also be seen from the deeply esoteric lectures Steiner gave during this period—such as those on *The Fifth Gospel, The Secrets of the Threshold,*

The Esoteric Foundations of the Bhagavad-Gita, and *Christ and the Spiritual World: The Search for the Holy Grail.*

By the following year, 1914, as if prophetically preparing for the wartime years, the center of Anthroposophical work had shifted to Dornach, where construction was in full swing and Steiner oversaw all aspects of the work. As a consequence, he was forced to reduce his lecturing activity, though he continued to research and speak on the Fifth Gospel, as well as on life between death and a new birth. It had been his hope to open the Johannesbau by December. However, with the inception of hostilities, following the assassination of Archduke Franz Ferdinand in Sarajevo on June 28, that of course did not happen. Events moved very fast, as the world caught fire. By the end of July, Austria-Hungary had declared war on Serbia, and Russia had ordered the mobilization of troops. On August 1, Germany declared war on Russia; on August 3 on France; on August 4, Germany invaded Belgium and Britain declared war on Germany. The die was cast.

Rudolf Steiner had long recognized what was coming. He understood that humanity was entering a great test. Since the deed of 1879, when the Archangel Michael—according to both Steiner's research and esoteric lore—overcame the Dragon, throwing him to Earth, and assumed the regency of the age, offering himself to human beings as their mediator and helper, the spiritual world had sought fiercely to manifest itself on Earth. Human beings meanwhile, for their part, sunk deeper into materialism and into the dragon's clutches. Evil had entered the world in a new way. Yet the call was to rise upward—to work one's way in freedom toward the spirit, thereby dissipating the evil, which in so many ways and in so much in human life now drew humanity evermore downward. From this point of view, the war came—or ought to have come—as a form of "hitting bottom." If ever an event should bring human beings to change their way of thinking and being, this was it. During the first six months of the year, therefore, Steiner, while continuing to focus on the building that would be the living manifestation of the anthroposophical spirit, sought above all to strengthen his students' spiritual resolve.

The reality of war had indeed changed everything. Suffering and death began to fill the air. Spiritual research, of the kind that Rudolf

Steiner had been doing, became difficult, if not impossible. In response to people's very heartfelt needs and the great confusion in the spiritual world, his focus narrowed. Thus, over the next few years, we find a greater emphasis on the vital connections between the living and the so-called dead, as well as on the esoteric historical currents underlying the ongoing carnage. On a more mundane level, travel, too, became more difficult. Steiner had to curtail his lecturing activity. Steiner's orbit would gradually become limited largely to Dornach and Berlin. Personal changes also ensued. His wife Anna (Schultz) Eunike (Steiner) had died in 1911. This left him free to marry his longtime co-worker and spiritual collaborator, Marie von Sivers, who was still a Russian citizen. With the War, the long-planned event became a necessity. Rudolf Steiner and Marie von Sivers were married on December 24, which meant that Marie Steiner, now with an Austrian passport, could travel freely to Berlin with her husband, Rudolf Steiner.

At the same time, Providence, establishing the new center outside the war zone, in Dornach, obviously provided a haven. While witnessing the horrific events going on in the rest of Europe, those in Switzerland were protected from them. This made it all the more important, as Steiner repeatedly stressed, for those whose fortunate karma had granted them this asylum to uphold with all their strength their spiritual ideals, manifesting them in their lives in the full existential resolution that the "Spirit will triumph."

The time for theory was over. The path to spiritual knowledge must be lived and practiced. Such is the context of the lectures collected here.

"Inner Reading and Inner Hearing," the first cycle, was originally intended to contain fourteen lectures. They were to be given during the rehearsal of Steiner's new Mystery Drama, which would have carried the previous four plays to a new level. This fifth play was to have been written during rehearsals in Munich, but the War made rehearsals impossible. It was never written. Nevertheless, in response to requests that he give the lectures anyway, Steiner gave what he had previously conceived of as a major and extended cycle of fourteen lectures in the shortened form of four lectures. Though, as he says, the War now made it impossible to say what he would have said in Munich—"it is just not possible to speak the highest truths into the storm"—what he did say, perhaps precisely because he was forced to speak at a "lower" level, is unusually clear, astonishing, and enormously instructive.

The tone is intimate. Steiner is speaking here not just as teacher, but also as friend and colleague, a coworker in a shared enterprise at a time of common—indeed, from a European point of view, near universal—grief and foreboding. But the War and its desolation are present only between the lines. Steiner's explicit theme is essentially meditation: the path to the spirit, to entering into relationship with spiritual beings—in the first place with the dead, but also with the angelic beings. Rather than instruction, he gives advice in the most remarkable, forthright, touching way, speaking not theoretically but directly from his experiences—which are often the most valuable teachings.

He begins with the in-itself-astonishing statement that "the essentials of spiritual science have been won basically through inner reading and inner hearing." That is to say, inner reading and inner hearing constitute the primary method of spiritual research. They are the way we come to and experience spiritual reality.

Such an "inner" phenomenology and hermeneutics, however, is very different to what we habitually practice in relation to the "outer" world. Steiner gives the example of someone who suggested that "seers" be gathered together to observe a group of people, each of whom was instructed to think and feel certain things. If then, based on seeing their auras, all the seers agreed and were correct in perceiving what the members of the group were experiencing inwardly, the validity of the seers' inner perceptions would be proved. In other words, this person has proposed a typical scientific experiment. But inner perception does not work like that. The spiritual world is not at the behest of our desires and intentions. Quite the contrary: it is always a gift: not a generic gift, but a gift given by a specific giver, a spiritual being. For the spiritual world is a world of beings—from the highest angelic hierarchies to the so-called dead. Spiritual knowing is not something we can take. It must be received. Therefore, to approach such knowing-receiving, we must silence our desires, purposes, and intentions and present ourselves in devoted, expectant, attentive, empty waiting. Whatever comes originates in the spiritual world, not in us. And that world is nowhere else but here, where we are. But we are unaware of it; we do not see it.

> Where are the beings of the elemental world; where are the beings of the spiritual world; where are the beings of the upper hierarchies? They are right where we are. They are all around us—where the table and the chairs are, where you yourselves are. They are everywhere all around us, but they are so thin and evanescent compared to the relationships and processes of the things of the external world that they escape our attention. We continually go straight through the spiritual world and do not see it; we are inattentive to the spiritual world because our disposition is not prepared for it.

The same, in fact, is also true for a right perception of the so-called physical or outer world. When we think, feel, and will in relation to the outer world, we usually think of ourselves as over "here" and the world as over "there." But, though we can certainly develop valuable capacities in approaching it in that way, reality is not like that. With regard to our soul and spirit, we are not skin-bound. When we see a rose, our astral body and our "I" are *in* the rose; and this experience is *reflected* back to us by our organism or body. We do not produce what we experience inwardly; we only reflect it. "With our soul-spiritual nature we are truly within the part of the world we observe, and we see it because our organism reflects it." But in ordinary daily life what we see is more or less ourselves reflected back to us. It is *maya* (or illusion) because we do not realize we are within what we see.

Perception of the spiritual world is even more complex, because (as stated in the above quotation) it is so fleeting and mobile compared to the fixity of the physical world. To begin to experience it, we must learn to forget ourselves as we do in meditation. Suppressing the *selfness* of the "I" enables us to sink down into the so-called astral body. But to have access to what we experience there, this experience too must be reflected—in this case, not by the physical organism but by the so-called etheric or life body, which is a body, we might say, of living thinking. To do this is more difficult than "reading" what our physical organism reflects, for what the etheric reflects is in continual movement—as it were, non-dual movement, outside space and time. This movement is a sign, which must be read or interpreted by "diving down" from the astral into the etheric body, "which is experienced as a fall into an abyss," in the process of which we separate into three parts (thinking, feeling, and willing), each of which has access to an "inner hearing" which reveals the meaning of what we have "read." The state of consciousness involved is akin to a conscious sleep state. It is the state of living consciously in the astral body, which enables us to experience the reflection of the spiritual world in the etheric body. But since this "reading" is actually a "descending into," the reading becomes something closer to "hearing." Then we realize how different true reality is from what we experience in the state of ordinary sensory-physical consciousness.

The process involved is one of identification. The fleeting world through which we encounter the spiritual world is one of images. First, we must clearly separate ourselves from these images. Then, in freedom we must plunge down into them, become one with them—in Steiner's striking metaphor "eat them." We enter their reality. Through this reality, the truth is heard. The phenomenon of "inner hearing" arises. But, in fact, it is not we that hear; more accurately, the image we have become "hears." This is a living process through which we really hear an objective spiritual being—Steiner's example involved communicating with the so-called dead—spiritually.

Much more, of course, is involved in all this than may be recounted here. Only the bare bones may be given. These lectures, in fact, which require close reading and even closer rereading, take us on a profound journey—one described in such precise and vivid language that we can sense something of the transformative magic that those listening to Steiner must have felt—from the sensory world into the experience of the spiritual researcher or meditant, and then back into the sensory world again.

Of central importance in the whole process is an experience of the Zodiac and the planets. When we dive into an image and identify with it, the image itself disappears. At the same time we feel diminished or reduced: we feel that we are only "a piece" of what we were before. As Steiner tells it, our experience is, as it were, a twelfth of what it had been: we feel ourselves in a circle, of which we occupy a twelfth. In other words, we have transformed ourselves into the Zodiac, through which the spiritual being, having penetrated through the image, speaks to us. We gaze, as it were, from the periphery inward—not, as in sensory perception, from the center outward—and discover there seven voices, corresponding to the planets. In other words, the astral body contains a twelvefold reflecting capacity and the etheric body a sevenfold reflecting capacity. Steiner then likens these two—the outer (astral, star-body) Zodiac and the inner planets—to vowels and consonants. In summary:

> We can say that we perceive a series of images. First we stand outside the series; then we dive down into it. In that process, through our devotion and sacrifice, we form a world sphere around what we wish to perceive. This world sphere contains within itself, like seven planets, the vowel system through which the being in question can speak with us when we ourselves, through the twelvefold nature of our being, form the system of consonants.
>
> We can only come into relationship with a being of the spiritual world by enclosing it; enclosing it in such a way that the enclosing gesture forms the cosmic consonants; the being itself can then address us in the cosmic vowels. And when the cosmic vowel system can work together with the cosmic consonant system, which we ourselves have formed, then reading and hearing work together. Then we penetrate into a particular region of the spiritual world.

These experiences must be reflected in the etheric body, where they may be cognized in the diluted, shadowy form of thoughts and ideas. If they were not so reflected, and we returned still bearing them into the physical, we would die: our body could not contain it. Indeed, Steiner stresses throughout that in the process of meditation and the encounter with the spiritual world, the threshold of death is ever-present, a danger that must be navigated cautiously and carefully.

What does it mean, we may ask, that we cannot directly apprehend spiritual realities? It means that we are protected; but even more it means that we are called to realize them in other ways, which takes preparation, a kind of continuous moral awareness, beginning with "the constant practice of loving interest in everything that surrounds us in the world." We must forego interest in ourselves. All the exercises in *How to Know Higher Worlds*, for example, have this as their consequence. Here Steiner gives some others, taking as his example ways of developing interest in other people. At a certain point in our development, we can enter into a completely different relationship with others, for instance, by taking a selfless, loving interest in their physiognomy, or the play of expression in their faces, or their gestures. Entering deeply into these three common realities, in fact, we have manifestations of three cosmic vowels. Later, Steiner will give clues to two more.

Throughout the first four of these lectures, Steiner speaks directly and candidly of his own research experiences—above all with the dead, but also, as the lectures unfold, with higher spiritual beings—in astonishing depth and detail. The lectures, therefore, ought not to be read for mere information about the spiritual world, but read and reread as a guide to our own inner and outer lives. Read in this way, readers will find them of almost inexhaustible wealth. In the last lecture, however, his tone changes. It is as intimate as before, but now it becomes more personal, as Steiner speaks, this time more out of his own life experiences than his research experiences, of the mission and task of Anthroposophy or spiritual science. What shines through here in a remarkable way, suffusing the text with a glow of warmth, is Steiner's enormous love for humanity, for the human project, and for individual human beings.

The second set of lectures, "How to Achieve Existence in the World of Ideas," follows on from the first, taking up several already-established themes, while giving them a somewhat different emphasis.

The call or injunction shifts from meditation and serious inner work to the consequences of such work for ordinary daily life. Common to both is the insistence that Anthroposophy not remain theoretical. One way of doing so is clearly to take up meditation. Another is to take up the spiritual realities discovered and articulated by those able to do the inner work, and put them into practice in one's life. Steiner is here concerned that Anthroposophists do not simply take up Anthroposophy as just another system of ideas to be schematized and philosophized about only intellectually. For him, Anthroposophy is nothing if it is not existential—if it does not change how we live. The second set of lectures thus builds in a new way on some of the spiritual realities touched upon in the first, as well as introducing others. It tries to show how, if people live their lives out of the conviction of their reality, their lives become different. Every spiritual fact adduced by the spiritual researcher has its application or extension in daily life. To live out of such conviction—in thought, feeling, and action—in fact constitutes a kind of second-order spiritual research. For when we take a spiritual fact as if it were a directive for life, and try to extend its reach by ordinary thinking, remarkable ethical and epistemological consequences appear in our lives and in our relationships with those we live with. They are changed fundamentally. Not nearly as dense as those preceding them, these lectures in their own way are equally astonishing. Time and again, as we read them, one senses "This is something I could do," and a new insight dawns.

The collection ends with two extraordinarily moving—and relevant—Christmas lectures—Steiner's first Christmas lectures of the war. Then, as now, as he puts it, "one can hardly think of a sharper mental contrast" than that between the desperate state of the world and the angels' proclamation to the Shepherds:

> Divine Revelation in the heights and Peace on Earth for people of good will.

Truly, these days the birth of the Christ child cannot simply be celebrated as usual; some deeper recognition is required, namely, that we face the reality that what entered the world at Christmas—and how it did so—is still not understood. The full meaning of Christ Jesus—and His birth, life, death, and resurrection—still eludes us. Though it has been slowly moving and evolving in human consciousness for two millennia, the reality and meaning of Christ's incarnation still has not penetrated humanity. It is perhaps the most difficult reality to grasp—and always has been. Historically, certainly, this is the case.

In the first centuries following the Mystery of Golgotha, for example, Mithras and the Mithraic Mysteries enjoyed great popularity. But Mithras was a very different being than Christ. Mithras could be encountered only in clairvoyant vision. He, too, was conceived of as a mediator between the spiritual world and the human soul, but he could not be conceived of as incarnating in a human body. He came down to Earth, but only in the imaginal realm. Ancient clairvoyance knew "The Future and Coming One," a Sun Being, Christ, and knew that he was approaching the Earth to dwell there, but it could not grasp that He would actually take on a human body and that the future of the Earth and the cosmos would thereby be transformed. People could not experience that "the great gift of cosmic Love, the Christ, from the God whom one calls the Father" had come to dwell with them, to unite His being through that deed with the whole future meaning of earthly evolution. For this, people had to learn to love Christ Jesus as their brother: they had to develop a relationship of the deepest intimacy with Him.

To some extent, indeed, over the centuries, human beings slowly did create such a relationship of intimacy and friendship, but now this intimacy—which is only half of the picture—must be broadened to include the cosmic and divine dimensions of Christ's work. Now Christ's cosmic nature must also become part of the new Christianity.

Ancient clairvoyance knew of the Cosmic Christ's work before Golgotha, but the Mystery of Golgotha itself came, as it were, as a stumbling block, which was aggravated by the general decline of spiritual vision. Thus, the great Mani, the third century founder of Manicheanism could see how Christ descended from the spiritual heights, but could not comprehend that He had penetrated the earthly world and dwelt in a human body, changing everything. And after Mani, even that knowledge of the descent grew weaker until it disappeared.

Ancient Gnosis, too, knew these things and its testament, as Steiner shows, is still most moving, but spiritual science can now see further and more deeply. In this spirit he gives a beautiful verse, which is far from the ancient Gnostic view, but oriented, like theirs, toward the living Cosmic Christ:

Light is love ... Sun-weaving
Love-radiance of a world
of creative beings —

which, through ages unheard-of,
holds us to its heart,
and which at last has given us
its highest spirit in the sheath
of a man for three
years: then He came into His

Father's legacy, which is now the Earth's
innermost heavenly fire:
that it, too, may once become Sun.

Now the task is to unite the Christ of Heaven and the earthly Christ in a single path of love, walked individually by each one of us. The attempt to do so, as Steiner says, will fill our souls, not only with love, but also and above all with humility. For by walking this path, we will begin to understand the enormity of the task of humanity, now and into the future: namely, "that human beings, as they go from incarnation to incarnation, must come more and more deeply to the understanding of what Christ really is."

To know Christ is always the most intimate, personal matter. It is the most inner affair and it occurs only gradually. Christ must be born in one's heart. That is why, as Christ becomes truly known, institutional Churches will wane and lose their purpose. For each individual must make the relationship, so as to give birth to Christ within; which means that the relationship is direct and requires no mediation. This path is contained in a verse of Angelus Silesius, much loved by Steiner:

> If Christ be born in Bethlehem a thousand times
> And not in you, you remain in eternal perdition.

INNER READING
AND
INNER HEARING

Rudolf Steiner